"I attribute my life to him," said L
operator, who was evacuate

This book is about Jon Cavaiani, stayed with his Pack, stared the Leviathan directly in the face, and who after his service, never dropped out and never quit. It's a story about a great man who, despite great trials and challenges, positively impacted so many lives.

Jon Cavaiani was proud of his heritage despite being left by his parents to the charge of an Italian farmer, moving to California from England. The lessons learned from his adoptive father, Ugo, and the hard work on the family farm as a young boy, revealed themselves later in life. Those acquired attributes would serve him well, and indeed may have saved his life. In Vietnam, he had a keen sense of duty, and proved that, as attributed to poet Dorothy Parker, "Courage is fear that has said its prayers."

Jon enlisted in the Army at 26 years old, he was initially rejected due to a malady with bee stings, yet convinced a doctor that "he wanted in." He breezed through Special Forces training and was assigned to MEDCAP, a program designed to further the "Vietnamization" program, providing medical care, veterinarian services, and agricultural betterment for the South's civilians living in rural areas. Cavaiani was known to the villagers as "Bac Si Jon" (Doctor Jon).

Read his citation. As all recipients of the Medal of Honor, they are all tough to swallow. Divine intervention, or a miracle, they were ordinary men, doing extraordinary things, under extraordinary circumstances. Refusing to be evacuated before all his men were on choppers, SSG Cavaiani stayed (after saving his platoon mates on three helicopters) with one SF Operator and his Montagnard "little people." Using his SERE training (Survival, Escape, Resistance and Evasion), he evaded the NVA for 11 days. Jon was considered MIA, and was awarded the Medal before he was shipped home March 1973 with his POW brethren. Captain Mike McGrath (USN-POW) told me all Army soldiers were labeled "lost sheep," as there was no contact among the others POW's while Jon was in captivity for 21 months.

Jon, the "Quiet Professional", favored a discussion about the person(s) he was with, rather than about himself. He was extremely humble. His scars were only known to his closest brethren. He was endeared, respected, and beloved by those who crossed his path, with the exception of the jealous, the envious, and the cowardly. To quote Mike Wallace, who knew Jon for almost 25 years, the SgtMaj was a "Renaissance Man." The Sergeant Major amassed a cadre of kinfolk, even though unrelated, throughout the country.

While training younger SF forces, he never complained, but taught, trained, and inspired his men.

The SgtMaj Commanded Delta Force before retiring in 1990. Becoming an expert Chef, helping Veterans, and a role model for all who met him. Because of his exposure to Agent Orange in The Poison Garden of Vietnam, he acquired MDS (Myelodysplastic Syndrome), a presumptive blood-borne disease that affects your bone marrow. Even through his challenging treatments, blood transfusions, and travel from California (Stanford University Hospital) to University of Penn in Philly, he never lost his mission to help people. His wife, Barbara, was his greatest cheerleader.

Jon became the yardstick for dealing with PTS and his medical condition, never relenting. On 29 July 2014, Jon joined his adopted son from Vietnam who was killed, along with all 22 orphans and 6 monks whose orphanage he both built, and cared for.

SgtMaj Jon Cavaiani continues to live on in our memories.

JON ROBERT CAVAIANI

A

WOLF

REMEMBERED

JFK Memorial Arlington, VA

John Siegfried and Dr. Michael B. Evers

First Edition

Year of First Publication: 2023

The events and conversations in this book
have been set down to the best of the
author's ability, although some names and
details may have been changed to protect
the privacy of individuals.

ISBN 978-1-959898-27-6 (eBook)

ISBN 978-1-959898-28-3 (Paperback)

ISBN 978-1-959898-29-0 (Hardcover)

ISBN 978-1-959898-30-6 (Audiobook)

Contents

JON ROBERT CAVAIANI circa 1970

"Jon Cavaiani was the epitome of the professional soldier."[1]

Col. Roger Donlon (MOH)

---

[1] Donlon, Roger, Col USA Retired (Medal of Honor Recipient; as stated in a conversation with Mike Evers; 24 September 2022

Dedication

To Those Who Never Returned

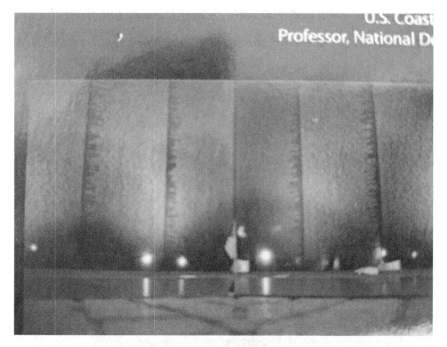

Night Photo of the Vietnam Memorial

*This book is dedicated to all who served, and especially, to those who did not return as represented by the honor of MIA Army Sgt. John Robert Jones, MIA 5 June 1971 / repatriated 2011. **Panel W3. Line 66 Vietnam Memorial***

SGT John R. Jones was the last American soldier killed on 5 June 1971, on hill 950 in Vietnam. He was fighting alongside of SSG Jon R. Cavaiani the last American alive after the battle on hill 950. Cavaiani escaped Hill 950 after Jones was killed, but was captured,

tortured, and held as a POW for 23 months. Jon never forgot his brother and returned to Vietnam in 2011, along with Larry Page, to help recover the remains. There are too many who have yet to be recovered and returned, not only from Vietnam, but from the many battles and wars that scar our history and leave lasting imprints on our souls.

In remembrance!

John Siegfried wears every day. (From Memorial Bracelets.com)

Photo of John Robert Jones, circa 1971, from G. Duane Whitman

files

Day is done, gone the sun,

From the lake, from the hills, from the sky;

All is well, safely rest. God is nigh.

Fading light, dims the sight,

And a star gems the sky, gleaming bright.

From afar, drawing nigh, falls the night.

Thanks, and praise, for our days,

'Neath the sun, 'Neath the stars, 'Neath the sky;

As we go, this we know, God is nigh.

Sun has set, shadows come,

Time had fled, Scouts must go to their beds.

Always true to the promise that they made.

While the light fades from sight,

And the stars gleaming rays softly send,

To the hands we our souls, Lord, commend.

Lyrics from TAPS

Acknowledgements

"A hero-I am not really sure who that is--except—that for ordinary men doing extraordinary things, under extraordinary conditions."
Doc Steve Knuboff. Company Medic. Americal Division. Passed-on 2016.

By writing the story of Jon Cavaiani we relied on numerous sources. Official records and documents provided detail upon which to build. But the meat of Jon's story has been preserved in the hearts and memories of those with whom he interacted.

The story of Jon, as it appears here, is as factual as we could make it, realizing that we had to rely on memories of past events, and the feelings that accompanied those events. Much of Jon's service record is sealed. Memories can become foggy, but by employing the eyes and ears of numerous people, we can peer into that fog and get a clearer picture of the man who survived shrapnel, bullets, beatings, other abuses, and PTSD to live and become a servant leader to others who, quite often, suffered the lingering effects of war as he did. And, who very likely finally succumbed to exposure from *"friendly fire"* effects of Agent Orange.

We owe a great deal to so many who contributed to our effort to convey the life of a humble but highly honorable man. We express great appreciation; because of their contributions to this herculean effort: Ray Celaya, Bill Chadwick, and Bob Chadwick, brothers who served with and became lifelong friends with Jon; to Jake Jacobson, who served with

Jon; to Dick James, who took extraordinary effort to care for Jon and his wife Barbara in later years; to Tacko; to Jim Shorten who instructed Jon in Recon Training to be a team leader; to members and friends of the Philadelphia Marine Corps--Law Enforcement Foundation (MC-LEF); to Captain Mike McGrath USN, Captain Ralph Galati USAF on their captivity for years in Hanoi; members of the Special Forces Association, and finally, to The Montagnards and Hill people who fought and died alongside our guys.

An especial thanks goes to Pete Laurence, who, through his taped interviews with Jon, was able to provide detail on the battle of Hickory Hill and Jon's survival, escape, resistance, and evasion efforts. Pete's notes were consistent with Jon's own words in an interview with Pritzker Military Museum and consistent with, but more detailed than-- Keith McKim's audio record of the battle of Hickory Hill, and with *The Assault on Hickory Hill* (as presented in *The Drop* - a Special Forces Association periodical). And to Jim Shields, who provided documents, photos, anecdotal information about of Jon's life as an advisor, and about Jon's life after retirement. Jim also provided leads to help us pull together a viable picture of the man we know as Jon Cavaiani, but whose family and high school mates called *"Bobby."*

There are many things of which I, John Siegfried, am honored to have been a participant. Nomination to the U.S. Army War College in 2012, interview on NBC in NYC @ 30 Rock, authoring my first book *Six Degrees of the Bracelet: Vietnam's Continuing Grip released 11/11/11*, having multiple speaking engagements with Korean and WWII POW's 19 September 2015, and 18 Vietnam "guests" of the Hanoi Hilton 13 September 2013, Release of *No Greater Love,* a book on Corporal Michael Crescenz, the only Medal of Honor recipient (posthumous) from Philly during Vietnam, just to mention a few.

Co-author Michael Evers, colleague, and collaborator with John Siegfried, is proud to be a former Green Beret, having served in the U. S. Army from 1967 until 1988. While in service Mike completed Command and General Staff College and later earned a doctorate in Educational Leadership from North Carolina State University. He is proud to have been a GS-13 Civilian Marine at Camp Lejeune, North Carolina where he worked as a Government and External Relations Officer.

Mike initially said he thought I (John Siegfried) should be the sole author of this book. How he contacted me was by sheer fate. But, after a lengthy conversation on both his interest, his contacts, and his work on Jon to date, along with Dick James, Jim Shields, and a host of SF operators emboldened to Jon, I insisted he co-author. His response: *"John; I would be honored."*

As proud as we are of our past experiences, the honor of researching and learning of the exemplary life of Jon Cavaiani is an honor of which we are deeply grateful. What we have learned from Jon's life and from being able to meet with and talk with those who shared their, quite often emotional, remembrances of Jon, is an honor that goes beyond our greatest expectations. We only hope that we have presented Jon's life in a manner that reveals just how great this man was – a man who, although he *"will never own this farm because you are an orphan"* – took ownership for his actions, and indeed his life.

Finally, thank you Colonel Harvey Barnum, for being patient with us as we stumbled our way through the initial phases of "finding the course," and for providing the *Foreword* to this story that needs to be told.

Foreword

"If not me, then who? If not now, then when?
Hillel The Elder (variation on original quote)

A Wolf Remembered reveals how a true American Hero, Jon Robert "Bobby" Cavaiani, confronted and overcame the challenges of being an orphaned child; the horror and fog of war as a driven, determined professional Special Forces non-commissioned officer; brutal existence as a Prisoner of War; the suffering and debilitating effects of PTSD; and finally, an ugly battle with Agent Orange. Jon's leadership and concern for his troops, U. S. and indigenous, was the backbone of his existence. He strove to ensure mission accomplishment by always doing the right thing, at the right time, for the right reasons. Upon retirement from the U.S. Army, Jon dedicated his life to assist his fellow man in confronting and dealing with PTSD. He challenged the Veterans Administration and Veterans' organizations to provide the services they proclaimed was their purpose. He worked to raise funds to support Veterans and the Marine Corps Law Enforcement Foundation, to provide scholarships to the future leaders of our great country, the children of fallen Marines, Federal Law Enforcement, and Philadelphia police officers.

To know Jon, was to love him. His low key, love of life attitude, coupled with his great sense of humor, humility, and his dedication to his brothers who wear or have worn the cloth of this great nation, identify him as an individual we should all try to emulate.

The authors set the stage for Jon's military service and accomplishments by including historical data about Vietnam, the politics of the war, and the background and functioning of Special Forces. With all this as a backdrop, the authors weave in Jon's rough childhood, heroics in battle, horrific treatment as a POW, ending with his struggle with PTSD and how he devoted his time to helping others. Jon fought right to the end as he battled cancer. He left an indelible mark on everyone he met. I miss him as he was truly My Brother.

H.C. "Barney" Barnum Jr
Colonel of Marines (Ret.)
Medal of Honor Recipient

Preface

"War loses a great deal of its romance after a soldier has seen his first battle. I have a more vivid recollection of the first than the last one I was in. It is a classical maxim that it is sweet and becoming to die for one's country; but whoever has seen the horrors of a battlefield feels that it is far sweeter to live for it."

Colonel John S. Mosby 1887

Precision can create enemies. Those who accept "close-enough" as a standard have difficulty dealing with those who are of an anal bent or obsessive-compulsive nature. Jon Cavaiani did not accept "close-enough" as an attitude or a standard of performance. In his mind "it is or it isn't; you do or you don't." When he observed things that were not precise and exact he spoke out and took action to make things precise. Whether it was a recipe, irrigation of crops, a training event, or an operation, Jon demanded precise standards be met. That is how he was taught, and it was instilled in his being. This created jealousies and animosities with those who accepted "close enough" as a standard.

So much of the war in Vietnam was based on an attitude of "close enough." Estimates of body counts were "close enough." Bombs dropped over various locations of Southeast Asia were "close enough." Estimations of KIA versus MIA versus POW counts were okay in newsprints, but for some, like Jon, it was unsatisfactory.

The effect that the Vietnam war had on those who served in Southeast Asia is demonstrable. Some of the remaining few are still suffering from their wounds, both internal and external. As Gary Maddox, the Phillies Hall of Fame center fielder (*SHOULD* be in the National Hall with eight gold gloves, and a Vietnam Veteran) said to a caustic radio friend (who changed his mind almost immediately) upon the idea to build the Philadelphia Vietnam Memorial: *"You have to separate the War from the Warrior"*[2] These warriors were not miscreants, malingerers, or reprobates. They were not Ronin. Most were men and women who wanted to stand tall, swear Allegiance to the Constitution, and fight for and serve, their country.

There was no Mama; no Papa; no Uncle Sam: just soldiers, Marines, airmen, guardsmen, seamen, flyboys, nurses, medics, doctors, and their buddies. Disregarded by the public and the previous generations, many of the returning Vietnam service members silently withdrew from society.

Returning home to the United States, many service members found an even greater disdain than they had received in Vietnam. The return was made worse by negative and misleading press and incorrect information. It was the media's negligence and collusion in defamation of those who served with honor that led to an increase in homelessness, suicides, and drug abuse in Veterans. Jon refused to succumb to such pressure and took action to encourage others to be strong.

Many Veterans returning from Vietnam dropped out of society, became homeless, or never told their partners, spouses, or children about their service. To make matters even more challenging, the WWII

---

[2] DeBella, John in interview with John Siegfried WIOQ July 2014, confirmed by Maddox October 2018

generation who had come home to parades and celebratory events lauding their victory, dismissed the call of duty to Vietnam. They dismissed the almost 20 years of combat, the more than 58,300 deaths, and the untold numbers of wounded warriors - not just physically, but psychologically and emotionally. They were for years shunned from joining both American Legion and VFWs throughout the country. Many of them silently withdrew from society – that in itself a form of PTSD.

Then there was the U. S. government-imposed plague brought upon U. S. service men and women by chemical agents used to *"aid in our ability to see the battlefield."* 'Operation Ranch Hand' not only destroyed vegetation in Vietnam (utilizing Agent Blue) and leaf borne trees (Agent Orange), it would slowly destroy the lives of many service members once they returned home. Agent Orange was the most well-known chemical to be sprayed indiscriminately throughout much of Vietnam and Laos. Those in Washington D. C. who made the decisions suffered none of the effects, but all too many Americans suffered long and painfully for the unanticipated consequences. And in recent years we have learned that the effects can be genetically passed on to follow-on generations of those who were directly subjected.

Dick Couch, a Navy SEAL, characterized Vietnam in 2016 as *"that long forgotten war."*[3] We need to keep both our men and women who served in that "conflict" front and center during their lifetime and beyond, just as we have done with the Greatest Generation 77 years later. Of the almost 10,000 nurses (ten are on The Wall: eight women),

---

[3] Couch, Dick, Tom Norris, and Mike Thornton; By Honor Bound: Two Navy Seals, the Medal Of Honor, and a Story of Extraordinary Courage; McMillan; New York; June 2017, pg.xxi

the vast majority have succumbed to Agent Orange exposure. *"The Army never even thought to keep count."*[4]

This book is about Jon Cavaiani, the Resilient and Uncompromising Wolf, who stayed with his Pack, stared the Leviathan directly in the face, and who after his service, never dropped out and never quit. It is a story about a great man who, despite great trials and challenges, positively impacted so many lives.

---

[4] Palmer, Laura; Shrapnel in the Heart: Letters and Remembrances from the Vietnam Veterans Memorial; Vintage; New York; 1988

Introduction

(Referring to Jon Cavaiani): *"I attribute my life to him,"* said **Larry Page**, a former Special Forces radio operator, who was evacuated off of Hickory Hill, 04 June 1971[5]

The barometer of a person's measure is what he believes in and fights for. Jon Cavaiani was a fighter, a survivor, and a winner. He did not tolerate laziness or shirking of one's duties. And he definitely believed in remaining loyal to those with whom you serve.

Jon Cavaiani was proud of his heritage in spite of being left by his parents to the charge of an Italian farmer in California after their move from England. The lessons learned from his adoptive father, Ugo, and the hard work on the family farm revealed themselves later in life. Those acquired attributes would serve him well, and indeed may have saved his life. In Vietnam, he had a keen sense of duty, and proved that, as attributed to poetess Dorothy Parker, *"Courage is fear that has said its prayers."*

Those who have seen war, the debris of battle, friends and comrades littered over an area of operation; only they know the horrors

---

[5] Langer, Emily; Washington Post 2 August 2014. Retrieved at:

https://www.washingtonpost.com/national/jon-r-cavaiani-dies-at-70-medal-of-honor-recipient-from-vietnam-war/2014/08/02/bcd24e5a-18bf-11e4-85b6-c1451e622637_story.html of combat. Cavaiani became all too familiar with this fact. As Cicero stated:" *Only the dead have seen the end of war.* " Jon, like so many in the Army who proudly wear their CIB (Combat Infantry Badge), could never forget what his eyes had seen, what his nostrils had smelt, what his ears had heard, and what his body and mind had felt.

Jon Cavaiani did not wear an epaulet like a field officer. But like a seasoned commissioned or non-commissioned officer, he may have seen the tactical situation on a day in June 1971 through a prism, that provides too many images that appear at once as he defended his tiny outpost atop Hill 950. Yet, in the end, he became the Shepherd of his unit. It was as if he, the Alfa Wolf, protected his Pack from the onslaught of demons ascending Hill 950.

Jon Cavaiani's actions on a particular day in June 1971, may have been like The Hyades in the Constellation, Taurus, to the men he was protecting. The "V' formed by this cluster of stars turned the tide for many in that battle from victims to evacuees. Some of the men he protected that day carry a heavy load of remembrance. They are alive today, in their words soon to follow, because of their team leader. Their boss had their back.

Cavaiani's military service has received some public notice. His courageous and heroic combat feats generally receive greater publicity than the fact that he fought trauma, PTSD, and wounds that civilians will never comprehend. Seldom do the facts of his great altruistic work for Veterans – especially homeless and those suffering from PTSD – come to the limelight. When his name is mentioned it is usually addressed only briefly with only basic details of his biography such as:

__Sergeant 5th Special Forces Group - Vietnam__

__POW__

__Medal of Honor Recipient__

__Delta Force.__

Jon, the "Quiet Professional," favored a discussion about the person(s) he was with, rather than about himself. He was extremely humble. His scars were only known to his closest brethren. He was endeared, respected, and beloved by those who crossed his path, with the exception of the jealous, the envious, and the cowardly. To quote Mike Wallace, who knew Jon for almost 25 years, the SGM was a *"Renaissance Man."* The Sergeant Major amassed a cadre of kinfolk, even though unrelated, throughout the country.

It is said that you are either born a willow or an oak. Jon was a hardwood tree with deep complex roots and an abiding faith who would not bend in the winds of convenience. Nor would he allow his maladies to slow him down after Vietnam. And, with every passing day after retiring from the Army in 1990, he continued to be firm in his beliefs, exacting in his performance, and true to the attitude of offering gratitude that he had made it through supreme torment and tragedy.

Prologue

"Our direct connections with the past are fading."
Dick Couch, *By Honor Bound.*

"We need to increase the brightness."
John Siegfried (following Dick's statement*).*

"Down these mean streets a man must go who is not himself mean, who is neither tarnished nor afraid. He is the hero; he is everything. He must be a complete man, and a common man; and yet an unusual man. He must be, to use a rather weathered phrase, a man of honor—by instinct, by inevitability, without thought of it, and certainly without saying it. He must be the best man in his world and a good enough man for any world.

He will take no man's money dishonestly and no man's insolence without a due and dispassionate revenge. He is a lonely man, and his pride is that you will treat him as a proud man or be very sorry you ever saw him.

The story is this man's adventure in search of a hidden truth, and it would be no adventure if it did not happen to a man fit for adventure. If there were enough like him, the world would be a very safe place to live in, without becoming too dull to be worth living in."

Raymond Chandler

An unusual caravan of vehicles sped south out of Philadelphia.

The flashing lights, occasionally accompanied by a blaring siren, drew the attention of those traveling on Interstate 95. To see a hearse followed by numerous cars is not unusual, but in this case, the make-up of the parading vehicles was quite unusual – and the length –the length seemed to be unending.

Those traveling north on I-95 probably slowed and wondered whether or not a dignitary was again, one last time, causing traffic congestion. Those traveling south were moved to the right lanes so that the commuter-lane was open and reserved for the convoy. They also saw on numerous overpasses, American flags draped over the rails as if to honor someone special; and guide them on their way. Several overpasses had people standing, waving Old Glory, with hand over heart or saluting.

Police and Highway Patrol vehicles leap-frogged ahead to block on-ramps until the line of cars, buses, and motorcycles could clear the area. The lead vehicle moved at a rapid but steady pace. At each state line a new set of Highway Patrol vehicles took the post of escort, both fore and aft.

Directly behind the lead vehicle was a hearse, and it was followed by a couple of limousines, which were then followed by two fully loaded busses, and numerous cars. Finally, there was a long line of motorcycles, rolling in off-set pairs down the highway moving at the same pace. Even more strange was that, or it so it seemed, at every on ramp, there were more motorcycles that joined the growing convoy.

Helmeted riders, many with beards showing the gray growth of older bikers made no gestures, no signs of festivity, or the usual signs of a biker rally. If one can ride a motorcycle in a respectful manner, almost at attention, these riders did so.

Those observing the event on that highway through Baltimore, past Silver Springs, and then along the beltway around Washington D. C. surely thought, *"Wow, who is that? Must be someone important."*

Had they known that memorial services had already been held in places like Columbia, Danville, and San Jose, California; in Michigan, Montana, North Carolina, and Wisconsin; and at a well-attended memorial in Philadelphia, with yet another service awaiting at the Arlington National Cemetery Chapel, they would surely have thought, *"That must have been one hell of a human being!"*

Indeed, my friend, indeed!

THE ROOSEVELT GATE AT ARLINGTON NATIONAL CEMETERY

CHAPTER ONE

Welcome To Chaos

"Those who had never seen a tribe of cats at war, or at least playing war games, would look upon what came next as utter chaos"
Jim Butcher

Jon Robert Cavaiani enlisted in the army in 1969 as the country was in turmoil, over whether to support the war or call it quits and leave Vietnam to whatever fate its karma would bring.

"Vietnam started out as a counterinsurgency between the North and the South. The South was primarily Catholicized and Buddhist; The North was Communist. It ended-up with the Americanization of the War."[6]

The French understood the Viet Minh fervor when defeated at Dien Bien Phu 7 May 1954, in what has been called "The First Indochina War." In August 1954, the Demilitarized Zone (DMZ) was established, dividing Vietnam into North and South. This became **THE** boundary between these two zones. It was established at the Ben Hai

---

[6] Summers, Harry G.; <u>Historical Atlas of the Vietnam War</u>. Pg 84; Houghton-Mifflin; Boston/New York; 1995

River, which enters the South China Sea at 17 degrees 0 minutes 54 seconds N latitude. The boundary followed the Ben Hai to its headwaters, about 55 km WSW, and thence to the Laotian border. The area within 5 km on either side of the border was declared to be a demilitarized zone. Troops of both governments were barred (in theory) from this area.

It was not like the bocage the Army had to navigate in Normandy, or even the flat terrain of Tarawa with its deadly coral reef, but similarly difficult due to double and triple canopy where helicopters and planes could not observe the terrain, temperatures that reached into the 120's in some areas, with humidity at a constant 80% minimum. Monsoon season--the wettest months--are from September through December, in most central parts of Vietnam (II – Two - Corps). In the southern portions, called III (Three) Corps (Saigon area), the dry season was December through April. In the North, I Corps (called "Eye" Corps), the temperatures could run the gamut.

Despite early in-roads to gain the trust of the Vietnamese, American presence became a nuisance to many Vietnamese as the war drug on without decisive engagements. Many service people found, upon arriving in country that they were, at best, tolerated. Those who worked more directly with the Vietnamese units and with tribal units such as Montagnard Tribes, were more welcomed. But, as events would prove, no one could feel that they were absolutely welcomed into Vietnam. There was always the eyes and ears of those "friendlies" who could sabotage any U. S. operation. Double and triple agents ran rampant.

Despite the setbacks of the late 1960's, the Communist saber-rattling continued. It was our media who turned the tide of the war by misrepresenting the actual status of on the ground events in Southeast Asia. Ho Chi Minh was willing to sacrifice 10 men for every US serviceman. It worked. Vietnam took the ugliness of war and exposed it in various ways. It was the first war covered on TV, and brought before our dinner trays and lounge chairs. Our Armed Forces had the Sword of Damocles hanging over their head. We had the CIA, the Phoenix program targeting VC and NVA key personnel from their air-conditioned environments and cushioned seats overseeing the war while the grunts, *"11 Bravos"* and muckers faced the enemy danger close.[7] 'Monday Morning' quarterbacks analyzed every operation, and many Americans became numbed to the daily reports as if they were watching a Hollywood production.

Special Forces advisors were present in Vietnam as early as 1955. Numerous Special Forces advisors attempted to convince the CIA and others that Ho Chi Minh was a nationalist who was interested only in Vietnam's independence and autonomy. Minh did not want his country colonized by a foreign government. They (Special Forces) advised that the U. S. should support Minh in his efforts for national sovereignty. However, political interests within the CIA and U. S. political circles promoted Ho Chi Minh as a Communist, and therefore advised against inviting him to any dialogue table. In essence; they drove Minh to the Chinese Communists.

Some have wondered why President Eisenhower sided with the South and why President John Kennedy eventually decided to side, first

---

[7] Webb, James; <u>Fields of Fire</u>; Bantam Books; New York; 1978

with Diem, and then with Premier Tho, who was a pawn of General Duong Van Minh who led a coup against Diem.

Speculation has it that the Catholic Church wanted to maintain a presence in Vietnam. That presence had grown with the involvement of the French in Vietnam for two decades. Kennedy was not a strong Catholic, but his wife Jackie was, and she was French. Influencers, through back-channels, attempted, with some success, to convince JFK to support a government that would be friendly to the Church and its mission endeavors, and more prone to have a dictator with democratic leanings.

In the aftermath of the 1 November 1963 coup that resulted in the murder of President Ngo Dinh Diem, it was Gen. Duong Van Minh, leader of the Revolutionary Military Committee of the dissident generals who had conducted the coup, who took over leadership of South Vietnam.

U.S. Ambassador Henry Cabot Lodge cabled President Kennedy and said: *"We could neither manage nor stop [the coup] once it got started...It is equally certain that the ground in which the coup seed grew into a robust plant was prepared by us, and that the coup would not have happened [as] it did without our permission."*[8] Lodge's words were more than a little disingenuous, since he had long been a proponent of removing Diem from power.

---

[8] This Day In History;

https://thisdayinusmilhist.wordpress.com/2014/11/06/november-6/

Following Diem's death, a Buddhist named Nguyen Ngoc Tho became Premier, but the real power was held by the Revolutionary Military Committee headed by General Minh. The new government earned U.S. approval in part by pledging not to become a dictatorship and announcing, *"The best weapon to fight communism is democracy and liberty."* However, Duong Van Minh was unable to form a viable government, and he was overthrown in a bloodless coup led by Gen. Nguyen Khanh in January 1964.[9]

The speculation that decisions were made based upon the Church's backchannels through Jackie are just that – mere speculation. But for whatever reason, JFK and his staff opted to support a volatile South Vietnam rather than leave South Vietnam to its own karmic fate.

James Schlegel, who served as an Army Specialist 5 in Vietnam reflected some forty years after the war and stated in an interview with John Siegfried the following:

"I've studied the Vietnam War, and it never should have happened. If you do your research and go back far enough, you will find that at the end of WWII, the French wanted to recolonize Vietnam when the Japanese were kicked out. In order to do that, they had to have the support of the United States

---

[9] History.com Editors, General Minh takes over leadership of South Vietnam; A&E Television Networks; November 16, 2009, updated November 4, 2019; https://www.history.com/this-day-in-history/general-minh-takes-over-leadership-of-south-vietnam

government. A Vietnamese, by the name Ho Chi Minh, who was not Communist at the time and who actually helped American flyers and supporters during WWII, begged Truman to keep the French out. Of course, France was the ally and France got our support."[10]

Perhaps it was easier for Presidents Eisenhower and Kennedy to just stay the course that had already been set in motion. According to the State Department's Office of Historian, President Lyndon Johnson and his cabinet fared much worse than previous U. S. Presidents in their attempts to control the future of Vietnam and Southeast Asia.

By August 1964, the Johnson Administration believed that escalation of the U.S. presence in Vietnam was the only solution. The post-Diem South proved no more stable than it had been before his ouster, and South Vietnamese troops were generally ineffective. In addition to supporting on-going South Vietnamese raids in the countryside and implementing a U.S. program of bombing the Lao border to disrupt supply lines, the U.S. military began backing South Vietnamese raids of the North Vietnamese coast. The U.S. Navy stationed two destroyers, the Maddox, and the Turner Joy, in the Gulf of Tonkin to bolster these actions. They reported an attack by North Vietnamese patrol boats on August 2, and a second attack on August 4. Doubts later emerged as to whether or not the attack

---

[10] Siegfried, J.; Six Degrees of the Bracelet: Vietnam's Continuing Grip, p. 98; Xlibris; Bloomington, IN; 2011. Republished 2023 with Amazon Books

against the Turner Joy had taken place.

Immediately after reports of the second attack, Johnson asked the U.S. Congress for permission to defend U.S. forces in Southeast Asia. The Senate passed the Gulf of Tonkin Resolution with only two opposing votes, and the House of Representatives passed it unanimously. Congress supported the resolution with the assumption that the president would return and seek their support before engaging in additional escalations of the war.

The Gulf of Tonkin incident and the subsequent Gulf of Tonkin resolution provided the justification for further U.S. escalation of the conflict in Vietnam. Acting on the belief that Hanoi would eventually weaken when faced with stepped up bombing raids, Johnson and his advisers ordered the U.S. military to launch Operation Rolling Thunder, a bombing campaign against the North. Operation Rolling Thunder commenced on 13 February 1965, continuing through the spring of 1967. Johnson also authorized the first of many deployments of regular ground combat troops to Vietnam to fight the Viet Cong in the countryside. The 3rd Marine Division intelligence estimated the combat strength of NVA and VC forces in the DMZ area in January 1968 was 40,943.[11]

"No different from the pundits planning WWI who failed

---

[11] Milestones, Office of The Historian; U.S. Involvement in the Vietnam War: the Gulf of Tonkin and Escalation, 1964; *https://history.state.gov/milestones/1961-1968/gulf-of-tonkin*

to learn that Civil War tactics would not work with the advent of munitions and ordnance, President Johnson and Robert McNamara never reasoned that nationalism among the Viet Minh, coupled with the guerilla-style warfare we walked into in the early years of the '60's, would not be supplanted by conventional military methods. The McNamara-led Defense Department miss-stepped in measuring both."[12]

In defense of Westmoreland who passed on in 2005, a reader of *The New Yorker* posed a question to the editor in the 12 June 1995 issue: "*If Robert McNamara wasn't smart enough to win in Vietnam, why should we now accept his view that the war was unwinnable?*" And when General Frederick J. Kroesen, who commanded the Americal Division in Vietnam and later served as Army vice chief of Staff, upon reading McNamara's memoirs published in a June 1995 issue of Army, stated:

> "*At no time does he mention the winning of wars; hence, despite President John F. Kennedy's intent to ensure success and President Lyndon Johnson's simple, emphatic 'Win the War' dictum, The Defense Department never produced or even addressed a plan to do so. Instead, all planning was designed to foment a negotiated settlement. Westmoreland's ideas were ignored, overruled, or considered irrelevant.*"[13]

---

[12] Summers, Harry G.; Historical Atlas of the Vietnam War. Pg 84; Houghton-Mifflin; Boston/New York; 1995

[13] Summers, ibid; pg 184

The NVA (North Vietnamese Army) and VC (Viet Cong or Victor Charlie) were the bane of the American ground and air forces in Southeast Asia. The VC also had regular units, just like the Army. The VC and the NVA assaulted our troops with both physical and psychological warfare. Punji sticks, AK-47's, sporadic mortars thrown at our positions in the middle of the night, IED's (Improvised Exploding Devices) made-out of any concoction available); they exemplified continuous hazards as troops were called upon to take terrain, only to leave it and allow the enemy to walk back in and claim it. Then, required weeks later to take the same terrain with more casualties and another retreat.

Sappers charged the basecamps. Their movement was difficult to detect. Often, they were so drugged, that a direct hit hardly slowed them as they kept charging forward. Some of these sappers wore suicide vests that were to be blown once inside the basecamps.

To exacerbate matters, it was difficult to determine who was and who was not an ally or who might be a double agent. U. S. Intelligence too often believed the reports handed to them by agents of the North and / or double agents. Jon Cavaiani would in the future learn this firsthand. Dick James, historian, diarist, and author of four books under the broad title of *Slurp Sends,* notes the following about the situation in Vietnam whereby sabotage, poor intel, disunity, jealousies, and politics undermined the efforts of servicemen on the front lines.

"On 20 June 1969 an event would occur, known as the 'Green Beret Affair,' that would rock the Special Forces community, and placed further vehement hatred in the minds of Green Berets far and wide, when it came to a leg tanker General

by the name of Creighton Abrams, who had always had a vendetta against Special Forces. He did not like airborne units, especially Green Berets. Every chance he got, he either snubbed us or tried punishing us in some fashion.

Among the many Greek-code-named special operations units within Special Forces in South Vietnam was Project Gamma, a covert intelligence collecting operation that focused on North Vietnamese Army and Viet Cong base camps in Cambodia, as well as Cambodian government actions aimed at aiding and abetting those same communist forces. Because Cambodia was, at the time, considered to be a 'neutral' nation, the actions of Project Gamma were thought by some, to be extremely sensitive, politically.

On 26 February 1968, 5th Special Forces Group Detachment B-57 had been transferred from Saigon to 5th Group Headquarters in Nha Trang, also being designated the unit in charge of Project Gamma. Project Gamma was so secretive that personnel assigned to it were given the 'official' cover job of Civil Affairs (CA) and PsyOps (Psychological Operations) officers, assigned to A-teams near the Cambodian border.

In early 1969, it became obvious that a problem had arisen within, or associated with, Gamma. Trusted intelligence agents and intelligence nets began disappearing. It was surmised that the operation had been somehow infiltrated, probably by a double agent. It wasn't until spring of that year that serious irregularities appeared. It was found that some

South Vietnamese Special Forces soldiers had been selling medical supplies and weapons to communist forces.

Shortly thereafter, a Special Forces special operations reconnaissance team operating across the border captured some documents and exposed film in a communist base camp. Upon its return to friendly territory, the film was developed. When analyzed, it appeared that one of the Viet Cong in the photographs appeared to be a Vietnamese Project Gamma agent by the name of Thai Khac Chuyen. In fact, Chuyen's handler, Sergeant Alvin Smith, a non-Special Forces intelligence specialist assigned to Project Gamma, identified Chuyen from the captured photo. It was ordered that Chuyen be interrogated, as well as be subjected to a polygraph (lie detector) test.

Strangely, Chuyen had not been so tested (as per standard procedures) when recruited for Gamma, especially given the fact that he was originally from North Vietnam, still had family there, and had bounced from job to job working with U.S. combat forces in South Vietnam (trouble following each departure). Chuyen was rigorously interrogated, and the polygraph tests administered.

The combination of polygraph tests and sodium pentothal injections (aka 'truth serum'), indicated that he was lying when he claimed he had done nothing that would compromise any Project Gamma security information. It also indicated that he was lying when he denied working for the Viet Cong. In addition, the sessions seemed to indicate that he also might have been working another job, for the South Vietnamese *intelligence service, as a triple agent.* "[14]

It is unlikely that Jon was aware of the historical backdrop of the War in Vietnam when he enlisted. It is likely that he received some training and briefings on the war while he was in the qualification course at the John F. Kennedy Center for Special Warfare located at Fort Bragg, North Carolina. But even with such information, which definitely had a U. S. Army bent to it, Jon was likely still very naïve about the chaos that he was about to enter.

There was no way Jon could see his future. Not only would he, for a while, see a non-combative type of role, which he did not desire but which paid dividends for his life, he would be thrown into a cauldron of hellfire that he could never have imagined. Then, he faced the devil himself in the way of a traitor.

After a fierce battle, a period of escape and survival, only to be captured by his enemy he would be led away by his captors to a life of torment and abuse. And it was then that Jon Cavaiani would come face to face with his betrayer on board a train to a prisoner of war camp. Learning that day that he and his fellow warriors had been betrayed caused the bile to rise in his throat and he vomited.

Such was the chaos in which Jon found himself as he as he disembarked from the airplane that had carried him away from the family farm life into the warzone in Vietnam.

---

[14] James, Dick; email to Mike Evers pursuant to phone conversations; 20 June 2022

CHAPTER TWO

Reflections on Growing Up

"Patience and perseverance have a magical effect before which difficulties disappear and obstacles vanish."
John Quincy Adams

What was it that enabled Jon Cavaiani to survive the hell of Hickory Hill and the torture and treachery while held captive by the egregious Communists Forces? What drove him to continue to fight and survive? Records in his high school yearbooks would indicate that Jon was a lad of strong faith as well as a competitive athlete. According to some, he was an Alpha Wolf. He was a tenacious, persevering individual, who, at times-- was considered domineering. He could be patient with those with whom he was training, helping, and befriending, but impatient with his own performance, or the performance of those who he thought might be slack in their duties. Perhaps we can find some hints as to his strengths and frailties in his early life experiences.

Little is known about Jon's early years. Several sources state that he was born in Ireland and soon thereafter was moved to England. His mother was British, and his father was an American Soldier. At an early age he found himself traveling across the Atlantic to the United States.

One can imagine a young boy traveling by ship across the Atlantic in the late 1940s. It is likely that the morning sun peered over the young boy's shoulder and brightened the skyline rising out of the ocean ahead. Standing at the rail of the liner, the lad was probably in awe. Jon would have likely been alive with excitement as he, his brother, and his mother, among others, sailed past the Statue of Liberty into New York harbor. His nerves must have been jumping with anxiety and his mind ablaze with awe.

His belly must have churned with the mystery of the unknown as the move was bold even for adults. Surely his eyes were bright with excitement: A new life in a new land gave hope of better days ahead. And it may be that, even at his young age, Jon felt the angst that comes with the onus of responsibility. He was the eldest man present in the family and he may have thought himself responsible for seeing after his mother, himself, and his younger brother as they made the long trek from England to California. Jon likely refused to allow his brother to see the doubt and concern that he felt. He would have had to have been the stalwart one of the pair.

Jon Robert Lemmons was the son of Orrin Arthur Lemmons and Dorothy Grace Gresty. The father, who was known familiarly as Pete, was a member of the United States Army stationed in England when he met and married Dorothy. Pete was seldom home as he was fighting in Normandy and France. Therefore, Jon's mother and father were estranged for significant periods of time after their marriage which occurred in early 1943. Jon was born 2 August 1943 and Jon's brother, Carl, was born the following year.

In 1946, Dorothy and the boys were sent by Pete to the United States to live with Pete's older brother, Vernon Lemmons. Vernon and his family lived in Riverbank, California which is now a suburb of Modesto. Adjustment was difficult, especially for his parents. Pete was seldom seen. It was a marriage that could not, and did not, survive the harsh realities of wartime and post wartime struggles. In fact, the father, after having sent his wife and sons to live with his brother, roamed about seeking lasting employment. He was seldom a presence in Jon's life. The parents divorced not long after their arrival in the United States.[15]

At some point, perhaps from birth or somewhat later on, Jon Cavaiani was called Robert, Bob, and Bobby. The use of his middle name (and its associated nicknames) was primary through high school and perhaps even beyond. This predominant name is verified by Pete Laurence, who interviewed Jon, and by Livingston High School Records and Yearbooks.

Jon and his brother Carl lived with their aunt and uncle in Riverbank for about three years. Perhaps those early years, gave Jon – or Bobby - his stoic, *"it is what it is"* attitude and allowed him not to be swayed by hardship and challenge. Those first few years of his life most likely played a key role in preparing him to cope with change, isolation, and hardship.

Jon's mother, Dorothy, met a widower named Ugo Cavaiani who was a farmer only a few miles from Vernon Lemmons' home. She remarried in 1950 to Ugo Cavaiani who took Dorothy and the boys to live at his home in Ballico, Merced, California. Ballico was about fifteen miles from Riverbank.

Life in Ballico was slow. Rather than villages with houses

---

[15] N Y Times and L A Times Obituary - Cavaiani 02 August 2014; and Pritzker Military Museum Interview; (https://www.thenmusa.org/biographies/jon-r-cavaiani/

abutting one another and a constant clamor of people in the streets as she had experienced in Ireland and England, there was but groves of trees and, except for farm equipment growling, silence. The nearest neighbor was a mile away and the workload on the farm was demanding. Breakfast preparation for family and farmhands started at four in the morning, and the food prep and cooking continued through lunch and dinner. She felt like a laborer rather than a wife.

Therefore, Dorothy would, in just a couple of years, divorce Ugo. She abandoned the boys so that the boys stayed on the farm with Ugo. Abandoned by both birth parents, the boys were in effect orphans.

Ballico California Town Center – Photo Mike Evers

Ugo would later marry a woman named Barbara. During a visit to Livingston and Ballico, Mike Evers met with a woman who had attended school with some of the Cavaiani children and she remembered Bobby vaguely. She remembered the girls her age better. Later the woman who Mike met at the Wolfs' Den said that she had been a hairdresser for Barbara S. Cavaiani, Ugo's wife after Dorothy. The hairdresser still referred to Jon as Bobby. She related that Ugo's wife Barbara was very active in the Red Hat Society, taught music, and sang in a women's acapella chorus. She also remembered that Barbara Cavaiani did not consider Bobby (Jon) and Carl to be part of the Cavaiani family. To her they were orphans and nothing more.[16]

It was not until late 1960 that Pete Lemmons gave his consent for Ugo to adopt the boys. Against his latest wife Barbara's wishes Ugo had done so. By this time Pete Lemmons (Jon's birth father) had started another family. Jon never knew his birth father well.

As Jon was growing up, Ballico was hardly even a community. It was more of a county sheriff's speed trap that happened to have a general store, eatery counter, and an icehouse. A few houses sat near the area, but most of the land area was farmed. Peaches, pears, almonds, walnuts were in vogue in the 1950s - 60's.

Santa Fe Road ran north and south through Ballico, and it was paralleled by a railroad track. A few crossing roads, mostly dirt roads, intersected Santa Fe Road and one of those was North Street. About a mile west of Santa Fe Road on North Street was a farmhouse, with

---

[16] Mercando, Elena interview with Mike Evers in Livingston CA. 16 August, 2022.)

several outbuildings. It was the first house on the left off of Santa Fe Road. According to Merced County land records it was built by Ugo Cavaiani in 1943 and was set back among the groves of fruit trees so that it could hardly be seen. The next house, the nearest neighbor, was about a mile further down the street. North Street was just wide enough for one vehicle requiring drivers travelling in opposing directions to negotiate, in a friendly manner, who would pull off to allow the other passage.

There was a small elementary school near the Ballico General Store and Post Office and so Jon and Carl could walk about one mile to school each day. But when they went to Junior High and High School, that required taking a bus into Livingstone. Livingstone, with a population of 2000 in 1960 was a metropolis compared to Ballico, and Livingston had a hamburger and milk shake joint (The Wolf Den) adjacent to the campus. For special occasions the Palms restaurant was a prime after school meeting place, but Jon and Carl seldom had time for those opportunities.

The campus was only about ten miles away, but the trip took almost one hour what with the erratic route to get to each farm family to pick up or drop off students. Tractors and other farming equipment often slowed the bus as it negotiated the narrow roads. Just south of Ballico ran the Merced River with a narrow bridge that required yielding by either of two approaching vehicles. An occasional flood or a broken-down vehicle on the bridge could delay the bus significantly. Jon and Carl lived near the terminal point of the bus route, so they were some of the first on and last off each day.

This required that they hustle each morning to get chores done before the bus came, and required that they get right to work when arriving home in order to have time to challenge homework and get something to eat before going to bed. Ugo employed about 80 people to work the farm and he depended on the boys to assist him in supervision.[17] One thing that Ugo stressed was that those who worked on the farm were to be respected, managed humanely and fairly, and treated as equals – as if they were members of the extended Cavaiani family.

It must have been these early years that toughened Jon. To have hardly known his father and to have been left behind by his mother. Then to be reminded often that he was not a citizen even though he stood for the National Anthem and recited the Pledge of Allegiance to the United States each day at school. And finally, to be told often, *"you are an orphan, you will never own this farm!"* The psychological scars of his early years may have played a role in his developing a drive to excel and survive.

In spite of these gnawing aggravations, Jon loved the man with whom he lived and who taught him so much about work and life. Ugo Cavaiani is the man that Jon credited with having provided a role model for him, and who helped shape his character more than anyone else.[18]

The boys were raised on Mr. Cavaiani's 600-acre farm in the fertile Central Valley of California. They were formally adopted by Cavaiani in 1961, the year before Jon graduated high school, which pleased Jon. He gladly took on the family name of Cavaiani, and had in

---

[17] Op Cit; Pritzker

[18] Op Cit; Living History and Pritzker

fact, even before the adoption, taken on that name with pride. Jon and Carl put in long hours of hard-work each day moving irrigation sprinklers before school, participating in athletics after school, and then performing necessary farm chores upon returning home. Ugo taught them to do what must be done, when it must be done, and in the way that it should be done. There was no procrastinating with nature and therefore farming. Being a farmer required patience with mother nature, but impatience with oneself and one's responsibilities when it came to getting the job done in a timely manner. And perseverance was what it took to succeed and survive in the agri-business world.

Moving irrigation sprinklers was not a "close is good enough" task. The job required precision. Too much water to a fruit bearing tree could cause root rot. Too little water could mean that the plants did not receive enough water and nutrients and would likely die. The loss of one fruit bearing tree was a loss of income. Distances between trees had to be precise and distances between the rows had to be precise. Timing the harvest was precise and movement of produce was precise. One had to do the tasks associated with the job when it was time to do the job. There could be no procrastinating.

Jon learned to be precise, and he learned to be timely. And he gained an attribute that would not let him tolerate laziness. He would call out slackers. If he encountered someone who did not take appropriate action (as he deemed appropriate) he did not hesitate to go past the slacker to the next level of supervision to force the issue. Later on in life, while in the Army he would encounter soldiers and senior Non-Commissioned officers who he termed as "slackers." These were individuals who would leave a job undone - leaving it to the next person.

While in high school, Jon played varsity football, baseball, ran track, starred in school plays, and was the Future Farmers of America Chaplain. In all sports he was a hard charger. The school mascot was, and still is, **"Wolf,"** and the student body is **"The Pack."** Perhaps Jon was the Alpha Wolf of Livingston and that attitude carried with him later in life. And, perhaps it was his faith, as revealed by his willingness to serve as chaplain, that served him well as he had fought for the lives of those with whom he served on Hill 950, fought for his life on Hickory Hill and afterward, enabled him, as a POW, to withstand tortures unimaginable to most, and carried him through the difficulties presented by PTSD and the agent orange induced cancer that he would face.

Number 8 In The Wolfpack Program (Jon) Bobby Cavaiani **(The Livingstonian 1962 –page100)**

Infielder/Outfielder

Bobby Cavaiani

(The Livingstonian

1962 Page 115)

VARSITY TRACK 1962

1st ROW: R. Howard, **R. Cavaiani**, J. Garcia, V. Cole
2nd ROW: R. Cherry, C. Cavaiani, S. Job, D. Ricketts, R. Lohman
(The Livingstonian 1962 – page 116)

FUTURE FARMERS OF AMERICA (FFA)

KNEELING: Left to Right

Oscar Bustamonte, Secretary

Stanley Morimoto, President
Robert Espinola, Vice-President

STANDING: Left to right
Ron McFarland, Treasurer
Alan Hamilton, Sentinel
Bob Cavaiani, Chaplain

(The Livingstonian 1961 page 71)

THE FARMER'S DAUGHTER PLAY
LEFT TO RIGHT: **Bob Cavaiani**, playing the bashful hero, and Grace George playing the role of the innocent heroine.

(The Livingstonian 1961 page 111)

An unusual weather occurrence in Jon's senior year may have foretold of what was to come. It snowed! There was quite an accumulation. Snow is unusual for the central valley of California, Any snow in the valley is very rare. Perhaps it was an omen of things to come for Jon "Bobby" Cavaiani. That such an event would occur in Jon's Senior year of high school, just as he was preparing to step into adulthood, may have been a sign that Jon would live an even more unusual life than he had encountered during his formative years.

Already he had traversed a good portion of the earth having come from the United Kingdom Isles to California, he had been left by both parents into the care of a fruit farmer in the middle of acres and acres of trees, been through all of his schooling as a non-citizen and had yet to be officially adopted into any family. What more could there be?

**THE WOLFS' DEN – A FAVORITE HANG OUT JUST
ACROSS THE STREET FROM LIVINGSTON HIGH SCHOOL
FREQUENTED BY JON, HIS BROTHER CARL, AND
FELLOW WOLVES**

Photo circa 1960 – copy presented to Mike Evers, 16 August 2022
by the owner of the Wolf's Den

Robert Cavaiani

Jon Robert Cavaiani 1962 Senior Photo with his "Fabian" Hairstyle. **(The Livingstonian 1962 page 19)**

Jon was one of one-hundred-thirty-four students in the Livingston High School graduating class of 1962. After high school graduation, Jon attended Modesto Junior College and then at California Polytechnic University studied phenology (the study of cyclic and seasonal natural phenomena, especially in relation to climate and plant and animal life with an emphasis in fruit trees).

Jon was into climate change studies before they became popular. He knew that climate and weather were never static, nor did these phenomena concern themselves with the laws passed in Sacramento or Washington. Climate and weather are constantly in flux and changing. However, climate, weather, and nature had cyclical trends and patterns that could be studied. The studies could lead to more precise timing of planting, more precise irrigation practices, and more precise forecasts, and hopefully more productive harvests. Further, these studies could assist in determining how human behavior impacted climate and potentially quality and yields of fruits and vegetables.

These studies would serve him well later when in Vietnam he assisted and advised the Vietnamese people about how to produce greater crop yields, especially rice.

Jon earned a comfortable job with Occidental Petroleum. One

may wonder how a phenology major would get a job with an oil and gas company. Phenology includes the study of rotting and fossilized plant materials. It also is very engaged in climate change studies, and as we have seen in recent times, perceptions of climate change have had a tremendous effect on the fossil fuel industries. Occidental, like other petroleum conglomerates, was trying to be at the forefront of what was looming on the horizon.

It was that year that Jon married Marianne Johnson. The marriage resulted in Jon's fathering two daughters, but the marriage lasted only four years. It was a difficult marriage from Marianne's standpoint, because Jon was so exacting and so precise in his every activity. Marianne was a bit more laid-back; willing to accept whatever came along and "not rock the boat."

The same year of the divorce, 1968, Jon had become a naturalized citizen of the United States at the age of 26. Some folks may have thought that it was the divorce that drove Jon to enlist in the United States Army, but in Jon's own words…

"I really believed in the United States. It had
given me so much when I did not have anything.
I believed in the National Policy regarding
Vietnam and that we had to try and succeed."

Jon had tried for a few years to enlist, but his 4F status prevented it until he was able to convince a doctor that a letter waiving his bee sting allergy was in the Doctor's interest as well as compliant with Jon's wishes.

President Johnson had upped the ante in Vietnam as well as the headcount of America's young people being sent to Southeast Asia. Jon wanted to serve.

CHAPTER THREE

From Valley to Hills

"The soldier's heart. The soldier's spirit. The soldier's soul; are everything."

General George Marshall

With the Vietnam War raging and the country in turmoil, rather than sit on the sidelines and merely watch as things fomented, Jon Robert Cavaiani felt that he should do his part. He had never been much of a spectator. He preferred to be engaged on the field, or court, of competition. He had played football, basketball, and baseball in high school and was the Northern California wrestling champ in his weight division as a senior in high school. The young man of 26 years of age from the San Joaquin Valley of California drove to Fresno and sought to enlist and serve. He wanted to participate.

> *"Joining the Army was something I always wanted to do. When I enlisted in 1968, they said I had the GT score to enter any career field. I said Infantry. They thought I was crazy. I was 26 years old and tough as nails,"* Cavaiani said, grinning. *"A farm boy."*[19]

---

[19] Baldi, Bob SP4; <u>SOLDIERS: "THE SAGA OF BOXIE (sic) JON"</u> Vol 40., No. 4; April 1985, page 50

In his interview at Pritzker Military Museum, Jon recounts that he was initially evaluated by the military as 4-F, because he was allergic to bee stings. That was enough to rule him unfit for military service. However, Jon was not one who surrendered his will easily. He was persistent in his efforts to enlist, and after a few medical appointments he was able to obtain an appropriate letter, written and submitted by a medical doctor on his behalf, and he was ruled fit for duty. To do so Jon had reminded the doctor that letters from him had aided several healthy young men to be disqualified from military service. Jon was accepted into the Army in 1969; and issued a bee sting kit (which he never used).[20]

Having quit his civilian job with Occidental Petroleum making $80 – $90 thousand dollars a year, he reported for duty at Fort Ord, California, and went through his initial training there. He then completed Airborne training (parachuting) at Fort Benning, Georgia, and then reported to Fort Bragg, North Carolina, for Special Forces training.[21]

The cold nights and hot days of the sand hills and muddy bogs of Camp Mackall, the mountainous terrain of the Appalachians, and the rigorous physical demands of the training, were not a tremendous challenge for Jon, even though he was a few years older than many

---

[20] Pritzker Military Museum and Library; Pritzker Military Presents with special guest MOH SGM Jon Cavaiani

https://www.pritzkermilitary.org/whats_on/medal-honor/medal-honor-recipient-jon-cavaiani-interview

[21] Pritzker, ibid

candidates. His hard work on the farm, coupled with his athleticism, had prepared him for these grueling physical demands.

The intellectual and psychological challenges of Special Forces training were a bit more daunting. Jon was a solid C student in school, but his tutoring by Ugo and the drive to excel instilled in him by his adoptive father proved invaluable as Jon completed the course with relative ease.

Jon's training led to two military occupational specialties (MOS) one of which was Weapons Sergeant. He had a working knowledge with weapons systems found throughout the world with knowledge about various types of small arms, submachine guns, machine guns, grenade launchers, forward-observer procedures, anti-tank missiles, and directing indirect-fire weapons (mortars and artillery). He was well versed in U.S. and foreign air defense and anti-tank weapons systems, tactical training, and range fire as well as how to teach marksmanship, and the employment of weapons to others. He was knowledgeable of conventional and unconventional tactics and techniques. He could function as a tactical mission leader. He had been trained to recruit, organize, train, and advise/command indigenous combat forces up to company size and would be expected to do so.

The other of Jon's MOS fields was medical sergeant. As a medical specialist he specialized in trauma management, infectious diseases, cardiac life support, and surgical procedures, with a basic understanding of veterinary and dental medicine. General healthcare and emergency healthcare were stressed in training. He had attended numerous days of advanced medical training.

Medical sergeants provide emergency, routine, and long-term

medical care for detachment members and associated allied members and host-nation personnel. They establish field medical facilities to support unconventional-warfare operations. They provide veterinary care. They prepare the medical portion of area studies, brief-backs, and operation plans and orders.

The result of the training was that he was awarded the Green Beret and sent to Vietnam as a Special Forces Soldier with extensive medical skills, weaponry skills, combat skills, and survival skills. He was well prepared and assumed that he would be placed on an A-Team and conducting combat missions within just a few days of his arrival in country. He was expecting that he would be a combat soldier.

Jon, like most soldiers on orders to a combat zone, was likely antsy. He had probably heard enough at Fort Bragg to know that already the number of wounded and dead were high. Perhaps the most anxiety creating events in life are those that we have yet to experience. He had studied and tried to prepare himself for the change to come but he was going into an orchard unlike any he had worked – it was an orchard of chaos.

What was difficult for many to grasp was the fact that South Vietnam was not as united as it needed to be in order to wage war in defense of its cultures. There were in fact numerous cultures: Vietnamese, Laotian, Cambodian, Thai, and Montagnard. The Montagnard tribes alone were thirty or more, each with its own unique nuances and lifestyles. These several cultures were revealed in the military structure of Vietnam. Jon was entering a land, an environment, that was rife with cultural clashes.

Within the South Vietnamese Military were various factions. In general there was the **Army of Vietnam (ARVN)** - *Lục quân Việt Nam Cộng hòa* - which was the ground force of the South Vietnamese military. At the time that Jon entered the country the ARVN, who had been reduced to playing a defensive role, was undergoing a transition called Vietnamization in order to upgrade, expand, and fulfill the role of national defense when the American Forces departed. Problematic was that the ARVN had a dual, sometimes conflicting role.

> *Unique in serving a dual military-civilian administrative purpose the ARVN had also become a component of political power and suffered from continual issues of political loyalty appointments, corruption in leadership, factional infighting, and occasional open internal conflict.[22] [23]*

Within the ARVN there was an elitist group of units that too often lorded themselves over other ARVN elements of the South Vietnam ground forces and the minority group forces. These units were the **Army of the Republic of Vietnam Special Forces (LLDB)** - *Lực Lượng Đặc Biệt Quân Lực Việt Nam Cộng Hòa*). The LLDB had unique missions and they were trained in intelligence gathering, sabotage and psychological operations (PSYOPs). Their main duties entailed the recruitment and training of one-to-four-man teams in intelligence,

---

[22] A Brief Overview of the Vietnam National Army and the Republic of Vietnam Armed Forces (1952-1975) (PDF). *Viet Nam Bulletin.* 1969. Archived from the original (PDF) on March 18, 2009. Retrieved July 24, 2022

[23] "Vietnam's Forgotten Army: Heroism and Betrayal in the ARVN". doi:10.1163/2468-1733_shafr_sim170070021.

sabotage, and psychological warfare missions in North Vietnam. Although some minor sabotage and unrest was fomented against the North, the success of these missions was limited and generally poor. Hanoi had declared that all South Vietnamese agents entering North Vietnam were to be captured, interrogated, and killed. Understandably, recruitment was difficult.

Finally, there were units that were made up predominately of minority group personnel. The **Civilian Irregular Defense Group program** (CIDG) was developed by the U.S. government in Vietnam to promote South Vietnamese minorities by way of irregular military units from local populations.

The generally accepted primary purposes for doing so were two-fold:

1. U.S. mission Saigon believed that the South Vietnamese effort to create localized paramilitary units under unified and similar training and operations needed to be bolstered. This could enlist the support of local tribal chiefs and elders who sometimes differed in their loyalties and approaches to the war. The U.S. was attempting an effort in "equalization" as part of its "Vietnamization" programs.

2. The U.S. feared that the Viet Cong (VC) would be able to recruit large numbers of minority troops. It was as if the thinking was: *"We'd rather have them inside our tent pissing out, rather than outside the tent pissing in."* (Legend has it that this was a quote of President Lyndon Johnson referring to a bloc of minority voters in the U. S., not to any groups in Vietnam, but it seems so appropriate here.)

The largest group of Hill People, the Montagnards, had always been treated as third class citizens by the Vietnamese government, which made them prime targets for Communist propaganda and recruiting.

The CIDG program had been devised by the CIA in early 1961 to counter expanding VC influence. US Army Special Forces A Teams (Green Berets) moved into Montagnard villages and set up Area Development Centers. Focusing on local defense and civic action, the Special Forces teams did the majority of the training. Villagers were trained and armed for village defense for two weeks, while localized Strike Forces would receive better training and weapons and served as a quick reaction force to react to VC attacks. The vast majority of the CIDG camps were initially manned by people of ethnic minority (mostly Montagnard).[24]

Montagnards, in general, did not trust and in fact disliked both the North and South Vietnamese, and therefore quickly took to the American advisers. The program was widely successful, as once one village was brought into "the tent," it served as a training camp for other local villages.

Clashes of cultures occurred when ARVN and or LLDB regulars disrespected tribal leaders, abused CIDG soldiers, or tried to relegate inappropriate authority over units made up of minority groups. U. S. Special Forces soldiers, and in fact, any and all U. S. military advisors, had to be astute in handling these clashes. But clashes between tribal

---

[24] Piasecki, Eugene G.; <u>Veritas, Civilian Irregular Defense Group, The First Years</u>; Vol 5, No, 4, 2009

groups of Montagnards could occur as well. R. A. Jones (Col., USA, Ret) in his book, *The Swamp: With an Army Ranger in the Mekong Delta*, tells of a time when two CIDG units almost went head-to-head in a firefight. Even as a solution was being worked out to ease tensions, one of the units set up an ambush to fire on the other as they moved away from the area. Fortunately, no shots were fired, and resolution came through reorganization and new leadership. Neither unit, being at odds with one another, had confronted the Vietcong.

Similarly, Ray Celaya (Maj. USA, Ret.) describes a Montagnard Uprising in 1969 at Trang Phuc where Rhade Montagnards rebelled against their LLDB counterparts and fired on the LLDB in their camp. In fact, the Montagnards executed two of the LLDB officers, in retaliation for abuse and maltreatment of their tribesmen." [25]

The chaos that Jon Cavaiani was entering as he went into Vietnam, and on to his assignment of working closely with people who were deemed to be by some Vietnamese elites as lesser people, or "little people," would require all of his skills. Not only those skills and competencies learned at Fort Bragg, but those learned back home in Ballico from Ugo Cavaiani, and some that he may not yet have developed. Military skills alone would not be enough. He would need the competencies of Cognitive Agility, Cultural Fluency, and Emotional Discernment.

Celaya describes these competencies as follows:

---

[25] Celaya, Ray; The Sit-Rep, Vol 30 Ed 3 May 2021, Montagnard Uprising Christmas Day 1969, Camp A233 – Trang Phuc; *The Clash of Culture*

"Cognitive Agility allows (Special Forces) teams to concurrently assess situations from many perspectives, so they develop the best course of action. Cultural Fluency lets us peek into our audience's cultural soul and its values. Understanding those values informs us how best to fit into their worldview. Emotional Discernment interprets behavior and emotions into cultural values, which are, for the most part, intangible. Understanding cultural values is the entry point to building trusting relationships."[26]

Did Jon possess these skills and competencies? If not, would he be able to develop them and hone them sufficiently to build trust of those with whom he would work? Would he be able to discern cultural values of Tribesmen who were considered "primitive" by some; and could he understand unique cultures that the French, and Vietnamese, had failed to grasp? Would he be the leader and Chaplain that he had been at Livingston high school? Would he continue to rely on his faith?

Because of his significant medical skills, his studies in phenology, and his experiences in agriculture while growing up on the family farm, Jon was initially assigned to a relatively dull position as a veterinarian and agricultural advisor for I Corps (pronounced as 'eye corps' – not one corps) in the mountainous northern region of South Vietnam.

The hills may have reminded Jon of days when he went to Yosemite and other highland areas of California. The hills of Vietnam have a beauty, not unlike the hills and mountains in the US, that

---

[26] Celaya, Ibid

constantly changes over the course of a day as light and shadow help paint nature's beauty. But these hills, in spite of their beauty had hostile side – war – that bred death and destruction of beauty.

The villagers were friendly enough, but Jon learned that there were unfriendly eyes watching and ears listening; he had to be careful. The agricultural and cooperative nature of the villagers may have reminded him of cooperative life in Ballico, so that he adjusted rapidly and fit in nicely. His adopted father had hired 80 – 100 workers, many of whom did not speak English, to tend the orchards back in Ballico, and Jon had been taught by Ugo to work with them, not use them; and to respect them and not belittle them.

The highlands of Vietnam were pockmarked with villages of a tribal people called Montagnards, or Hill People. Jon was comfortable with the small villages because he grew up in a small village. Like Ballico, the younger farmers relied on their elders to advise them on planning, planting, harvesting, and marketing their crops or caring for and raising livestock. The people worked in harmony and cooperation to eke out a living by drawing from what mother nature could provide. The elders were respected and honored just as in Ballico.

His job was to conduct the Medical Civic Action Program (MEDCAP), which is to take the actions necessary to provide veterinary and medical care to the local populations. Throughout the region, he assisted Vietnamese farmers with land agriculture and animal farming, while at the same time he helped treat the local villagers regarding human medical and health concerns. That included delivering babies. This was during the period of the War called "Vietnamization:" to win the hearts and minds of the population, many of whom were native tribespeople.

> *"I left (Fort Bragg) for Nam in late '69. When I got there, they asked: 'Special Forces Medic?' And I said: 'Yep.' They asked: 'Farm boy, right?' I said: 'Yep.' Then they said: 'Well, you are now the agriculture advisor for Military Region One (I Corps) – slash – veterinarian.'* His job was to assist local indigenous populations with their agricultural endeavors. *"We had pig projects and chicken projects. We taught them how to raise more rice on an acre and how to use fertilizers. I did not know a damn thing about chickens, or pigs, or cattle . . . . I mean nothing. But I learned out of manuals and didn't have any major catastrophes. I used to go into their villages and treat their water buffalo then turn right around and treat their children."* Cavaiani said: *"I was naïve as far as the war went. I just did not see much of it."*[27]

Ray Celaya, a Special Forces Medic who served in Vietnam, provides some insight into how Jon might have used his military, medical, and farming skills to win the trust and friendship of the indigenous people with whom he worked.

> *"Interwoven into our training and operating methods was relationship building with the CIDG, the community, and the LLDB. Each team member trained and coached a cadre of CIDG in their specialty. For me, that cadre was the CIDG medics, 8 to 12 of them. As they provided medical services to the*

---

[27] Baldi, Op Cit. Pg 50

broader CIDG group and villagers, we supervised their activities, interacting with that wider group. While not distinctly separated, relationship-building strategies lived within our training and operating methods.

Patrolling operations were, on average, 10 to 15 days long and usually included a CIDG Company, one SF Team member, and one LLDB member. In addition, a CIDG interpreter that spoke both Rhade and English was SOP on all operations. Patrols gave SF Team members ample time to strengthen relationships with the CIDG. We were more than advisors; we were becoming part of their community."[28]

There were 30 different tribes in the Central Highlands of both Vietnam and Laos. The Montagnards, or 'Yards' as their Special Forces/Advisors called them, are a tribal people of the Malayo-Polynesian and Mon Kymer language groups. Between 1962 and 1972, the Montagnards' mountain domain was the scene of some of the most intense fighting in the Vietnam War. Members of both 1st Special Forces and 5th[h] Special Forces Groups (Green Berets) fighting there often bonded with the 'Yards' militia, who were regarded as courageous fighters and fiercely loyal friends. Before the POW/MIA bracelets were introduced nationally at a hotel in 1971 by two women in California, these mountain people issued bracelets to their SF friends. These bracelets were given to U. S. warriors prior to their leaving Southeast Asia, as a memento for their service to them.[29]

---

[28] Celaya, Ray; Interview with Mike Evers, 22 July 2022

[29] Siegfried; Op Cit -The Six Degrees of the Bracelet; pg. viii

With the collapse of the Vietnamese government in April 1975, Montagnards who had cooperated with Americans were viewed with suspicion by officials of the Socialist Republic of Vietnam, often subjected to persecution, imprisonment, or death. Many fled to Cambodia, where they organized a resistance to Communist rule but were ultimately persecuted by the Kymer Rouge.[30]

"Yard" Fighters with a Special Forces operator.

---

[30] Surry Roberts, *Montagnards: NC Pedia,* edited by William S, Powell, UNC Press; Chapel Hill; 2006

Steven Rogers and Carl Thomas pose for a picture with two indigenous personnel. Interestingly enough Rogers is holding a modified RPD machine gun and the "Indig" trooper on the right holds a PPSH-41 submachinegun.

Montagnard Cross Bow, given to John Siegfried 2014 by USA SGM James Meador (from Virginia). Meador taught General

Schwarzkopf artillery at West Point in 1952, while also serving in Korea. A Vietnam tribal chief gave it to Jim, thanking him for providing services to his village. The SGM passed-on 28 October 2014, shortly after gifting it at 84 years old.

Jon endeared himself to the Montagnards, the Hill People of Vietnam. Unlike the Chinese, Vietnamese, and French who tried to take them out of their traditions, Jon, like most other Special Forces soldiers who lived with and worked with them, honored their tribal traditions, respected them and their tribal elders and worked with them to improve their plight as "other people." The Vietnamese, in general, looked down on Montagnards and held themselves to be superior. In return, the Montagnards did not have much trust in the Vietnamese, both North and South of the DMZ.

Jon assisted the villagers with improving yields of rice, a staple of the local diet. And he helped obtain treatments to reduce diseases in water buffalo and chickens. He showed the villagers how to inoculate or otherwise treat their animals for diseases. He found ways and means to provide needed medicines and materials to help improve the health and well-being of the people.

> *"Oh, once in a while I would get a message like, 'Help, my pigs got a hole in it.' So, I would go out, dig out the shrapnel, do a little minor surgery, and put the pig back together."*[31]

Rather than dictate to them what to do and walk away, he

---

[31] Baldi, Op Cit,; Pg 50

listened to them and advised accordingly. Jon lived with and became accepted and trusted by the people with whom he worked and lived. Each village welcomed him as he moved through the region.

"I even started an orphanage while I was a veterinarian. That was ultimately the reason I ended up getting out of the agricultural advisory business."[32]

---

[32] Baldi; Ibid

Montagnard women

Because of the war, there were many orphaned children in the villages. A CIDG Sergeant Major with whom Jon had developed a friendship was brutally murdered by Viet Cong. The Sergeant Major, prior to dying, asked Jon to adopt his son. He did so and then Jon built an orphanage that cared for as many as 30 children. He enlisted monks to serve as teachers and to provide daily care for the orphans. He "scrounged" materials to build and maintain the orphanage.

> *"I knew some guys at CORDS (The Office of Civil Operations and Rural Support, a civilian aid agency under the Command of U. S. Military Assistance Command, Vietnam). They told me that an orphanage was really needed up near Nong Son. I used to travel a lot in that region, so I started one. Bodai monks and nuns ran my orphanage and were caring for 30 orphans. Charlie (the Viet Cong) came in and killed all the kids and all the monks except one, whom they left alive with a warning, 'Bac Si (sic) Jon, stay out of our area. Bac Si (sic) means 'doctor.' Like I said, I was relatively naïve about the war. (Authors note: Bác Sĩ is the appropriate spelling of the Vietnamese word for 'doctor')."* [33]

In addition to CORDS, the Counterinsurgency Support Organization (CISO) – an agency that specialized in meeting the needs of SOG units and indigenous forces – was in country to provide support specifically to Special Forces and SOG, and the indigenous soldiers with whom they worked. Ben Baker spent several years in Vietnam. CISO operated outside of normal military supply chains and often met special needs requests when the bureaucratic logistics agencies could (or did) not.

Baker, a WW II veteran served briefly in General Douglas MacArthur's headquarters staff before putting his skills at organization and logistics to work in the field. In 1963 he was working in Okinawa, when Special Forces Capt. David E. Watts worked to develop the

---

[33] Baldi; Ibid

Counterinsurgency Support Office (CISO) in anticipation of needing to equip thousands of CIDG troops as the Vietnam War escalated. With more than 80 trips to forward base camps in-country to determine specific needs of those forward units, Baker traveled often to numerous countries in an effort to find the most effective suppliers of materiel. Part of CISO and Baker's immense value was their ability to provide support that was both within and outside of normal military channels without the interference of power politics which was rife within the military procurement process.

Baker played an instrumental, and hands on roll in the research, development and production of new highly specialized weapons, uniforms, rations, and equipment. The end users were principally US Special Forces, SOG, other Federal Agencies and indigenous forces operating within and from the Republic of Vietnam. Baker was happy to assist with building orphanages and other such positives.

While the regional veterinarian position was not the warrior role that many imagine all combat roles to be, it was a worthwhile undertaking that won the hearts and minds of the local people. The bond that this young farmer from the Central Valley of California built with the indigenous population he served would pay big dividends later.

Sadly, Vietnam was indeed a war zone. Jon worked very closely with the Montagnards and called them his *little people.* As stated, he had built and developed an orphanage for South Vietnamese children. In retaliation, the Vietcong killed six of the seven monks who ran the orphanage and the more than 20 children to include the Montagnard boy that Jon had adopted. They left word that this was done as a warning for him to get out of the area. This was the pay back for his having worked with the Montagnards and for their support of and fighting alongside of U. S. forces. Many Montagnard villages were attacked by the North Vietnamese Army and the Viet Cong. It was such retaliation that resulted in the killing of many "Yard" orphans, and monks that U. S. personnel had worked with, provided for, and cared for … which included his adopted Montagnard son. Jon mourned heavily for the young boy and reminisced at times later in life about the boy.

Such was the environment that Jon Cavaiani volunteered to enter when he enlisted into the Army. However, the "dull, boring" assignment as a region veterinarian was about to end. Jon would soon find himself going through Recon Training, then lead a platoon on a forlorn hill overlooking Laos.

Numerous reports had come from the outpost located on Hickory Hill (Hill 950) that stated the North Vietnamese units were amassing in the area. Higher echelon commands and the CIA would write off the field reports of such enemy movement as improbable or impossible. The U. S. intel community did not believe the reports from hill 950.

To exacerbate the dangers of duty atop Hill 950, the regular army did not have a plan to provide needed indirect fire in support of the outpost. Those who served there would exist on a 1000 square meter (roughly two basketball courts) outpost without effective artillery support. They would have to declare, "*Molon Labe: Come and get our weapons.*"(as attributed to King Leonidas I in reply to the demand by Xerxes I that the Spartans surrender their weapons). A battle was inevitable, and for the survivors of the battle to come, they would have to engage the enemy, endure an unforgiving environment, and, for those who survived, carry with them the trauma that attacks one from deep inside for the rest of their lives.

Montagnard soldiers setting-up in an A-Team Forward Observation Base (FOB)

For those serving in Vietnam there were a variety of arms that were available for carry. From Colt 45s, .38 calibers, shotgun, grenade launchers, over and under M-16s with M-79 Grenade launchers, and CAR 15s. Some SF hearty souls carried a M60 machine gun. The preferred weapon of many of our Special Forces soldiers was the CAR 15.

Jon Cavaiani with his CAR-15

CHAPTER FOUR

Hickory Hill

"It doesn't take a hero to order men to go into battle. It takes a hero to be one of those men who goes into battle."

General H. Norman Schwarzkopf

Soon after the massacre of orphans and monks, Jon was transferred to the Military Assistance Command Vietnam – Studies and Observations Group (MACV-SOG). His commander was aware that Jon was distraught over the massacre and tried to get Jon to return to the States, apply for OCS, and take a commission. Jon opted to re-enlist, gain a stripe to Staff Sergeant, and remain in Vietnam. He completed one-zero (reconnaissance leader) training, and became involved in clandestine missions across the border of South Vietnam into Laos, Cambodia, and North Vietnam. His instructor in the course was Jim Shorten, who told Mike Evers that Jon was the best soldier in that group of new Recon Leaders.

"I met Jon in late 1970 when he came to B-53 for 1-0 school (Special Operations Team Leader Course). Jon came across as a country boy, well versed in the out-of-doors. Toward the end of the course of training, I was his lane grader

on the field mission. There were eight men on the team, all from CCN (Command Control North) at Da Nang, Vietnam. "We were compromised in the field by the enemy, so I called for extraction. The first chopper came in and picked up 4 men via the STABO Rig. These are 120-foot ropes dropped from a motorized pully inside of the helicopter that we hooked to the top of our shoulder harness. The chopper then would pull us up through the jungle and fly us out to safety. The next chopper came in but there were 5 of us left, so Jon and I hooked up together on one rope. As we lifted up, we saw the enemy on the ground, Jon commenced to fire his CAR 15 at them causing us to go into a spin. Jon was having a great time while I was getting dizzy. I started shooting in the other direction to calm the spinning.

When we returned to base camp, B-53, the camp commander wanted me to make sure all the men were ready to be 1-0 team leaders. I told the camp commander, no way, these men need combat time under their belt before I would make then team leaders. I also told him that Jon Cavaiani was the only one who was close to being a good team leader, but SOG missions are a lot more dangerous than running missions in Vietnam, and they needed to be seasoned SOG soldiers first."[34]

---

[34] Shorten, Jim; Jim Shorten (Jones) <theemeraldsea@aol.com> Date: Mon, Aug 15, 2022, 4:58 PM

Subject: Re: SGM Cavaiani

To: john@johnsiegfried.com <john@johnsiegfried.com>

There were times when, on recon, the teams had to lay low and just let a large force walk past them. Being significantly outnumbered there was no wisdom in engaging the enemy in a firefight. On one occasion, Jon's team came across an unexploded bomb that was designated as extremely sensitive. So as not to set the bomb off, the members of the team dropped all of their equipment, stripped down to bare butt nakedness and called for a helicopter extraction at a point well away from the bomb. Their radio call for extraction ended with, *"Be on the lookout for the naked guys running to the PZ (Pickup Zone)."*[35]

Later, on another recon mission Jon was wounded. He was sent to a field hospital for treatment and recuperation. After convalescing, he voluntarily extended his tour of duty in South Vietnam for another year.[36]

Jon's next assignment was to lead a platoon at a remote outpost called "Hickory" which was near Laos where it meets what was the border of North Vietnam and The Demilitarized Zone (DMZ). "Hickory" was perched just below Hill 1015 and above Hill 915 and was designated as Hill 950. Hills in Vietnam were measured in meters. A U.S. Marine unit had previously held the camp but determined it to be untenable. Prior to Jon's assignment to Hill 950 ("Hickory"), Sergeant First Class Robert Noe had the dubious assignment of security

---

Forwarded to Michael Evers evers.michael.b@gmail.com Oct 6, 2022 for insertion

[35] Pritzker, Op Cit

[36] Living History of Medal of Honor Recipient Jon Cavaiani; interview at: ***https://youtube.com/watch?v=4SeTr-itHkc&feature=share***

responsibilities on that hill for a period of time. His comments, regarding the site follows:

"During the briefing before I assumed command of the defense of Hickory, I was told that when it is 'socked in,' the only fire support we could call on would be the 175mm Self Propelled Gun Battery stationed at Camp Carroll. These guns had a 20-mile (sic) range. When I plotted the distance from Camp Carroll, I discovered Hickory would be at the outer limits of the field of fire and thought to myself, who the hell would call in 175[mm] at this distance unless it was absolutely the last resort as any attack on Hickory would be in close, I mean Very Close, so any thing (sic) being fired from a long distance would not be that effective or precise for the needs of anyone defending such a small spot. Often while on Hickory, I would look to Hill 1015, realizing it gave outstanding indirect fire onto Hill 950 and could not for the life of me figure out who the hell would occupy the lower hill, giving any advantage to the enemy if he were to occupy 1015. Little did I know that the Marines had lost 950 for the same reason and later SOG would also. During my stay, I kept all my mortars directed toward the top of 1015 and conducted random firings on it and over the other side and other areas on 1015. Once Khe Sahn fell to the North Vietnamese in June of 1968, Hickory was a [solitary] very small dot on the map and deep in enemy held territory and anytime the enemy wanted it, they could take it, there are many times the hill was completely 'socked' in by low clouds and there would be no air support and you couldn't see crap, much less hill 1015 where the

enemy would surely position themselves to take Hickory. The enemy could lock down the Americans on Hickory by indirect fire, walk down 1015 and across to Hickory. To me, it was just a bad place to be, a bad, if not impossible hill to defend, but that is the way it was. My tour on Hickory was June thru mid-July 1970. "[37]

Hill 950 or Hickory Hill (formerly named Lemon Tree) was located north of the abandoned Khe Sanh Combat Base. It was CCN's top secret radio relay outpost atop of hill 950 established to observe enemy movement and monitor and relay radio transmissions from SOG teams' operating in Laos. It was the final allied presence in the northwest South Vietnam after the siege of Khe Sanh during the summer of 1969 (Captain George R "Randy" Givens of CCN was given the mission of re-establishing Hickory as a CCN radio relay site, the site also housed the Army Security Agency's Top Secret "Explorer" system and was monitored by two ASA personnel) until it was finally abandoned on 5 June 1971 when it was over-run by enemy forces. Jon Cavaiani was the Security Force Commander that fateful day, putting up a fierce counter-defense for two days.

Authors note: On 4 June 1971 Captain Valersky was the ASA officer responsible for the operation of the Explorer system and he had two readers on site with him. Jon Cavaiani was the person responsible

---

[37] Noe, Robert L.; et al; *The Drop: Assault on Hickory Hill, June 1971;* Special Forces Association Fall Ed.; Fayetteville, NC; 2013

for security of that three-man team and the top-secret equipment. Cavaiani had a few other Green Berets, and about 60 Bru Montagnards for which he had leadership responsibility.

Map of Vietnam

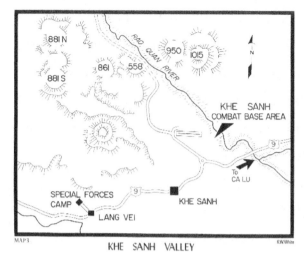

Hickory Hill (950)
Near Khe Sanh
and the DMZ
(The Assault on
Hickory Hill: Noe)

Hickory, (April/May 1971)

Authors' note: The following account of the battle of Hickory Hill is a compilation from numerous sources to include: Interview notes presented by Pete Laurence; *The Assault on Hickory Hill – June 1971.*" as it appeared in the Special Forces Association's Fall 2013 edition of periodical "The Drop"; Living History of Medal of Honor Recipient Jon Cavaiani video*; Interview with Jon Cavaiani by Pritzker Military Museum; Library of Congress; BOARD OF INQUIRY: SGT CAVAIANI;* McKim, Keith; *Vietnam: Green Beret SOG Medal of Honor Recipients*; Yucca Creek Records, 2015; Medal of Honor recipients – Vietnam (A-L)". United States Army Center of Military History https://www.youtube.com/watch?v=4SeTr-itHkc&authuser=0;

The National Museum; https://www.thenmusa.org/biographies/jon-r-cavaiani/; various obituaries regarding Jon; and the Citation as presented to MOH Recipient Jon Robert Cavaiani. No slight is intended toward any previous recounting of this battle, and we hope we have compressed the thoughts of many into these few pages. Additional citations presented as appropriate.

A saddle ridge connected the two hills of 1015 and 915 with a small rise in between designated as hill 950. These were about six kilometers north of Khe Sanh, a sight of several fierce battles, the most famous being The Siege that lasted 77 days before the Chinese New Year in January 1968. With a commanding view of the terrain for miles, the mission of the occupants was to conduct reconnaissance, maintain a radio relay site, and monitor enemy movement into South Vietnam.

The tiny camp was about 20 meters wide and 50 meters long, clinging to a ridgeline like an old saddle on a bony nag. There were steep cliffs on two sides, a fairly sharp-drop-off on the third side, and on the fourth side a gentle upslope toward the peak of Hill 1015.

Vegetation along the rocky ridgeline consisted of trees (single canopy) with lush undergrowth. The vegetation was sparse enough to allow for unobstructed view of the valley floors on three sides. The camp was surrounded by rolls of concertina wire and a thick earthen berm. In the perimeter, there were tall radio antennas, a small helipad, and a few sandbagged bunkers for storage, sleeping, and protection.

The purpose of the tiny outpost located within enemy held territory was to monitor movement of enemy forces into and out of south Vietnam. Sophisticating sensing devices enabled a small team of Americans to monitor the sensors, read the data coming into the "Explorer" system and report findings to higher headquarters. Captain Valersky was the senior individual of that team and he had two readers, Specialist 4 Robert Garrison, and Specialist 4 Walter Millsap.

Jon and his platoon had responsibility for providing security for this team and for ensuring that the highly sensitive equipment of "Explorer" did not fall into enemy hands. The Russians and Chinese Communists had been trying for years to get this technology and would have paid a hefty price to North Vietnam officials for the capture of one of these systems.

When Jon arrived, the camp was in desperate need of much work to fortify and strengthen its defenses. Jon called for and received a team of Seabee's (US Navy term for the Combat Engineers) to assist with fortifying the small encampment by replacing concertina wire, rebuilding the berms and bunkers around the small encampment, and reinforcing perimeter barriers. With Cpt Valersky's calls to his higher headquarters a team of army engineers also came to help fortify the bunkers and berm around the perimeter, but for some reason the request for more concertina wire was not honored. All of this in June 1971.

Hill 950 – Hickory Hill – After Jon and his crew fortified the hill.

Jon's "Pack" of warriors responsible for securing the listening team and the position to which they were assigned consisted of Sgt Robert Jones (John Robert Jones), Sgt Roger Hill, SGT Ralph Morgan, Sgt. Larry Page-- all Special Forces qualified; a forward observer, 2nd Lieutenant George "Skip" Holland (attached from A Battery, 8/4th Field Artillery) and finally about sixty Bru Montagnards. The forward observer was there to communicate with artillery support units and call for artillery fire as needed. A significant problem was that Hickory Hill was at max range for supporting artillery fire. Significant artillery fire support was unlikely, and gunships were a poor option due to time on target and quite often, limited visibility.

The Explorer team reported significant movement of men and equipment coming from the north and moving south. These reports were either ignored or disbelieved, for no interdiction was taken by U. S. or South Vietnamese forces. After about one month, the team on Hickory had strong indications that the enemy had plans to attack and take the hill as they saw significant enemy activity in the area.

Despite being at an elevated location, or perhaps because of the elevation, fog, at times, would set in limiting visibility. The morning of 4 June 1971 was such an occasion. During the night, a heavy fog had limited visibility around the perimeter. Even when using night vision goggles designed to see in limited light – such as starlight on a moonless night – the visibility was almost nil.

That morning the fog was reluctant to burn off as if wanting to hang over the hill like a blanket of fluffy snow. The winds were too light to move it away and the sun was slow in dissipating the mist. Sgt Roger Hill and three others were outside of the perimeter checking security around the lower helipad. Visibility began to improve and that is when they began receiving small arms fire. NVA forces atop Hill 1015 started firing rockets down into the area. Sgt. Hill was wounded in the hand.

Ralph Morgan grabbed his M-16 and began returning fire to provide the four men opportunity to rush back into the perimeter. He rushed to an M60 machine gun that offered greater suppressing fire against the enemy on Hill 1015. Sp4 Millsap manned another machine gun and began to place fire onto the hill and saddle ridge. He then assisted a wounded officer and protected him when a rocket round exploded nearby.

In the early hours of the battle, Cpt Valersky, 2nd Lt Holland, Specialist Millsap, and Sgt Hill Were wounded.

Sgt. Roger Hill from Jon Cavaiani's picture Files

As visibility improved in the morning light, the men inside the perimeter of Hickory could see Chinese-made claymore mines facing them, placed just outside of the perimeter wire. The lifting of the fog allowed them to see, what appeared to be a battalion of enemy (700 plus in number) dug in only forty meters away!

On this day, the farmer from Ballico, California who had enjoyed working with local villagers in their farming endeavors, and who was trained to provide medical care and who had done so much for the indigenous people of nearby villages, would be required to do things he never dreamed of doing. He would have to fight for his life and for the lives of his fellow Special Forces members, and for the people of the Montagnard villages who he had grown to love.

The battle was fierce! The green clad enemy were scampering, firing, and charging ahead in a mélange of terrifying assaults. Some of the enemy had gained the ridge above the camp and this high ground allowed them an unobstructed view of about seventy percent of the camp. Those on this high ground rained direct fire down onto the camp.

Rocket propelled grenade (RPG) launchers poured rockets into the perimeter. These also included B-40's and 2.75 rockets, as well as rifle and machine gun bullets. The rounds peppering down limited the Green Beret men and their indigenous mates from maneuvering into better positions to gain advantage and return well-aimed fire.

(Later in life Jon would reflect, saying; *"I couldn't outrun 'em, so I had to fight 'em!"*). And fight he did.

Jon immediately jumped to the .50 Caliber machinegun and began firing at the claymores to neutralize them. This also prevented an all-out rush by the enemy. The .50 Caliber quickly overheated due to the rate of fire, and Jon had to stop to adjust the headspace and timing. As he was doing so, Specialist Milsap, the ASA reader stepped up and asked if he could man the .50 caliber weapon. Jon asked if he had ever fired a .50 caliber machine gun and Milsap responded in the negative, *"But you're a Green Beret, you can teach me in three minutes."*[38]

Milsap was a large man who wore coke-bottle glasses, but Jon quickly instructed him on how to operate and fire the weapon and told

---

[38] Pritzker; Op Cit

him to keep the thing pointed at the enemy. As he then turned the big gun over to Milsap, he realized what the young soldier had done; he had essentially sent a message to Jon to get back to commanding the defense of the hill. Jon raced from position to position. It was doubtful that Jon knew at the time, but it mimicked the actions of Captain Roger Donlon on 6 July, seven years earlier, at Camp Nam Dong. Captain Donlon was the first Army Medal of Honor recipient of the Vietnam War.

At each position he quickly assessed the men, their supplies, and their medical needs. As he moved, he coordinated air-support, provided medical treatment, re-supplied the men with ammunition, and encouraged them to keep fighting. He seemed to be everywhere, all at once.

At one stop he grabbed a M-79 Grenade Launcher and lobbed a dozen or more grenades at the scurrying enemy. Then he grabbed a M-60 machine gun and threw it up onto the berm; when no return fire was observed he rose, aimed, and fired. He repeated this move a few times, but on one such occasion his face was bloodied by shrapnel from a grenade. Still, he continued-on, ignoring any pain or discomfort.

Jon ran back toward the .50 caliber machine gun because it had stopped firing. As he approached he saw that the berm had been hit just in front of the gun and it had fallen forward. Milsap, a rather large man, was standing up hugging the gun and trying to pull it back into position. Jon arrived and helped him and then saw that Milsap had taken quite a bit of sandbag fiber and sand to his face. It looked as if Milsap's face had been sandpapered. Milsap told him that he could not see. Jon reached up and took Millsap's coke-bottle thick glasses off his face at which time Milsap told him *"Ah, that's a little better."* Jon asked if he had a second pair and Milsap told him they were located in his bunker, so Jon ran and got them. With replacement glasses Milsap once again manned the big machine gun.

At one point, Jon recalled that some of their ammunition was still near the helipad and exposed to the enemy. Braving a torrent of bullets and explosions, he led a few men to the helipad, and they pulled the ammunition into a bunker.

Then the enemy began zeroing their mortar rounds, which had been off target, into the camp showering shrapnel and debris everywhere. More than one-hundred mortar rounds impacted in the small camp.

Jon realized that the only way to get any relief from the barrage was to return counter-battery fire on the enemy mortars. He counted the number of thumps from the mortars on the hill which told him how many rounds had been fired (three). When the third mortar round exploded, during a brief pause in the explosions, he raced out with a stick and a compass to poke holes in the impact point of the last round. This effort would help determine a reverse azimuth on the enemy mortars lobbing rounds into Hickory. It was an expedient, not a precise, method. With this type of expedient direction and distance guide to help estimate the locations of enemy mortars, he directed the four-deuce (4.2in) and .81mm mortars at the enemy mortars. The process was a long shot, but the effort was successful in silencing at least one of the North Vietnamese mortars.

Jon was wounded several times, by shrapnel. The camp's antennas had all been blown down, parts of the berm were destroyed, and a supporting Cobra gunship (an attack helicopter) had been blown out of the sky. Though they fought determinedly, fending off continuing assaults, the camp was pulverized. Nightfall was approaching. These conditions led Jon to a decision to have as many survivors as possible extracted by air.

The position had become untenable. Cpt. Valersky directed Sgt. Page to call for medivac, then rapidly changed the direction to full extraction. Page called the Special Forces Mobile Launch Team requesting immediate assistance. To Sgt. Page the call for extraction was a demand, but to a desk jockey sipping on a cold Pepsi in an air-conditioned structure, it was a request. Shortly they received a response from a voice on the radio to go ahead and prepare for extraction; choppers were on the way. Three helicopters were dispatched.

Cobra gunships and F4 Phantoms preceded the medivac helicopters and placed suppressing fire on the enemy positions. Two medivac helicopters rolled in, one being *My Brother's Keeper* and the other *Curious Yellow*.

On the ground, Jon's "pack of wolves" skillfully provided covering fire as Jon guided the choppers, one at a time, into the camp, to extract the men out of the camp. Just prior to climbing on board the first chopper, Cpt Valersky directed the destruction of the Explorer equipment and all sensitive items in the bunker. Jon directed Sgt. Page to do so, and Page immediately ran to the site and ignited the prepositioned thermite sheets fed by oxygen tanks that lay atop the equipment. The equipment in the bunker was soon reduced to ash, slag, and melted plastics.

As Warrant Officer Dave Hansen lifted off in *Curious Yellow*, some men were hanging onto the helicopter skids, but none-the-less, they got on board safely. While on the ground the chopper had taken a few rounds and shortly after liftoff a white smoke began to tail the chopper. Chief Warrant Officer 2 Steve Woods watched Curious Yellow as it left a trail of vapor. Woods aborted his descent into Hickory and followed the damaged chopper. Hansen was able to make an emergency landing and *My Brother's Keeper* touched down nearby to take on all been on board *Curious Yellow*.

Later in the day, slicks (unarmed UH-1H helicopters came in and took a few more off of the hill, even as the battle still raged. Sgt. Page, Sgt. Morgan, and SP4 Garrison were included in those who were evacuated. Morgan later said that he tried to convince Cavaiani to leave the hill and leave the Bru Montagnards behind.

> *"[I] did not understand why they (Cavaiani and Jones) refused to leave because the Hill was going to fall. There was no way it could be defended any longer as . . . [I] was the last defender on the east, facing Hill 1015, fighting with a M-60 [machinegun]. Now there was nothing defending the saddle between Hill 1015 and Hill 950, and the enemy could just walk across... Cavaiani directed the helicopters that evacuated U.S. servicemen and indigenous Vietnamese who were fighting with them. But he remained behind. 'That will tell you the most about Jon,'* Ralph A. Morgan, a sergeant in the Special Forces who served with Cavaiani on Hickory Hill, said in an interview."[39]

Photo left: Ralph Alexander Morgan who was 1-1, 1-0, of RT

---

[39] Langer, Op Cit

[Reconnaissance Team] Rhode Island, and 1-0 of RT [Reconnaissance Team] Connecticut 1970-1971. Morgan was on Hickory with Jon Cavaiani.

Note: 1-0 designates a trained Recon Team Leader and 1-1 designates Recon Ream Radio Operator. Morgan had trained in and was designated as capable of serving in either role.

For the eighteen defenders remaining on Hickory Hill the odds were estimated to be 23 to 1.[40] At about sixteen-hundred hours a U. S.

---

[40] McKim, Keith; *Vietnam: Green Beret SOG Medal of Honor Recipients*; Yucca Creek Records, 2015

Airforce "Jolly Green Giant" helicopter was seen coming towards them out of Thailand. That chopper was more than sufficient to pick-up the remaining force on the hill. Jones, Cavaiani, and the Montagnards remaining on the hill could load as the helicopter hovered with the blades spinning and the ramp lowered near or on the ground on the backside of the hill.

But then, the chopper turned around and with only a brief message via radio turned and departed without final approach to Hickory Hill. Some write ups said that the Jolly Green Giant was called back due to inclement weather. In his interview with Pritzker Military Museum, Jon recalled that he could see the bird clearly, he was sure that the pilots could see the hill, and even as the sun set that day, Jon had no problems with visibility. It was a clear afternoon.

The pilot, with seemingly tears in his voice, had told Jon that the mission to pick them up was aborted; the pilot and crew were under threat of court martial by the commander who called off the recovery craft. A "territorial commander" had called for the chopper to "cease and desist." That commander's feelings had apparently been hurt, because no one had asked his permission for the helicopter to enter "his space."[41]

Richard Whitaker and his team sat aboard several slicks ready to go in and extract the few men remaining on Hickory Hill. The blades were turning, and they were armed and ready. The craft never lifted off. The extraction mission was aborted, and no reason for the abort was provided.

---

[41] Pritzker; Op Cit

Morgan had asked that he be allowed to stay with them, but Cavaiani, the ranking NCO, ordered him to leave, saying that he and Jones would remain with the Bru pack. The last chopper to leave the hill that day was full. There remained with Jon and Jones sixteen Bru Montagnards. As night was coming on, and with it the blinding fog accompanying it, there would be no more attempts at extraction from within Vietnam.

Jon and his fellow soldier Jones could have been on one of those loads that departed Hill 950 that day. The Americans could have left the Montagnards to fend for themselves and then escape and evade as best they could. But Jon chose to remain behind with his remaining few men. In an interview with Pritzker Military Museum much later in life, Jon essentially stated, in essence, that *"Because my little people (Bru Montagnards) bleed just like I do, I was determined to remain on the ground to help them."*[42]

As daylight faded into darkness and with increasing enemy fire, there were no more helicopters coming for further extractions. Eighteen residents of "Hickory" remained to defend the small bit of ground through the night.

Jon's actions throughout the day had led to the evacuation of most of his men and now to a prolonged defense of the outpost with but a few men. It seemed immanent that an overwhelmingly larger enemy force was sure to annihilate those who remained on the ground atop Hickory. Still fighting for their lives were sixteen Montagnards, another Special Forces Sergeant from Texas named John Jones, and Jon

---

[42] Pritzker; Op Cit

Cavaiani. Jones may have tried to make a joke of the situation by saying, *"This is our Alamo."* But if he did so it was unlikely that anyone laughed.

In an attempt to hold onto the back half of the camp, Jon crawled to the front half and prepared a boobytrap to greet the next assault wave. He rigged a 105mm artillery round so that he could detonate it at the appropriate time. He placed mortar rounds and other equipment around it so that these too could cause harm and/or be damaged beyond use by the enemy. Any remaining equipment that might be useful to the enemy, he destroyed using thermite grenades.

Then, for the first time in Jon's combat experience, he strapped on a steel helmet. He then issued more ammunition and encouraged the men to dig a little deeper. It was his intent to make it very costly to the enemy when they again assaulted. Perhaps it was *"Alamo,"* Vietnamese style.

At about eight o'clock in the evening, just as the sun was setting, the enemy renewed its assault on the small camp. The few men remaining in the camped braced themselves and returned fire as best they could. The odds were about twenty-three to one in the NVA's favor. A front row of enemy fired automatic weapons while a second row lobbed grenades over their heads as they advanced. The Montagnards and two Americans returned fire, but the advancing enemy breached the wire, crawled up and over the berm and swarmed into the front part of the camp.

That was when Jon detonated the artillery round creating a huge crater and literally blowing several of the enemy off the ridgeline. With that huge blast the enemy retreated. During this lull, Jones rose from his position near the mortar pit and scampered back to Cavaiani's position on the western perimeter. They then moved to the remnants of a bunker to try and consolidate their efforts.

However, about two hours later, the North Vietnamese and Viet Cong renewed their assault. At first, they came in groups of about ten or twelve, moving more cautiously than before in case there were more boobytraps. As their confidence grew, they began to send wave after wave of about fifteen attackers every fifteen-minutes or so.

Because Jon had set the few remaining men in positions that created a crossfire along the bottlenecked entry into the back part of the camp, many enemy soldiers were killed and wounded. It was a long night of human wave assaults. It was danger close. After each assault, during the few moments of respite; wounded would be tended to, and ammunition redistributed.

There were no bombers or fighter aircraft available for support. However, Jon was in contact with a Stinger orbiting overhead. It was a C-119 with a Gatling Gun that would put bursts of 7.62 rounds on the perimeter. The Stinger also dropped illumination flares. The flares gave an eerie effect to the life and death drama.

Jones manned the radio communications, while Jon and the Montagnards fought gamely. Jon used the machineguns and focused the direction of fire of the remaining few. Through the night they withstood the incessant barrage of rocket fire, mortars, and small arms fire; they beat back wave after wave of charging enemy.

Shortly after 0500 hours, but just prior to the NVA breaching the perimeter in mass, Jon and Sgt. Jones passed the word to the Montagnards to try and escape off the mountain. Knowing that they could not hold out much longer, Jon ordered the Montagnards to *"di di mau"* (boogie out of the camp) and had Jones call for the Stinger to fire on their position. As they all headed over one of the steepest slopes of the hill, Jon was shot in the back near the spine. His men came back to help him, but he ordered them to go. He covered their escape with blazing M-60 machine gun fire.

When the enemy took control of Hickory. Jon had Sgt. Jones contact the Stinger and have them fire on the camp again as they dove into a sandbagged bunker. For some unknown reason, the Stinger did not fire on the enemy swarming the hill. The fire power of the Gatling Guns on board the stinger would have likely annihilated the swarming NVA and allowed Jones and Cavaiani to escape. With no Stinger support firing directly on the hill, the two Americans huddled in the small bunker, about seven-by-seven feet in size, and waited. The bunker had a thick sandbagged cover and only one trench-like slit for entry and egress. Patiently they waited for the inevitable moment of their discovery, preparing to kill silently with their knives or more likely, to be killed by the enemy.

The enemy death toll was somewhere between three and four hundred. The North Vietnamese were initially so excited about taking the hill that they failed to search the bunkers. But then, two of them came to the access and entered one at the time. Jon let the first man go past him, then swiftly killed the second man with his Gerber. Jones took on the lead man, but in that struggle, despite killing the North Vietnamese soldier, shots were fired, which alerted the enemy above. One of these two NVA soldiers was the son of a NVA Colonel. Jon would pay dearly for that later.

Hearing the rifle fire, the enemy soldiers above reacted quickly. A grenade was thrown into the bunker, and it was deafening. Jon was wounded, again, by the grenade's shrapnel, and Jones was wounded severely. Realizing that they were surely trapped, Jones crawled out of the bunker to surrender, but he was killed immediately by a North Vietnamese soldier. Another grenade was tossed into the bunker to finish off anyone else inside. Only Jon remained and the blast deafened him and caused more hemorrhaging. It also destroyed the last line of communication for Jon back to his friends at it tore apart their one remaining radio. Up until that time, Americans in the Stinger above and back at Special Forces Headquarters had been monitoring the entire battle, hearing everything up to the final grenade.

Hours later, after morning fog had burnt off, reconnaissance aircraft could see the outpost and confirm that it had indeed been overrun; Hickory Hill was now in the hands of the enemy.

Per records of the Library of Congress under the heading of BOARD OF INQUIRY: SGT CAVAIANI, JON R., JONES, JOHN R., WITNESS STATEMENTS[43] the following gives a clearer picture of the chaos in which Jon Cavaiani and John Jones found themselves.

On 3 August 1971, a Board of Inquiry was convened to determine the status of Sergeants Cavaiani and Jones. Witness statement

---

[43] *Congress, Library of; MANUSCRIPT/MIXED MATERIALBOARD OF INQUIRY: SGT CAVAIANI, JON R., JONES, JOHN R., WITNESS STATEMENTS (e-location at -*
https://www.loc.gov/item/powmia/pwmaster_76566/

had been gathered from U. S. personnel and Montagnard personnel who had been evacuated from hill 950. These were presented to the board and reviewed. A document dated 9 June offers that 11 CIDO's were interviewed and that nine of the eleven had seen SSG Cavaiani under intense small arms fire and B-40 rocket fire. One CIDO stated that he saw SGT Jones lying on the ground near a mortar pit. None of the CIDOs could confirm the death of either Cavaiani or Jones. Several of the statements appear below:

Major Herold B. Quarino provided the following:

> *"Last contact with US personnel was established 0505454 (sic) Jun '71, at that time the radio operator stated in a whisper, 'They are two feet from me, out.' A FAC [forward air coordinator] came on station 0506034 (sic) but could not establish radio or visual contact at that time. On 051250 – 051305H Jun 1971 a UH-IH flew a VR [visual reconnaissance] over the site with good visibility and observed no personnel or bodies. On 051525H a UH-1H flew within 150ft of the site. On 051730 an attempt was made to insert a rescue force on the site. The attempt was aborted due to heavy enemy ground fire. The E&E [escape and evasion] route was not flown on 06 Jul due to unworkable weather."*

Larry Page's statement reads:

> *"When I left the site Sgt Jones and Sgt Cavaiani were in good condition. Sgt Cavaiani had suffered a minor frag wound to the left side of his face at approximately 1700hrs. Both men were located at the west perimeter organizing their people for*

extraction this time was approximately 1630. (sic) [pen and ink correction made to reflect hours and initialed]."

Roger Hill's statement reads:

"The last time I saw SGT Jones, and SGT Cavaiani was on or about 1130 on 4 June 1971. Both were in good health and spirits. They were both in the process of re-organizing troops and ammo, while also taking care of the wounded."

A transcription of Ralph Morgan's statement follows:

"At approximately 1945 on 4 June I departed the radio relay site, on the last extraction of the day. At this time, I saw SGT Cavaiani and SGT Jones both in good health. However, SGT Cavaiani had suffered a fragmentation wound to the face and both men were in low spirit. I was the last American to see either of these men."

A statement taken by a U. S. Army officer from a Montagnard soldier named Tung states (through a translator):

". . . . CMD Tung states that he witnessed one American with a mustache (Sgt Cavaiani) being shot by an NVA, from close range, with remaining American at the vicinity of a mortar pit, receiving a heavy volume of SAF(small arms fire) and hand grenades."

A different soldier named Tung wrote his own statement and signed his name in cursive:

"At 0400 hours I was in a bunker on the west side of the radio

relay. I saw SGT Cavaiani fire his CAR-15 at an NVA soldier and kill him. Another NVA, approx. 3 meters from SGT Cavaiani fired an AK-47 and I saw SGT Cavaiani fall to the ground. At approx. 0500 hours I saw SGT Jones crawling to the mortar pit in the center of the perimeter. The last time I saw SGT Jones he was near the mortar pit and receiving many hand grenades and small arms fire. The hilltop was covered with fog, and I could not see well. I left the hill at 0510 hours."

Yet another CIDG soldier named Ai-Ta provided the following through an interpreter about what he observed on the morning of 05 June 1971:

"From his bunker on the western perimeter, CIDO AI-TA OBS one American lying on the ground near a mortar pit inside the perimeter. He observed a possible B-40 rocket, or mortar round explode 2 to 3 feet from the American. CIDG AI-TA also observed one other American lying near the western perimeter, and SAF [small arms fire] fire being placed on and around the American."

A CIDG soldier named A Van provided the following:

At 0530 hours 5 June 1971 I saw enemy advancing and saw SGT Cavaiani kill or wound 25-30 enemy with M-60 MG fire. Approximately 2 minutes later SGT Cavaiani was wounded by a B-40 rocket and was screaming. A second B-40 rocket hit the position and there was no sound from SGT Cavaiani. The last time I saw SGT Jones he was in the mortar pit. I left the hill at 0545 hours."

From one named KINH:

"At 0530 hours 3 [sic] June 1971 I saw enemy advancing and SGT Cavaiani fired on them with the M60 MG killing or wounding 20-30 enemy, SGT Cavaiani continued to fire for 1-2 minutes. A B-40 rocket was fired into SGT Cavaiani's position and I heard him scream. I saw SGT Jones lying two meters from the mortar pit. At 0545hours I left the hill after yelling for SGT Cavaiani and getting no answer."

Similar reports were rendered by CIDG personnel A-Vat, Phong, Xang, Quang,Nui, Va-Chuai, Quai, and A-Cum. These individuals reported that it was still dark and foggy when they departed the hill about 0540 hours.

Having considered the statements presented, the board prepared a document dated 20 August lending closure to the investigation. The document bears the concurrence the Commanding General, United States Army, Vietnam that Sgt. Jon R. Cavaiani and Sgt. John R. Jones should be listed as missing in action.

Soon thereafter, for having held out so valiantly, for having saved so many lives of his men, and for having killed so many of the enemy, Jon was recommended for the Medal of Honor. Cpt. Valersky submitted the recommendation as a *posthumous* award.

Sadly, for Sergeant John Jones the board was incorrect. **However, the board was correct in Jon Cavaiani's case, for he was not yet dead.** After the last grenade, Jon had played dead which wasn't too difficult at that point. A North Vietnamese soldier had entered the bunker and checked him out, then threw Jones' dead body on top of him.

The tarp paper that lined the bunker was then set on fire. Using his willpower, Jon stayed inside, as long as possible, withstanding the choking smoke and boiling heat that seared his hands, back and face.

Forced by the unbearable situation, he finally crawled out of the bunker to face whatever fate awaited him. Fortunately, the group of enemy soldiers that had burned the bunker had moved on to other interests. This allowed Jon time to crawl into yet another bunker.

The "new" bunker had been partially destroyed by a rocket, so Jon hid among the debris. He was still determined to eliminate any enemy who might find him. As daylight began to appear in its foggy form, he watched legs pass back and forth for what seemed like an eternity.

Eventually a soldier entered the bunker and began to probe around. When he pulled the cover off Jon, he was shocked and too surprised to speak or yell. Jon's knife went forcefully into the man's heart. Muffling the man's gurgling, Jon tried to pull the knife out, but it was stuck in the man's sternum. As he pulled, the burned meat of his hands started to rip. Leaving the knife protruding from the man's chest, Jon crawled under a bunk that had survived the night, then passed out.

When Jon came to, there were two enemy soldiers in the bunker. Again, Jon feigned death. One of the enemy soldiers sat on the bunk and reached down, grabbed Jon's leg, and raised Jon's leg by the ankle. The man turned Jon's foot slightly, studying the size of his boots perhaps for fit on his own feet. It must not have been a good fit, for the man dropped the leg and continued rummaging in the bunker. He left shortly thereafter.

Summoning all his strength, Jon stealthily crawled out into the fog, slithered over the earthen berm, and down the steep sides of the mountain. Shot, torn by shrapnel, badly burned, yet scared enough to overcome the pain, he headed through the jungle toward Dong Ha.

"By this time, I was crazy. And just did not want to get caught," Jon would later recall in an interview with Soldier magazine.[44]

Photo of Hill 950 0n 5 June 1971 taken by W.O. Dave Hansen during Recon Flight to determine the extent of damage and ascertain the potential for locating U. S. personnel who might have survived the battle.

Deafened by the grenade, he moved only at night. He tried to re-call and use the Escape and Evasion training received in the Special Forces course at Fort Bragg (called SERE: Survival, Evasion,

---

[44] Baldi; Op Cit; page 51

Resistance, and Escape). Hunger, sleep deprivation, and self-reliance had been part of that training; but now it was real – this was his life that he was fighting for – not just a medal or certificate. He reflected on his life on Ugo's farm. To survive, chores needed to be done. There was no choice.

During Jon's interview at the Pritzker Military Museum interview, he told the audience that, and we paraphrase here, he learned that when eating insects, it is best to first remove their legs. Otherwise, the critters would try to crawl back out.

By moving only at night, he avoided the enemy over the next few days, covering several kilometers, and finally approaching Camp Fuller. He elected to await daylight so as not to be mistaken for an enemy saboteur/sapper. But while waiting for daylight to make his presence known, a Vietcong soldier who had been tracking him and others who had crawled down the slopes of Hill 950 stumbled upon him. The Vietcong soldier looked to be about sixty years old and was shaking as he pointed his rifle at Jon. Because of the man's nervousness, and because Jon was exhausted, he did not resist. At gunpoint, Jon was marched all the way back to near Hickory, and to enemy interrogation in a Vietcong encampment. The march back was not easier, but it was faster in the daylight.

Jon imagined what might be in store for him. He recalled an earlier time when he had found the remains of a Special Forces friend who had been captured by the communists. Found two days after the capture, the body was still warm but dead. They had popped the soldier's eyes, perhaps with sharpened bamboo sticks that lay nearby and bloodied, gutted his intestines so that they were still attached but dangling outside his body. There were signs of other grotesque indecencies to include severing his penis and testicles. All surely culminated in a most agonizingly slow death.

Near Hill 1015, Jon's arms were tied behind his back and a T-Bar was slid through so that he was hoisted off the ground. Spasms of pain coursed through his already torn and bloodied body. They beat him and pounded him as he hung suspended. Each blow to his body brought excruciating pain, not only to the targeted spots, but to his arms and shoulders as he bounced up and down in his suspended state. But all Jon would provide was his name, rank, and serial number. After long and excruciating amounts of abuse, Jon still refused to provide the North Vietnamese Army (NVA) interrogator the desired response. The interrogator then had five Bru Montagnards brought forward. These were five of the men who had served with Jon at Hickory. They, too, had been captured. The interrogator told Jon to respond to all questions or he would kill each of these men in turn.

Jon responded with, *"Cavaiani, Jon, Staff Sergeant..."* when he was cut off by the noise of a pistol being fired. As Jon started to speak, the Interrogator had casually raised his pistol and shot the nearest Bru Montagnard. Jon said, *"You can kill them all and me, too, but you still will get nothing from me."* The NVA officer again raised his pistol to the temple of a second Bru and pulled the trigger.

Jon remained silent. Seeing that this method was not making Jon talk, the North Vietnamese officer had the beating resumed. In defiance Jon said, *"My grandmother hits harder than that."* They then went to hitting him with rifle butts, pistol whipping him, and kicking him. In doing so they fractured three vertebrae in his neck and three in his lower back. Repeatedly, he fell unconscious from the blows.

Eventually, Jon was lowered to the ground where, after some time, he regained consciousness. When he did so he noted that his facial wounds and hands had been rudimentarily bandaged and that he was dressed in an American flight suit. He was then forced to stand and walk in a specified direction. It was when they approached a village below the Vietcong encampment that he realized that he was to be paraded through villages as if he were a pilot of a US jet that had been shot down. The bandages were designed to show that proper treatment was being provided.

> *"So, this political officer (North Vietnamese) had the villagers all riled up (because there had recently been U. S bombing raids in the area). – The political officer had announced to the villagers that he was bringing a U. S. pilot though their village – a pilot who had recently bombed their region - They all had their sticks, and they were going to beat this pilot as he was paraded through their village. But the political officer screwed up because he removed the flight helmet that had been placed on me. Well, this little old grandma got right up into my face, and all of a sudden, she let out with a loud, 'Boxie (sic) Jon!' 'She had recognized me.' Jon had helped deliver four babies in that village and one of them was the grandma's grandchild. Well, the political officer lost face (with the villagers.) because he had lied."*[45]

---

[45] Pritzker, Op Cit

(Author's note: Lying and falsification are unacceptable behaviors in most Asian cultures and brings significant shame upon the person and the family.)

Local farmers joined in waving to him and calling to him. They recalled how that "Bác Sĩ Jon" had helped them with their farming techniques. The villagers knew how he had cared for their children and had delivered some of them into this world. They knew that he was not a jet pilot. They knew him as a caring and compassionate farmer and medic. That he had been in the dull position of regional veterinarian was cause for the villagers to have fond remembrance of him. Their calling to him on that day may well have saved his life.

With the NVA political officer having lost face for putting on a pretense, Jon was spared. As he departed the village for a new, but unknown destination, Jon saw the Political Officer one last time – he had been tied to a tree.

Jon marched on foot across the DMZ. After a time, he was placed in the back of a truck for a short distance and then placed on a train for the long trip to Hanoi. While on the train Jon recognized some of the Bru Montagnards who had been with him on Hill 950. There was hardly a handful. He quietly whispered to one but there was no response. He then asked why they would not speak with him. One quietly responded, *"The train has many eyes and ears."* About 20 miles short of Hanoi, the train stopped and the Montagnards who had served with him were taken away; hopefully to a prison camp for South Vietnamese but probably to a re-education and indoctrination camp. It is likely that none survived.

As the Montagnards were moved off the train, Jon saw a

Vietnamese man who he knew to be an interpreter on Hill 950 step from the train and, discarding his South Vietnamese Army jacket, donned a North Vietnamese jacket bearing the rank of Lieutenant. He was both welcomed and saluted by the North Vietnamese. Bile rose in Jon's throat and he vomited.

Over the next twenty-three months, he was held in such infamous prisons as Plantation Gardens, The Zoo, and the Hanoi Hilton.

To the Army Jon was presumed dead but listed as MIA. To some of his hopeful family and friends he was missing. To himself he was just worn down, aching, and tired - but happy to be alive. His wounds were crudely bandaged, but the bullet lodged in his back was not removed. As for the numerous fragments of shrapnel in his flesh, he was forced to sharpen a bamboo stick and remove as many of them as he could himself. Some fragments, fibers, rocks, and sand would have to wait for extraction at some later date or just stay in place.

CHAPTER FIVE

Just a Plain POW

"Suffering is in proportion to the strength which has been accorded to a person. In other words, the weak suffer more, where the trial is the same, than the strong. In addition, what are the elementary principles, we may ask, which compose human strength? Is it not - more than anything else - exercise, habit, experience?"

Alexandre Dumas, *The Man in the Iron Mask*

Jon was not a 'prized' POW. He was of little value to the North Vietnamese. Had he been captured a few years earlier he would likely have been killed and dumped into a mass grave. However, with peace negotiations having begun in earnest, the North Vietnam government did not want any incidents that would create negative publicity on the international front and thus jeopardize their chance for victory.

He was not the most senior of POWs held by the North Vietnamese. He was not an officer. He was not the son of an officer or politically appointed or elected official. Jon, being a mid-level NCO was not a significant catch for the North Vietnamese. That alone would be sufficient to segregate him from senior ranking POWs. Plus, the NVA did not place much value on Army personnel. They wanted pilots. Except, of course, in Lieutenant Colonel Jim Thompson's case, or, like Jon Cavaiani, when you kill a North Vietnamese Army Colonel's son, then extended retribution and abusive punishment was deemed appropriate. The other POWs called their Army counter-prisoners "lost sheep". According to Siegfried's interview with Captain McGrath, they were seldom seen while in captivity. *"Our Army POWs were rare commodities among the camps in the North.* [46]

Add to that the routine of keeping all prisoners segregated and infrequently allowing them to converse, it is unlikely that he had interactions with very few other POWs. And considering the number of prison locations located across North Vietnam, it is likely that the total number of POWs known to him personally was hardly more than a small portion of those housed at The Plantation.

Nor was Jon's stint as a POW nearly the longest. His almost two years pales in comparison to some of the longer held POWs. That is not said to diminish the effects of the ordeal that he suffered, but merely to provide perspective. The "old hands" had suffered terribly under the tortuous treatment of the North Vietnamese earlier during the war. By the time Jon was captured, some of the more horrendous treatments had subsided. Again, that is not said to diminish the effects of Jon's suffering, but to stress to the reader that duration and severity do not determine the extent to which traumatic damage is done to an individual's psyche. And these do not give measure to how far one must travel in rehabilitative efforts to return to some level of normalcy.

The legendary stories of Lieutenant Commander John McCain, and Lieutenant Everett Alvarez are well known to many. But the longest held POW, Lieutenant Colonel Floyd (Jim) Thompson is lesser known.

---

[46] Galati; Ibid

Their stories provide us with insight into what mind-set had to be established in their lives in order to survive and continue on after their return home.

Because McCain's and Alvarez's stories are more widely known, we focus here on Thompson's story. And, like Jon, Jim Thompson was Army, almost escaped capture, and was a Green Beret.

On March 26, 1964, an Air Force observation plane arrived at Thompson's camp [and] Thompson went aboard for a quick reconnaissance of the outlying area, searching for signs of Vietcong activity. Spotting what appeared to be a footbridge, he asked the pilot, Captain Richard Whitesides, to descend into the valley for a closer look. When they dropped below the ridgeline, small-arms fire struck the aircraft, sending it into a dive. A bullet grazed Thompson's cheek. The plane hit the ground and exploded. Thompson was thrown free of the wreckage. Thompson later described his capture: *"V.C. guerrillas found the crash. I regained consciousness when one of them grabbed my hand. He had a knife and was about to slice my finger off to get at my birthstone ring, a ruby. I got the ring off myself and handed it to him. They'd already stripped me of weapons and everything I had in my pockets. I was tied to a litter and carried down the mountain. When I regained consciousness, that night or the next, I was tied spread-eagle on the floor of a Montagnard hut."*

During the first weeks of Thompson's captivity, the Vietcong moved him from camp to camp. For more than a month, he was unable to feed himself because of his injuries. His captors kept him alive on rice gruel, treated his wounds, and gave him penicillin. His back was so badly damaged that he couldn't walk. With great effort, he began to wiggle his toes and stretch his limbs. Gradually, he recovered the ability to stand. By June, he was able to gather wood for a fire and make his own meals. His captors told him that the National Liberation Front never maltreated prisoners of war, but he did not feel reassured.

"I was in mental anguish over my family, particularly about what had happened to my wife and baby," he recalled.

"When were the Vietcong going to put the pressure on me? Before my capture, I had heard of all kinds of atrocities at the hands of the Communists.

Then one morning I woke up at peace. I knew that the baby had been born.

Knew that it was a boy. I knew that both Alyce and the child were doing fine.

And I knew that I would survive."

In June, two interrogators arrived in the camp. Both spoke excellent English. Initially, they presented themselves as teachers. *"They began with the history of Vietnam, going back some five thousand years and moving forward through the Mongol invasions and various other conflicts,"*

Thompson recalled. *"They told me what a grand and glorious tradition the Vietnamese people had, fighting for independence and freedom. The lectures lasted four to eight hours a day. They said that, as soon as I understood their side of the war, I would be allowed to go."*

After six weeks, however, their tactics changed. The interrogators kept Thompson awake until he was exhausted, fed him meagerly, and restricted smoking. *"Their method was to alter the pressure,"* Thompson said. *"If you put pressure on somebody and hold it on, he can learn to live with it. But alternating a hard day with an easy day causes mental pressure to build up."*

Thompson still had a great deal of back pain while the NVA forced him to sit through long interrogations. It was *"pure torture."* He had also contracted malaria and dysentery.

During Thompson's first month of captivity, he made three attempts to escape, simply walking away from his guards when they fell asleep or (when they) were distracted. Each time, after travelling a short distance, he came upon other guards, signaled that he had to defecate, and was returned to his hut. On his fourth attempt, Thompson left a dozing guard outside his hut one morning, encountered no other guards, and kept walking. Late in the afternoon, he came to a river.

"I was free," he recalled. *"Even the air seemed different- just breathing without a guard over my shoulder. I had visions of a big beer bust in the club at Da Nang. I would call home and tell my wife that I was all right. I would find out I had a son. I thought what a relief it would be to hear Alyce's voice. Then I'd get back to where the V.C. had held me to clean their clock."*

At dusk, he decided to cross the river, and he was knee-deep in water, then spotted by a group of Montagnards who were friendly to the Vietcong. They lit torches and screamed at Thompson. A Vietcong soldier appeared and fired at him. He was captured and taken back to the camp, where the commander had him tied up and beaten until he lost consciousness.[47]

Because of the consistent attempted "breakouts" by U. S. POWs during the '60's, which were sanctioned by the Military Code of Conduct, Admiral Stockdale grew concerned that these would lead to harsher punishments for the POWs. Initially, no senior official said "no" for an escape attempt. Ultimately, Stockdale demanded via the "tap code" that there would be no further attempts.[48]

During the next month, the interrogations became more severe, and he was deprived of food, sleep, and warm clothing. *"The pressure now got as high as it could without killing me,"* he recalled. *"I had lost forty to fifty pounds in three months. It was an effort to put one foot in front of the other. I had to move very, very slowly or I would pass out."*

In the third week of August, he was presented with a statement to sign. It said that the Vietcong had given him excellent medical care and had treated him kindly. It praised the National Liberation Front as freedom fighters, who sought only peace, democracy, and neutrality for their country. And it called for the withdrawal of all American forces from South Vietnam.

"I sat there with pen in hand as they shouted at me to

---

[47] Philpott, Tom; The bitter heroism of America's longest-held P.O.W. (Jim Thompson—Longest Held POW): New Yorker, April 2, 2001, Pg. 52, Annals of War: The Prisoner

[48] Galati, Ralph; interview with Siegfried; 7 July 2022

write," he recalled. *"They altered their approach, from trying to convince me I should write to cajoling me. Periodically, they hit me with bamboo. They kept at it for eight, ten, twelve hours a day. I would almost lose touch with reality. When I finally signed the thing, it was as if I were standing to the side, watching myself do it. As soon as I signed it, the pressure stopped. The next day, they brought me back and told me to rewrite the statement in my own handwriting and sign it. Which I did. Then they put a microphone in front of me and said, 'Read it.' And I read it."*

For the next six months, Thompson was left alone. *"I spent most of my time in a bamboo hut, six-foot square, with absolutely nothing to do,"* he recalled. *"A guard sat out front. If I had to leave, I asked permission. I could go down to the creek and wash or go to the latrine. If I needed wood, the guard handed me an axe and told me to go cut it. No reading material. Nothing to write with. "I invented all manner of things to pass the time. One was building houses."[49]*

Edward Alvarez was listed by the media and the Pentagon as the first Prisoner of War. He was, in fact, the first **pilot** shot down, but Alvarez was second to Colonel Thompson as POW. Lieutenant Everett Alvarez, Jr., had been shot down over North Vietnam on 5 August 1964.

Nine years later, when the P.O.W.s came home, Alvarez took part in a nationally televised celebration of the repatriation, presided over by Bob Hope, in Oklahoma City. Among those at the event was an Army Special Forces officer, Lieutenant Colonel Floyd (Jim)

---

[49] Philpott, Tom; Op. Cit.

Thompson, who had been captured in March 1964, more than four months before Alvarez. Colonel Thompson's ordeal had been unusually severe. He had spent the first five years of his captivity in solitary confinement, mostly in remote jungle camps in the mountains of South Vietnam and Laos. He had endured beatings, disease, and starvation, and five times had tried, unsuccessfully, to escape. He was not allowed to join other American Prisoners of War until 1969, when he was near death.

A dinner was held for the Prisoners of War the night before the taping of the Hope hosted show. In 1986, Alvarez said:

> *"Jim Thompson was at a separate table. I was awed to be in Jim's presence. Earlier that day, we had some rehearsing to do. The TV people brought captions that would be superimposed on the screen. They wanted to make sure they spelled our names right. Below mine, it said, "Longest-held P.O.W." "Wait a minute," I said. "I'm not the longest held. He is."*
>
> *"Who is he?"*
>
> *"Colonel Thompson." (I declared!) 'Oh.' Was the response. To me, Jim was a hero. Yet people still referred to me as the longest held prisoner."*
>
> *"I wondered why. Well, that night I asked him. "Jim," I said, "how come they don't call you the first?" He did not answer me."*[50]

Perhaps his answer was not necessary. Duration, severity, circumstances of capture, rank, and branch of service were no longer of

---

[50] Ibid

importance. Those few who were held, maltreated, and traumatized were a unique band of brothers. First, last, most senior, most junior were of little concern.

Jon Cavaiani may have been present at the Bob Hope salute to POWs in Oklahoma City. Later he was with his fellow POW brothers when President Richard Nixon hosted the largest formal dinner at the White House to welcome them home. And again, after having been awarded the Medal of Honor, Jon was present with his brothers in 2013 at the Nixon Presidential Library Reunion for Vietnam War POWs.

That they may not have known one another while in captivity, they knew one another now by their scars. They knew one another by their spirit, they knew one another by their common bonds.

The experiences and insights presented by those Prisoners of War who have, over the years, shared their trauma, pain, depth of faith, and determinations to survive provide a basis upon which we can better understand the type of conditions that Jon Cavaiani encountered as a prisoner of war. Although each one has his own account of the traumatic events, there exists a commonality that no other group of human beings can share.

Jon Cavaiani was one of those who unfortunately was fated to enter that unique fraternity. And, like Jim Thompson, when asked to compare his experience to that of others who are in that fraternity, he did not answer. The experience was not about comparison, but about the unity of brotherhood.

CHAPTER SIX

Prisoner of War Cavaiani

"I am the harvest of man's stupidity. I am the fruit of the holocaust. I prayed like you to survive but look at me now. It is over for us who are dead, but you must struggle, and will carry the memories all your life. People back home will wonder why you cannot forget."

Eugene B. Sledge, *With the Old Breed*

Jon was originally listed as missing in action and paperwork for awarding him the Medal of Honor was being prepared. Then, his name was mentioned on a Viet Cong radio program. He was a Prisoner of War and would be held and tortured as a POW and from 5 June 1971 to 27 March 1973. Jon was in solitary confinement a good portion of the time, but his beatings that began in June continued with regularity for much of his imprisonment.

When he first arrived in North Vietnam, he had almost 120 shrapnel punctures and several bullet holes in his body. He said that was when all of his worst nightmares came true. He called what happened next as *...the rude, crude, and socially unacceptable interrogation techniques.* By his own account in his own words, Jon gives us an idea of the man and what sustained him:

"An individual must at least attempt to keep his mind occupied, to retain his sanity, otherwise, the enemy will enter. Therefore, I decided what were the things I believed in: God, America, and my family. Yes, they had always been in my mind and then when

I needed them most, they stood by me as a shield against the enemy.

As a prisoner I was to meet some of the most heroic men I have ever or will ever hope to encounter, men who never let their country or families down, when so many people in the United States were letting us, the POWs, MIAs, and almost all our country, down. Well, by God, regardless of what some people said about the war, we did our jobs as men and kept the faith in our President and country."[51]

Jon was moved from camp to camp. He was at the "Plantation", the "Hilton," and the "Zoo." *"Since they were not getting anything out of me through beatings, they let the bedbugs do the nasty work,"* Jon would years later quip. He then continued on, saying: *"When they interrogated me I would try to piss them off so that they would knock me out. I traded pain for time."*[52]

The NVA administered their wrath, in what the poet Robert Burns (*Poem: Man was made to Mourn: A Dirge in 1784*) wrote as *"Man's inhumanity to Man."* It is possible that Burns reworded a similar quote from Samuel von Pufendorf, who in 1673 wrote, *"More inhumanity has been done by man himself than any other of nature's causes."*

---

[51] Wyatt, Frederick (USN) Ret'd) and Barbara Powers Wyatt; <u>We Came Home</u>; POW Publications; Toluca Lake, CA; 1977 (Text is reproduced as found in the original publication (including date and spelling errors).

[52] Baldi; Op Cit; pg. 52

Prisoner of War pajamas worn by Cavaiani during his captivity in Vietnam. (The National Museum: https://www.thenmusa.org/biographies/jon-r-cavaiani/)

A typical day at Plantation Gardens was a mixture of boredom intermingled with pain and terror. *"You'd get up about 7:00 every morning, fold your stuff a certain way and sit on your bed and tap-talk to the other guys,"* Cavaiani later recalled. As for breakfast? *"It had a little bit of everything from rat feces to string and cockroaches in it."* Like other Americans, Jon was tortured and undernourished to the brink of starvation. Jon was transferred for a period of time to the Zoo.

> *"It was at the Zoo that I was "exposed to 'Dumbo'* (and Oxford educated English Speaking interrogator). *"A very good interrogator"* Cavaiani recalled. With his voice then a bit softer Jon went on to say, *"I ended up getting worked-over bad there. You might say they used the bell ringer on me for electrical shock."* .... *I was returned to Plantation and placed in an eight-man room but wound-up spending most of my time in isolation for breaking camp rules. . . . We all wanted to be released, but we all wanted to come out with our heads held high. This is something we all felt, not just a few."*[53]

In time, the harsh treatment eased a bit. The POWs were not aware that negotiations had begun to end the war and their ultimate release. It was then that in some of the prison camps prisoners were able to play cards, read, and talk with one another. Still the smallest infraction could lead to 124 lashes with a rubber hose. When the guards were feeling lenient, the prisoners were permitted to drink beer. Cavaiani related to Pete Laurence, well after his retirement, that he remembered that *"we finally celebrated Christmas, Tet, and the Fourth*

---

[53] Baldi; ibid

of July – but not Thanksgiving, because they didn't think we had anything to be thankful for. The camaraderie amongst the POWs during those last few months was really about the only good part." Cavaiani summarized.

Though Jon was a prisoner of war, the North Vietnamese did not initially report him as such. The American Government, although processing documentation for the Medal of Honor posthumously, had not found his body on Hill 950 and thus listed him as one of the 2,646 Missing in Action (MIA). That number included both POWs and reportedly Killed in Action (KIAs) and was based upon a "body not recovered" status. Jon had become another statistic in a body-count war. To some of his family and friends, Jon was (hopefully) still alive. To official government statisticians, he was missing. To those who saw the destruction of Hickory Hill, he was surely dead.

Eventually his name was broadcast over North Vietnam speakers, but there was no way for the U. S. to confirm that Jon was still alive. Was he dead? Was he missing in action? Was he a prisoner of war? No one was sure. It was during the largest prisoner of war swap in the Vietnam War that Jon was finally fortunate enough to be accounted for, and rejoin the living. He was released by the North Vietnamese 27 March 1973.

Cavaiani remembered seeing a C-141 airplane arriving at Gia Lam Air Base, where the prisoner exchange took place. Cavaiani called *it "the greatest sight in the world"* when he first saw the approaching aircraft. Weighing a little more than half his pre-captivity weight, Cavaiani limped toward the aircraft until (someone) grabbed him, and his *"legs went to rubber."*[54]

> *"I can remember when they took me out to the airplane at Hanoi Airport. We walked up and saluted the Vietnamese General, who then turned us over to a Colonel in the U. S. Air Force."* One by one an aide would call a name and *"Thump, our name would be checked off a list."* . . . . *"I started walking out to the airplane . . . . and, aw, man, I was really trying to walk upright and really proud; and this (American Captain or Crew Chief) grabbed me and said, 'You're alright now, Sarge. I've got you.' My knees just turned to rubber. Seeing. that C-141 landing with the American Flag on the tail. There is nothing like it. I came back with a hell of a deeper pride for America."*[55]

When Jon returned home, he was told of a remarkable incident that had given his family some relief and hope when he was reported as MIA and recommended for a posthumous award.

A labor foreman who worked on Ugo Cavaiani's expansive farm had approached Jon's adoptive father the day after they had received news of him being listed as MIA. The foreman's name was Ramon, and he had always called Jon "Bobby." Ramon said to Ugo, *"Bobby is okay! I saw him in a dream last night, his face was bloody, but he is alive and okay!"* Twenty-one months later, Jon proved Ramon's dream to be true.

---

[54] National Museum – United States Army:

https://www.thenmusa.org/biographies/jon-r-cavaiani/;
retrieved June 26, 2022

[55] Baldi; Op Cit. pg. 52

A video-taped interview entitled **Living History of Medal of Honor Recipient Jon Cavaiani** with Jon occurred a few years later in which Jon himself discussed his captivity. A transcript of that interview is below. The interview can be viewed on https://youtube.com/watch?v=4SeTr-itHkc&feature=share.

Jon: I was adopted in 1950 and raised in an Italian family. I enlisted in the service at 26 and was 4F, which means they would take my mother before me. Found a doctor, who said a couple of guys he claimed were 4F. I wanted to enlist in the selective service, would like to check them out. He goes *"what do you want, Jon?"* and I said *"IN."* So I got into the service.

Narrator: Jon Cavaiani enlisted in the army in 1968. Although originally turned away due to an allergy to bee stings, the young soldier eventually qualified for the elite special forces; and was sent to Vietnam in 1970. Once there, he forged a special bond with the South Vietnamese people.

Jon: I had befriended a Vietnamese Sergeant Major. He was shot and mortally wounded. It was a Med Cap operation (Medical Civic Action Program - the care of the indigenous civilians by U.S. military medical personnel during the Vietnam War.) I adopted his son and built an orphanage for 7 monks and 22 kids. And I continued running Med Cap, was getting ready for the holidays, and went down to visit the orphanage. I was told my son was dead. My kids were killed. 6 of the monks were killed. They told me NOT to go down there. Stay out of the area.

Apparently, I had been very successful winning the hearts and minds of the people. Loved my son and the orphanage. It was now smarter for me to go to a different unit.

Narrator: In the summer of 1971, still reeling from the loss of his adopted son, Sgt Cavaiani took the assignment to lead a mixed platoon of native Montagnards and American soldiers, the former whom he affectionately referred to as his "little people." Together, the men were deployed to a dangerous radio relay site located deep within enemy territory.

Jon: I went up there to make sure communications could be made from Laos and North Vietnam through our relay site down into headquarters. I got up there and the camp was a disaster. So, we fixed the camp up. Installed all the wire (concertina wire) and all the access points, mined it, and everything else. We started to see more and more activity from the NVA. I reported down to my unit which they came back that our assets don't tell us that. They continued questioning, while we were seeing 1,000 men a day in rucksacks, and helicopters, and they still didn't want to believe it. Finally, I decided that I know we are going to get hit. And sure as heck, we were surrounded. Everywhere around the perimeter there were Chinese claymore mines sitting all the way around the camp. Well, I grabbed a machine gun and placed the weapon over the side of the berm and shot them up, continued around the perimeter of the camp blowing up the claymores. I destroyed all the mines. Next thing I knew they flip up their bunkers and came out of their charley holes (that is what we called them) and started firing at us. Managed to get all my people back into the camp, and wound-up quieting all the guns. Then, they started firing rockets, and we counter-batteried their position. Then I realized we were going to lose the camp. I've got to destroy all the sensitive equipment that we have, so I set off all my additional ordinance, burned all the equipment up and started back to assist my guys.

Narrator: Sgt Cavaiani directed his remaining troops to a helipad where he provided covering fire for the three helicopters coming in to extract his men, which was the majority of his endangered platoon. Night began to fall, Cavaiani defied orders to evacuate himself, opting instead to stay behind with a small group of Montagnards who remained on the ground

Jon: I had already been ordered to get off the hill, take your people get out of there, or leave the Montagnards. I said shit-you have to be freaking joking: I was a reconnaissance team leader before; the first man on the ground is the last man off the ground. So, sorry, I am not obeying that order. When you come to pick up all my little people then you will see me on the helicopter. Likewise, I continued to strengthen out defenses; we had at least half the camp, and me with a Montagnard planted a 106 round, set it up, booby trapped it, so when they tried to make one breach in the wall, whom ever was there on it would be killed. That went off, and the first attack wave was all killed. I told my Yards to pull back. We had the helicopter pad in between the two ends of the camp. I set up upon one side, had the Montagnards set up on the other side. And we now had the enemy in a crossfire. We just annihilated them-- they never knew what hit 'em. Then we hadn't had anything happen in 45 minutes, so I knew they were getting ready to hit us big, so I pulled the Yards back and told them to all move out and about the time the whole world came running at us on that end. I grabbed the machine gun got up on the bunker and began shooting at anybody that was moving. My Yards were starting to take off the back side of the hill and all of a sudden, I got a sanity attack because I said what the hell are you doing up here. Turned around to bend-over to get off the hill and took a bullet in my back which stopped just below my neck. The remaining Yards came over to help me get out and I said no, get out of here. I crawled into the bunker, and the next thing I know a grenade pops in rolling in-- it was one of ours. I kicked it up towards the radio and it went off took out my radio and that was the last time anybody heard from me. I had to fight to play dead. And remember watching- I am laying-out and there is a guy sitting on the cot, feet hanging down and he's got my boot. Going like this--- checking to see if it would fit and I guess he figured they were too big. He must have figured I got killed when the grenade came through and he got up and walked out. It sobered me up real fast. Did a nice, neat, low crawl to the door then out the side and past the berm and started escaping and evading.

Narrator: Unarmed, badly wounded, and completely alone, Sgt. Cavaiani traveled through the jungle for 11 days before being captured by North Vietnam troops, then taken to a POW camp where he remained for 23 months. Jon was still considered missing in action when his Medal of Honor was awarded in 1973, he was repatriated later that year, and returned to America where he received the Medal from President Gerald Ford.

Jon: People ask me what I got the medal for in that battle. I said I couldn't outrun them, so I had to fight them. And I'll leave it there. I was just doing my job: Did whatever any one of my guys would have done, because we all felt the same about the Montagnards. Many of times I put my life on the line for my Yards. And a number of them died for me, so it's reciprocal.

JON's WORDS ABOUT HIS POW ACTIONS AND REFLECTIONS AS TOLD TO Robert L. Noe, Cpt, USASF (Ret) are provided below and can be found at: http://www.macvsog.cc/jon_cavaiani's_pow_&_peace_committee_experience.htm

"During the attack on Hill 950, I had killed the son of the "NVA" commander with a Gerber knife and his father was ready for me when I was returned to his camp with a Gerber sheath strapped to my leg. My interpreter, Thant, told me I should answer all their questions but that was not a part of the Code of Conduct, therefore, I couldn't give out any information.

Four days Later, after I was taken for my first formal interrogation, I faced, the rude, crude and socially unacceptable interrogation techniques. My captured Montagnards were put on their knees, and I was asked about our unit and our modes-operandi. I gave them my name, rank, and serial number. They then put a pistol to one of my seriously wounded Montagnard's head and said give me name, rank, and serial number again and I will kill your man. They killed my man then moved on to one of my other Montagnards and made the same request; they killed him as well. I told them to kill the rest of my Montagnards and come on back and kill me; for if I was ever going to tell them anything they could forget it now.

Understand one thing about me. My Montagnards were closer than my own brother. I told the interrogator go ahead and kill me and my men as I wasn't going to say anything that would put another person in harms' way. They proceeded to break many of my ribs on the left side and when they cut me down, they fractured three vertebrae.

I was moved to Vinh, North Vietnam, with my interpreter and eight other Montagnards. As we moved to the rail yard, I noticed my interpreter push several of my Yards and at the time it didn't mean much. Once we were on the train for about eight hours, I moved over in the cattle car and asked one of my Yards a question and he said, "The train had many eyes." I move away from him until we reached a camp about two to two and a half hours from Hanoi. The train stopped and the Montagnards were taken off the train at what I can only describe as a North Vietnamese re-education camp for my Yards.

When Thant leapt from the train and a North Vietnamese friend of his presented him with his Sub-Lieutenant uniform, I knew he was a North Vietnamese soldier, and he knew every operation I was on with him.

I stayed on the train for another two hours before being taken to a camp about an hour from Hanoi. I was to spend six days in this camp and was interrogated every night but one. While I was there, the two Canberra pilots in the cell next to me never came home.

I was then moved to Plantation Gardens for one night then moved to the Zoo. I was interrogated by "Dumbo", an Oxford University, England, graduate who spoke fluent English. I again met "Jeff" in the "Mutt and Jeff Interrogation techniques". Later I was moved back to the Plantation Garden's until I was transferred to the "Hanoi Hilton"; December 27,1972

After about a year at the "Plantation Gardens" I was ashamed by the conduct of the "Peace Committee" (PC'S). The soldiers in the PC's were flipping off and giving our, Senior Ranking American Officer, (SRO) Ted Guy total disrespect of his command. This was totally unacceptable to me.

During my stay in isolation, for pissing-off the political officer, I noticed that the drop site for our messages was compromised and was forced to send LTC Guy (SRO) a message stating that our safe drop was compromised. The only way I could do this was to get a message to him. I told the guard that my bread was sour and that it should be given to Ted Guy. The guard made sure that our SRO got the message. Months later, LTC Ted Guy told me that he got the message but almost got caught as he always destroyed the bread he didn't eat, and the guard was looking in when he took a bite of the bread and pulled out the note I had hidden in the bread, and it was stuck between his lips. All he could think to do was ask for a light. We laughed over that one.

Insulted by the actions of the PC's I decided to join them and break them up. Old Special Forces Training. I felt that I could succeed in disrupting the PC's. I felt that the Political Officer "Cheese" would see right through my attempt to infiltrate the PC's, but he didn't catch on.

Once I joined the PC's, I saw that the guys in the sick room were better fed. I was obligated to do what I had to do to continue living with the PC's. After about a week with the PCs, I was asked to sign a letter that protested the war in Vietnam, which I reluctantly signed, wanting to continue breaking up the PC's. I continued my stay in the PC's room and documenting gratuities received, statements made and in general creating dissension amongst the PC's (divide and conquer). Eventually, I had the PC's fighting in the compound.

It wasn't until the Vietnamese told the PC's that the war was about to end that the PC's got together and talked about what they were going to do. They talked to one another and realized that I had created dissension in their ranks. It was at this time when I got to meet my first North Vietnamese General who explained to me that if I broke one camp regulation that I would be executed in front of the men in the camp.

Three weeks later, the 27th of December, we were moved to the Hanoi Hilton and about a week later I had learned that Le Duc Ta and Kissinger had signed an agreement and immediately tapped out, that the "war was over" to LTC Ted Guy, Major Montague and CWO Ziegler. LTC Guy Tapped me back and asked me to let all the other POW's know. I did and LTC Guy and I were in with other POW's when we were notified by the Vietnamese Commander that we were to be released.

"Ted Guy asked me to be a witness against the PCs. CW2 Ziegler also contacted me and asked me if I would testify against the PCs. I told him yes. I was officially debriefed as to the violations of the Code of Conduct that the Peace Committee violated. and therefore, had conversations with the Army CID.

I don't know if I was on the list of witnesses, but Col Guy knew I was available."

**Sergeant Major, (then SSG Jon R. Cavaiani), TF1AE, MACVSOG.
Dated: 15 December, 2009**

While in captivity, he and three other POWs helped the camp's Senior Ranking Officer, Colonel Ted Guy, to infiltrate a U. S. military collaborators' group called the Peace Committee. The Peace Committee were POWs who had opted to side with the North Vietnamese, in order to gain special treatment. The Peace Committee collaborators sided with the North Vietnamese by disavowing loyalty to the United States and by sending radio messages designed to undermine U. S. Troop morale and their will to fight. Jon and the others conducted psychological operations to disrupt the collaboration of the Peace Committee. In a divide and conquer method, Jon sought to pit one collaborator (deserter) against another. James A. Daly, wrote a book called *Black Prisoner of War, a Conscientious Objector's Vietnam Memoir.* at pages. 214-219, 232, 258-9, 262, 264 on how Jon disrupted the organization of the 8 men who collaborated with the enemy.

Following are excerpts from *BLACK PRISONER OF WAR, A CONSCIENTIOUS OBJECTOR'S VIETNAM MEMOIR,* by James A Daly and Lee Bergman, University Press of Kansas that describes the frustration of the Peace Committee with Jon's disruption of their "harmonious" existence with the North Vietnamese

Chapter 19 of the book (noted hereafter as **BPOW,COVM**) describes the Peace Committee and notes that James A. Daly joined the Peace Committee on December 28, 1971. Another individual joined shortly after him for a total of 8 active members (five Army, three Marines) who were together in the Plantation Gardens Prisoner of War

Camp. The commander of the American Prisoners of War was the Senior Ranking Officer, Colonel Theodore Guy. The members of the Peace Committee were Pro-Communist and aided the North Vietnamese, even to the point that all eight members signed a letter to the North Vietnamese Camp Commander stating they were willing to join the North Vietnamese Army to fight against Americans, An earlier incident before Daly (according to Daly) joined involved AF Captain Edward W. Leonard, Jr, who had ordered them to "stop" their Anti-American activities wherein the Peace Committee members gave him the middle finger.

"It continued like this, easy going and friendly, even after Fred Elbert came in and joined our group," wrote Daly *(Note: Elbert made the 8th member). Within a short time of each other four more joined the PC following Fred Elbert: Don MacPhail, Jon Cavaiani, John Sparks and Dennis Tellier. Branch had been dead set against admitting any of them. We should have listened to him. After the trial period and interviews, Branch was not at all convinced that the four were sincere in why they wanted in--and, actually, we all had our doubts. We wondered if they'd understand our studying books by Marx and Lenin. We even considered the crazy possibility that maybe they were put up to joining the Peace Committee as spies for Colonel Guy."*[56] (Page 214, BPOW,COVM).

"Thinking back on it, it's easier to understand how Cavaiani

[56] Daly, James A. and Lee Bergman; BLACK PRISONER OF WAR, A CONSCIENTIOUS OBJECTOR'S VIETNAM MEMOIR, University Press of Kansas, Lawrence, KS; October 2000

began to influence some of the guys the way he did. In most POW groups, there was one guy who was especially looked up to, usually because he was the brightest. Then a guy like Cavaiani would come along--older, wealthy, college-educated. One of the first things, I noticed was how after Cavaiani started to work in the camp flower garden every day. it was no time before Riati went out with him to mess with the flowers. Then you'd always see the two of them together. Soon Kavanaugh and Rayford began to hang around with them all the time, and, before long Sparks and MacPhail, too. Little by little, they started to stick by themselves. The split started without any of us realizing it, and we only found out later why it kept getting wider. What we didn't know was that Cavaiani was going from one guy to another, spreading rumors, like telling someone that he was being put down by someone else in the other room, things like that. Before long, half the guys were carrying grudges against somebody. The atmosphere was seldom ever friendly, the way it had been. And though there still weren't any out-and-out arguments or fights at that time, we were really split right down the middle. One room didn't visit the other, and soon we weren't even eating at the same table. Then the idea got around that maybe all of us in the PC had really been brainwashed by the North Vietnamese after all, that they only let us believe we were making our own decisions about things. I was really surprised when I heard Riati and Kavanaugh talk like that, and my guess was that Cavaiani had got them thinking that way. Next thing, fighting started. Even among guys in the same room. Stupid fights, over nothing."[57] (Pp 215-216 BPOW,COVM)

---

[57] Daly; Ibid

Jon would have been a key witness in the court-martials of the collaborators if Secretary of Defense Melvin Laird had not decided against prosecuting the known traitors after one of them committed suicide. This has been substantiated by several sources, including one of the members of the peace committee who was a POW and became a conscientious objector.

Jon was moved on 27 December 1972 to the *Hanoi Hilton*. He weighed 198 pounds when he was captured and 92 pounds when he was released having lost 106 pounds during his incarceration.

CHAPTER SEVEN

U. S. Prisoners of War in North Vietnam

"Fear knocked at the door. Faith answered. No one was there."
From above the fireplace at Hinds' Head Hotel, near London

To add further perspective to Jon's stint as a POW we include a discussion on North Vietnam's war prisons and some insight into the treatment of POWs. In Vietnam there were many prisons used to hold American POWs. Several were in close proximity to Hanoi, with a few of the more well-known jails located directly in Hanoi. American prisoners spent years living in these uninhabitable cells enduring the pain and suffering oftentimes inflicted upon them by the Vietnamese guards. With the end of the war and the release of the POWs, some decided to tell their stories about life as a prisoner in Vietnam.

As a prelude to Jon's capture and years as a POW, it is of note to recall that efforts were being made to recover and free POWs in North Vietnam, or at least reduce the torture and suffering that they were subject to.

James N. Rowe successfully escaped from North Vietnamese captivity. On 21 November 1970, U.S. Special Forces launched *Operation Ivory Coast* in an attempt to rescue 61 POWs believed to be held at the Sơn Tây prison camp 23 miles (37 km) west of Hanoi. Fifty-six commandos landed by helicopter and assaulted the prison, but the prisoners had been moved some months earlier and none were rescued. While the raid failed to free any POWs and was considered a significant intelligence failure, it had several positive implications for American prisoners. The most immediate effect was to affirm to the POWs that their government was actively attempting to repatriate them, which significantly boosted their morale. Additionally, soon after the raid all acknowledged American prisoners in North Vietnam were moved to Hỏa Lò so that the North Vietnamese had fewer camps to protect and to prevent their rescue by U.S. forces.

> *"The Pentagon developed a strategy to raid Son Tay. Developed in early May 1970 where intel confirmed where they were PRIOR to June of that year. After months of planning, over forty SF operators attacked the compound with no American loss of life. But the POW's were gone. Faulty intel was the culprit.*[58]

As summer arrived in Vietnam in June 1970, the NVA knew the war was in its final chapter. They moved prisoners away from areas like Son Tay, which was about ten miles away, into other structures. Even with pre-raid recon, we didn't know POWs were in a different location. The post-raid consolidation brought many prisoners who had spent years in isolation into large cells holding roughly 70 men each. This created the "Camp Unity" communal living area at Hỏa Lò. The increased human contact further improved morale and facilitated greater

---

[58] Seals, Robert D.; USASOC History, *Operation IVORY COAST: A Mission of Mercy;* December 2020; https://www.army.mil/article/241352/operation_ivory_coast_a _mission_of_mercy

military cohesion among the POWs. At this time, the prisoners formally organized themselves under the 4th Allied POW Wing, whose name acknowledged earlier periods of overseas captivity among American military personnel in World War I, World War II, and the Korean War. This military structure was ultimately recognized by the North Vietnamese and endured until the prisoners' release in 1973.

Nevertheless, by 1971, some 30–50 percent of the POWs had become disillusioned about the war, both because of the apparent lack of military progress and what they heard about the growing anti-war movement stateside. Some of them became less reluctant to make propaganda statements for the North Vietnamese. Some refused to be dissuaded and did not cow-tow to their tormentors. Some were so defiant they held church services and made efforts to write letters home that portrayed the camp in a negative light. These defiant prisoners were usually sent to a camp reserved for "bad attitude" cases.

The horrific treatment of POWs continued through the balance of 1970. After the much-heralded Son Tay Raid, the NVA, knowing the war was in its final chapters, began treating the men with better grace: Windows were opened, rations increased, prisoners were allowed to be in groups for camaraderie in the same area, and hygiene improved. This was a political move to "fatten-up" the men who all had encountered significant weight loss. And no torture was administered from that time forward.[59]

Members of the United States Armed Forces were held as prisoners of war in significant numbers during the Vietnam

---

[59] Seals; ibid

War from 1964 to 1973. Unlike U.S. service members captured in World War II and the Korean War, who were mostly enlisted troops, the overwhelming majority of Vietnam-era POWs were officers. Most were Navy, Air Force, and Marine Corps airmen. A relatively small number of Army enlisted personnel were captured, as well as one enlisted Navy seaman, Petty Officer Doug Hegdahl, who fell overboard from a naval vessel. Most U.S. prisoners were captured and held in North Vietnam by the People's Army of Vietnam (PAVN); a much smaller number were captured in the South and held there by the Việt Cộng (VC). A handful of U.S. civilians were also held captive during the war.

Thirteen prisons and prison camps were used to house U.S. prisoners in North Vietnam. The most widely known was Hỏa Lò Prison (nicknamed the "Hanoi Hilton"). The treatment and ultimate fate of U.S. prisoners of war in Vietnam became a subject of widespread concern in the United States, and hundreds of thousands of Americans wore POW bracelets with the name and capture date of imprisoned U.S. service members.

American POWs in North Vietnam were released in early 1973 as part of *Operation Homecoming*, the result of diplomatic negotiations concluding U.S. military involvement in Vietnam. On February 12, 1973, the first of 591 U.S. prisoners began to be repatriated, and return flights continued until late March. After *Operation Homecoming*, the U.S. still listed roughly 1,350 Americans as prisoners of war or missing in action and sought the return of roughly 1,200 Americans reported killed in action, but whose bodies were not recovered. These missing personnel would become the subject of the Vietnam War POW/MIA issue.

American pilots continued to be captured over the North between 1965–1968 as part of *Operation Rolling Thunder*, the sustained aerial bombing campaign against North Vietnam. After President Lyndon Johnson initiated a bombing pause in 1968, the number of new captures dropped significantly, only to pick up again after his successor, President Richard Nixon, resumed bombing in 1969. Significant numbers of Americans were also captured during *Operation Linebacker 1* between May and October 1972, and *Operation Linebacker II* in December 1972, also known as the "Christmas Bombings". They would have the shortest stays in captivity.

The "Little Vegas" area of Hỏa Lò Prison, built for American POWs in 1967. Shown in a final inspection in 1973 shortly before the Americans' release.

Beginning in late 1965, the application of torture against U.S. prisoners became severe. During the first six years in which U.S. prisoners were held in North Vietnam, many experienced long periods of solitary confinement, with senior leaders and particularly recalcitrant POWs being isolated to prevent communication. Robinson Risner, and James Stockdale, two senior officers who were the de facto leaders of the POWs, were held in solitary for three and four years, respectively. The Alcatraz Gang was a group of eleven POWs who were held separately because of their particular resistance to their captors.

The POWs made extensive use of a tap code to communicate, which was introduced in June 1965 by four POWs held in the Hỏa Lò: Captain Carlyle "Smitty" Harris, Lieutenant Phillip Butler, Lieutenant Robert Peel and Lieutenant Commander Robert Shumaker. "Smitty" Harris had remembered the code from prior training and taught it to his fellow prisoners. The code was simple and easy to learn and could be taught without verbal instructions. In addition to allowing communication between walls, the prisoners used the code when sitting next to each other but forbidden from speaking by tapping on one another's bodies. Throughout the war the tap code was instrumental in maintaining prisoner morale, as well as preserving a cohesive military structure despite North Vietnamese attempts to disrupt the POW's chain of command. During periods of protracted isolation, the tap code facilitated elaborate mental projects to keep the prisoners' sanity.

At times I was *"chief of communications in the camp. And of course, passing messages was a big, big sin. So, I got in a lot of trouble over that."*[60]

The "Tap" Code Matrix

	1	2	3	4	5
			C/		
1	A	B	K	D	E
2	F	G	H	I	J
3	L	M	N	O	P
4	Q	R	S	T	U
5	V	W	X	Y	Z

Colonel Carlyle "Smitty" Harris USAF (Ret.) wrote in his book: *"Tap Code: The Epic Survival Tale of a Vietnam POW and the Secret Code That Changed Everything."* The following:

"So, is it genius? With the letter 'K' removed, the 1st tap would be the first row. The 2nd tap would be the letter in the row. It was brought to the POW committee by a friend of mine, and without going into the gory details, I was finally, after three days in the jungle, captured, I was taken to Hanoi for a couple of months. So, I got up to Hanoi, and for about 9 months I was totally isolated: Not only alone, but I had no way to have contact with anyone. You had to tap softly so the guards wouldn't hear; we would pass info amongst ourselves—where we were from, what college we attended, and aside from 'speaking' to each, we would give each other encouragement. And if they caught you communicating, which we did all day long, they were very rough

---

[60] Baldi; Op Cit. pg 51

on you. I was finally moved from Hanoi Prison (it wasn't an actual prison), and the guy next to me was a young sailor name Doug Hegdahl. He began teaching me the code using three-code with one alphabet, so he taught me the tap code: 25 letters; no K. Then we could tap to each other. It was great for me, since I had been isolated for those 9 months—it was the first time where someone wasn't beating me up. And I have to tell you that that is really rough in an environment where the only contact was somebody else who was hostile, a la beatings. So that really hits you. Human beings like to be around people, and they like to be around nice people. Being in touch with someone, and then of course even if you were in bad shape, it was uplifting getting messages thru the walls. You had to hang in there for that sort of thing. I was in 9 months, and I resisted no differently then— than when I was in different quarters. Spiritually, you get very, very, weary, and tired, because you have no constant human contact. Sometimes we just tapped "GBU," - God Bless You."[61]

John M. McGrath, (Lt. Cmdr) a young Navy pilot who was captured in 1967 after being shot down over Vietnam, vividly presents a straightforward and compelling tale of survival, of years of suffering, and of the human will to endure. During the era of the unpopular

---

[61] *Harris, Carlyle "Smitty" (Col. Ret'd) and Sara W. Berry; Tap Code: The Epic Survival Tale of a Vietnam POW and the Secret Code That Changed Everything; Lemuria Books; Jackson, MI; 2019*

Vietnam War few issues united the American people as did the emotion-laden problem of POWs and MIAs. When the peace treaties were finally signed and the POWs returned to American soil, the nation was collectively relieved by their safe return. A self-taught artist, the starkness of McGrath's drawings underscores his remarkable and moving chronicle of the lives of these prisoners, who were constantly in peril, attempting to survive a brutal captivity almost unimaginable in civilized times.[62]

Drawings below by Captain Mike McGrath: *Prisoner of War: Six Years in Hanoi.*

Admiral Stockdale, POW and Medal of Honor Recipient, *said "No man alive can beat THE ROPES."*

(Admiral Stockdale Statement on Medal of Honor interview on DVD *within Medal of Honor book.* Collier Press.*)***

---

[62] McGrath, John M.; Prisoner of War: Six Tears in Hanoi; Naval Institute Press; November 2011

Various items the POW's had in their "rooms." *McGrath.*

McGrath drawings

NVA Captors Spook, Rabbit, and Spot. As named by the POW's.
Source: Mike McGrath

U.S. prisoners of war in North Vietnam were subjected to extreme torture and malnutrition during their captivity. Although North Vietnam was a signatory of the Third Geneva Convention of 1949, which demanded "decent and humane treatment" of prisoners of war, severe torture methods were employed, such as waterboarding, strappado (known as "the ropes" to POWs), irons, beatings, and prolonged solitary confinement. The aim of the torture was usually not acquiring military information. Rather, it was to break the will of the prisoners, both individually and as a group. The goal of the North Vietnamese was to get written or recorded statements from the prisoners that criticized U.S. conduct of the war and praised how the North Vietnamese treated them. Such POW statements would be viewed as a propaganda victory in the battle to sway world and U.S. domestic opinion against the U.S. war effort.

During one such event in 1966, then-Commander Jeremiah Denton, a captured Navy pilot, was forced to appear at a televised press conference, where he famously blinked the word "T-O-R-T-U-R-E" with his eyes in Morse code, confirming to U.S. intelligence that U.S. prisoners were being harshly treated. Two months later, in what became known as the Hanoi March, 52 American prisoners of war were paraded through the streets of Hanoi before thousands of North Vietnamese civilians. The march soon deteriorated into near riot conditions, with North Vietnamese civilians beating the POWs along the 2 miles (3.2 km) route, and their guards largely unable to restrain the attacks.

In the end, North Vietnamese torture was sufficiently brutal and prolonged that nearly every American POW so subjected made a statement of some kind at some time. *"Unbearable to most, our POWs endured some of the cruelest torture methods known to mankind — solitary confinement, malnutrition, rope binds, irons, beatings and constant threat of being killed including being kneeled with a gun to their head if they did not talk to name but a few — and this by a country that had supposedly signed the Geneva Convention,"*[63] As John McCain later wrote of finally being forced to make an anti-American statement: *"I had learned what we all learned over there: Every man*

---

[63] Crowell, Bob; Northern Nevada Business Weekly, May 2, 2018

has his breaking point. I had reached mine. "[64] Only a small number of exceptionally resilient prisoners, such as John A. Dramesi, survived captivity without ever cooperating with the enemy; others who refused to cooperate under any circumstances, such as Edwin Atterbury, were tortured to death. James Stockdale, fearing that he might reveal details of the Gulf of Tonkin incident if tortured, attempted suicide, but survived; he never revealed this information to the enemy. Under these extreme conditions, many prisoners' aims became merely to absorb as much torture as they could before giving in. Leo Thorsness later described the internal code the POWs developed, and instructed new arrivals on, as follows:

> *"The internal code for our POWs was take physical torture until you are right at the edge of losing your ability to be rational. At that point, lie, do, or say whatever you must do to survive. But you first must take physical torture."*[65]

After making statements, the POWs would admit to each other what had happened, lest shame or guilt consume them or make them more vulnerable to additional North Vietnamese pressure. Nevertheless, the POWs obsessed over what they had done, and would years after their release still be haunted by the "confessions" or other statements they

---

[64] McCain, John S. III, Lieutenant Commander USN 1973-05-14
(reposted under Title: "John McCain, Prisoner of War: A First-Person Account", 2008-01-28)

[65] Thorsness, Leo (2009-06-07) "Surviving Torture". The Philadelphia Inquirer. Retrieved 2009-06-27).

had made. As another POW later said, *"To this day I get angry with myself. But we did the best we could. [We realize], over time, that we all fall short of what we aspire to be. And that is where forgiveness comes in."*[66]

The North Vietnamese occasionally released prisoners for propaganda or other purposes. The POWs had a "first in, first out" interpretation of the Code of the U.S. Fighting Force, meaning they could only accept release in the order they had been captured, but making an exception for those seriously sick or badly injured. When a few captured servicemen began to be released from North Vietnamese prisons during the Johnson administration, their testimonies revealed widespread and systematic abuse of prisoners of war. Initially, this information was downplayed by American authorities for fear that conditions might worsen for those remaining in North Vietnamese custody. Policy changed under the Nixon administration, when mistreatment of the prisoners was publicized by U.S. Secretary of Defense Melvin Laird and others.

---

[66] Farrell, John Aloysius (2008-01-23) *"A Refining Experience"*. The Boston Globe

The Hanoi Hilton in a 1970 aerial surveillance photo.

At the "Hanoi Hilton," POWs cheered the resumed bombing of North Vietnam starting in April 1972, whose targets included the Hanoi area. The old-time POWs cheered even more during the intense "Christmas Bombing" campaign of December 1972, when Hanoi was subjected for the first time to repeated B-52 Stratofortress raids. Although its explosions lit the night sky and shook the walls of the camp, scaring some of the new POWs, most saw it as a forceful measure to compel North Vietnam to finally come to terms.

Former POW Lieutenant Colonel Myron Donald stated that they (the POWs) were too often times misled about going home. The NVA would bus them to Gia Lam airfield only to return them to their prisons. This time it had all the trimmings of being real.

Captain Ralph Galati, the second youngest POW, was on his potential "ride" out of North Vietnam on 28 March. He later became a good friend of John Siegfried, and John asked him, what his thoughts were when he saw the C-141 (jet) taxing down the runway:

"My group was lined up in two columns. Ahead of us we could see a table with Vietnamese military members and what appeared to be a US military officer - at least someone dressed in an American military uniform. Again, was this just another hoax or propaganda stunt by our North Vietnamese captors? We wanted it to be real, we wanted it to be legitimate. After all, the uniforms looked proper; the C-141 that just landed was certainly one of ours! No shots were fired.

"One-by-one our names were called, we were saluted by the American Officer, and then escorted across the tarmac to the waiting C-141. It was rather peaceful, and very orchestrated - no sense of hostility. After we were all onboard, and it looked like we might actually be leaving, we started to relax a bit. We then taxied, then had an uneventful takeoff. I remember looking down, and seeing a terrain littered with bomb craters. After about 20 minutes, the pilot announced we had cleared North Vietnamese airspace, and were over the Pacific enroute to Clark Air Base in the Philippines. It was at this point we were finally able to erupt in cheers. The entire group of us were in a state of unbridled euphoria. The Hanoi Taxi was taking us home."[67]

---

[67] Galati, Ralph; interview with John Siegfried; 11 June 2022

Ralph's Plane upon leaving Vietnam airspace 28 March 1973. He is behind the man in the 3rd row with his right hand in the air.

There were fifty planes (C-141) that transported our guys from Gia Lam to Clark AFB in the Philippines. Support planes (C-130) carrying additional medical staff arrived at Gia Lam as well. One of those had Jon Cavaiani aboard.

Released at Gia Lam Airport, Hanoi, North Vietnam at 1555 hours and arriving at Clark Air Base, Philippines at 1851 hours:[68]

Name Rank SVC		
Allwine, David F.	SSG	USA
Anshus, Richard C.	CPT	USA
Anzaldua, Jose J. Jr.	SGT	USMC
Chirichigno, Luis G.	CPT	USA
Cavaiani, Jon R.	**SSG**	**USA**
Daugherty, Lenard B.	SP5	USA
Daves, Gary L.	CIV	CIV
Elliott, Artice W.	LTC	USA
Gauntt, William A.	CPT	USAF
Hefel, Daniel H.	SGT	USA
Henderson, William J.	CPT	USAF
Horio, Thomas T.	SP5	USA
Jacquez, Juan L.	SP5	USA
Kientzier, Phillip A.	LCD	USN
Kobashigawa, Tom Y	SGT	USA
Kroboth, Alan J.	1LT	USMC
Malo, Isaako F.	SP5	USA
Meyer, Lewis E.	CIV	CIV
Mott, David P.	CPT	USAF
Murphy, John S. Jr.	CPT	USAF
Nowicki, James E.	WO2	USA

---

[68] Mac's Facts no. 48.... Hanoi Taxi, Operation Homecoming 1973.

Olsen, Robert F.	CIV	CIV
Parsels, John W.	CPT	USA
Prather, Phillip D.	WO2	USA
Purcell, Benjamin H.	COL	USA
Rander, Donald J.	SFC	USA
Reeder, William E. Jr.	CPT	USA
Rushton, Thomas	CIV	CIV
Tabb, Robert E.	SSG	USA
Tellier, Dennis A.	SGT	USMC
Thomas, William E. Jr.	WO2	USMC
Willis, Charles E.	CIV	CIV

Lieutenant Colonel Myron Donald, USAF (Ret.), a POW in Vietnam, spoke with John Siegfried in 2010 and recounted that:

"In late January 1973, our captors read the Paris Peace Accord to us. In unison, we retorted, 'Oh, bullshit!' We had been through this quite often. After countless times of this banter and misinformation, with us not believing them, we played it off. Then one day, they paraded-us into a room that had some pretty crappy-clothes - jackets, pants, shoes, socks, and shit. So, we all picked-thru stuff and got dressed. Then we waited.

Finally, after parading us to Gia Lam Airport, we saw that a C-141 (a jet plane) had begun its descent, then taxied, stopped, and then the door opened. I could smell the flight-nurses perfume all the way across the ramp. After the smell of the North Vietnamese camp for over 5 years, I was in seventh heaven. "[69]

Jon Cavaiani possibly had the same frame of mind as the LTC. On 27 March, Jon was on a plane to Clarke AFB in the Philippines.

---

[69] Mac's Facts no. 48.... Hanoi Taxi, Operation Homecoming 1973.

January 9, 2020 (Note: there are 50 pages to this document)

CHAPTER EIGHT

Recognition

"True heroism is remarkably sober, very undramatic. It is not the urge to surpass all others at whatever cost, but the urge to serve others at whatever cost."

Arthur Ashe

The Medal of Honor, the nation's highest award for bravery, has been awarded to men who defended their friends against overwhelming odds, or who stayed behind to evacuate the wounded, or even those who suffered in prisoner of war camps for years on end. Rarely is the Medal given to one man for all three actions. Jon R. Cavaiani was one of those men.

(National Museum – United States Army:

https://www.thenmusa.org/biographies/jon-r-cavaiani/)

On 12 December 1974, President Gerald Ford placed the Medal of Honor around Jon's neck. Jon Robert Cavaiani received the United States Congressional Medal of Honor for "*distinguishing himself by conspicuous gallantry and intrepidity at the risk of life above and*

beyond the call of duty in action in the Republic of Vietnam on 4 and 5 June 1971. Several years later Betty Ford related the story of how *"Jerry (President Ford) was so impressed with Jon."* The President had told Mrs. Ford, ***"He shouldn't have made it off that hill, and definitely should not have survived as a Prisoner of War, so don't ever bet against that guy!"***

President Ford was so correct in his assessment.

Staff Sergeant Cavaiani's official
MEDAL OF HONOR CITATION:

S/Sgt. Cavaiani distinguished himself by conspicuous gallantry and intrepidity at the risk of life above and beyond the call of duty in action in the Republic of Vietnam on 4 and 5 June 1971 while serving as a platoon leader to a security platoon providing security for an isolated radio relay site located within enemy-held territory. On the morning of 4 June 1971, the entire camp came under an intense barrage of enemy small arms, automatic weapons, rocket-propelled grenade and mortar fire from a superior size enemy force. S/Sgt. Cavaiani acted with complete disregard for his personal safety as he repeatedly exposed himself to heavy enemy fire in order to move about the camp's perimeter directing the platoon's fire and rallying the platoon in a desperate fight for survival. S/Sgt. Cavaiani also returned heavy suppressive fire upon the assaulting enemy force during this period with a variety of weapons. When the entire platoon was to be evacuated, S/Sgt. Cavaiani unhesitatingly volunteered to remain on the ground and direct the helicopters into the landing zone. S/Sgt. Cavaiani was able to direct the first 3 helicopters in evacuating a major portion of the platoon. Due to intense increase in enemy fire, S/Sgt. Cavaiani was forced to remain at the camp overnight where he calmly directed the remaining platoon members in strengthening their defenses. On the morning of 5 June, a heavy ground fog restricted visibility. The superior size enemy force launched a major ground attack in an attempt to completely annihilate the remaining small force. The enemy force advanced in 2 ranks, first firing a heavy volume of small arms automatic weapons and rocket-propelled grenade fire while the second rank continuously threw a steady barrage of hand grenades at the beleaguered force. S/Sgt. Cavaiani returned a heavy barrage of small arms and hand grenade fire on the assaulting enemy force but was unable to slow them down. He ordered the remaining platoon members to attempt to escape while he provided them with cover fire. With one last courageous exertion, S/Sgt. Cavaiani recovered an M60, and with fire directed at him, and began firing the machine gun in a sweeping motion along the two ranks of advancing enemy soldiers. Through S/Sgt. Cavaiani's valiant efforts with complete disregard for his safety, the majority of the remaining platoon members were able to escape. While inflicting severe losses on the advancing enemy force, S/Sgt. Cavaiani was wounded numerous times. S/Sgt. Cavaiani's conspicuous gallantry, extraordinary heroism, and intrepidity at the risk of his life, above and beyond the call of duty, were in keeping with the highest traditions of the military service and reflect great credit upon himself and the U.S. Army.

Medal of Honor recipients – Vietnam (A-L)". United States Army Center of Military History

President Gerald Ford's Remarks on Awarding the Congressional Medal of Honor to WO Louis R. Rocco and S. Sgt. Jon R. Cavaiani, United States Army.

12 December 1974

"Secretary Schlesinger, Secretary Callaway, our distinguished recipients, Ladies and Gentlemen:

"It is, of course, a great blessing that the last American soldier is home from the battlefields of Vietnam. Our landing ships again, fortunately, have long since departed those distant shores. And our planes have long ago flown their last mission on the war across those faraway jungles.

"Let us, individually and collectively, fervently pray that Vietnam was, indeed, the last---our last war.

"We are, however, reminded of Vietnam today--of that long and painful time--by two men who lived it and whose actions will never die in the annals of the United States military history. For the Nation they served bestows on them today the Congressional Medal of Honor for *their acts of courage above and beyond the call of duty.*

"United States Army Warrant Officer Louis Rocco--Sergeant First Class in Vietnam--and Army Staff Sergeant Jon R. Cavaiani, by the courage of their acts, carried forward the long and very proud military tradition of selfless dedication to the cause of freedom.

"Army Warrant Officer Louis Rocco distinguished himself on May 24, 1970. He volunteered to help evacuate eight critically wounded South Vietnamese troops under attack. His helicopter crash-landed at the evacuation site under intense enemy fire. Ignoring a fractured wrist and broken hip and severely bruised back, Warrant Officer Rocco pulled the unconscious survivors from the burning wreckage. His hands were severely burned, causing him excruciating pain. He nevertheless carried each of his unconscious comrades more than 20 yards through enemy fire to friendly positions. Trained in first aid, he administered to them before collapsing into unconsciousness.

"Warrant Officer Rocco's bravery was directly responsible for saving three of his fellow soldiers from certain death. His gallantry, disregarding his own pain and injuries, is in the highest tradition of self-sacrifice and courage in our military service.

"And I say to his family here today, you also walk in the respect and admiration of your country and of your President.

Sergeant Cavaiani was presumed to have been killed in action when recommended for the Medal of Honor. It was only later learned that he had been captured. He was a prisoner of war for more than 2 years and was repatriated on 27 March 1973.

On June 4 and 5, 1971, he served as a platoon leader, providing security for an isolated radio relay site within enemy-held territory. The

Sergeant's unit was attacked by a superior enemy force. For those 2 days, firing with different weapons, Sergeant Cavaiani directed the evacuation of some of his platoon by helicopter while ordering the others to escape. Many were able to do so. He remained, however, exposing himself to heavy enemy fire. Sergeant Cavaiani was wounded numerous times, finally falling to his captors."

We are honored that the Sergeant's family is here with us today. The President of the United States wishes to tell them in person that Sergeant Cavaiani is an American of extraordinary heroism, and his valor reflects well on all of them.

This day is witness to the fact that the bravest of the brave still rise from among our people, that freedom and that justice have survived and will survive, that peace is still our most precious and enduring goal, and that we the American people will forever cherish the noble deeds, the noble ideals entrusted to us these past two centuries by our forefathers.

These ideals do not sleep. They are not silent. They live among us here today in the presence of Jon Robert Cavaiani and Louis Richard Rocco and their families.

The Secretary of the Army will now read the citations.

[At this point, Secretary of the Army Howard H. Callaway read the citations. The President then resumed speaking.]

"Thank you very much, Secretary Callaway, Secretary Schlesinger, Ladies and Gentlemen. I thank you all for being here.

"It is a very wonderful occasion paying tribute and honor to two very gallant and wonderful soldiers in the very highest and the very best traditions of the United States military service.

"I suggest now that we all might go into the State Dining Room and have some refreshments."

SSG Jon Cavaiani is congratulated by President Ford after receiving the Medal of Honor at the White House in 1974. (Frank Johnston/The Washington Post)

President Ford and Staff Sergeant (MOH) Cavaiani

A young Major with the Capitol Honor Guard, briefs Major Blair and Staff Sergeant Cavaiani on proper protocols. Jon's look says, *"You've got to be shitting me Major."*

Jon celebrating his Medal of Honor with Ugo Cavaiani and his brother Carl and a couple of other friends

Jon congratulated on his MOH by Sergeant Major of the Army Leon Van Autreve

Later in his life, Jon would admit to not remembering much about the ceremony due to his being a bit hung-over from having spent the previous evening with a fellow Medal of Honor recipient, Warrant Officer Louis R. Rocco. They had attempted to drink Washington D.C. dry and had failed. But they were proud of their effort.

After the ceremony at the White House and even before joining family and friends over drinks and a meal, Jon made his way to Arlington National Cemetery. He asked to be dropped off and said that he would return shortly. He then walked to the center of the expansive grounds filled with markers that identified heroes of a sometimes-grateful nation, yet too often, an ungrateful and uncaring mob of humanity. He saw the flickering flame ahead and, as if marching to his commander to render a report, he drew near the flame that marked the resting place of John Fitzgerald Kennedy, 35th President of the United States of America. Jon halted and saluted. No one heard his words if he spoke. No one knew his thoughts. But it was as if he were saying, *"Sir, I have returned, I have fulfilled my mission, and I am ready for your next order. I am a soldier here to serve."*

Medal of Honor Grove
Freedoms Foundation
Valley Forge, PA

The Medal of Honor Grove is located on the campus of Freedoms Foundation at Valley Forge. It is a 42-acre natural woodland and is designed as a living memorial to over 3,500 recipients of our nation's highest military decoration, the Medal of Honor. A section of the Grove is designated **for each of the fifty states**, including our territories Puerto Rico and the District of Columbia. Each Medal of Honor Recipient is identified by a stainless-steel marker with the name and military organization of the Recipient and the date and location of the act of valor. The recipient's name is inscribed on the state obelisk of which he/she entered service.

Two additional memorials are at the entrance. One is the AOH Memorial which honors over 150 immigrants who received the Medal of Honor but, because they were not citizens, could not be honored in a state. The second is the Chaplains Memorial that honors 9 chaplains who received the Medal of Honor.

In 2011, the Friends of the Medal of Honor Grove, a 501c3 were created by community members to maintain and enhance the Grove. Since that time, the Friends have updated all the recipients names in their accredited state or territory, re-paved all the roadways, became a level 1 Arboretum and is currently removing hundreds of dead or diseased trees. The Friends are a 100% voluntary organization depending on private donations to keep the Grove in the honorable condition it is in. Over 800 people volunteer to work in the Grove yearly with company and community service days.

The images below are all currently located at "The Grove" in the California Section, honoring SgtMaj Cavaiani.

ARMY — AIR FORC

BACA, John Philip, Sgt.,
Cav. Div. (Ft Ord) (b. R.I.)
BELLRICHARD, Leslie A., Pfc.,
8th Inf. Div. (Oakland) (b. Wis.)
BROPHY, James, Pvt.,
8th U.S. Cav. (Stockton) (b. Irela
CARTER, Edward A., Jr., Staff S.,
U.S. Army (Los Angeles)
CAVAIANI, Jon R., S/Sgt., U.S.
Vietnam Tr. Adv. Gp. (b. England
CRAFT, Clarence B., Pfc.,
96th Inf. Div. (Santa Ana)
CROCKER, Henry H., Capt.,
2d Mass. Cav. (b. Conn.)
DAVILA, Rudolph B., 2d Lt.,
7th Inf. (Los Angeles) (b. Tex.)
DEAN, William F., Maj. Gen.,
Inf. Div. (b. Ill.)

SSGT JON R. CAVAIANI
US ARMY

VIETNAM TRAINING
ADVISORY GROUP

REPUBLIC OF VIETNAM

4 AND 5 JUNE 1971

Congressional Medal of Honor Grove
Freedoms Foundation at Valley Forge, PA

CHAPTER NINE

Though Worn and Abused - Still a Soldier

"Success is not final. Failure is not fatal. It is the ability to continue that matters."

Winston Churchill

Due to the secretive nature of his service, much of Cavaiani's military record after Vietnam is unknown. (National Museum – United States Army: https://www.thenmusa.org/biographies/jon-r-cavaiani/

Cavaiani was released from POW imprisonment 27 March 1973, after spending six-hundred-sixty-one days in captivity with much of his confinement in a solitary cell. He would later state that he *"was not the most cooperative of prisoners. "*

Much of what Jon did in his Army career beyond his POW experience and recovery years is still not available to the public. His service beyond Fort Devens, and up until assignment as an ROTC Instructor, are not presented or discussed. What can be related regarding his military service follows in this chapter.

After enduring twenty-two months of being a non-existent being – since he could not, with certainty, be determined as MIA / POW / or KIA - Jon proved Ramon's dream to be true. He was indeed, against the odds, still alive.

Upon his release by the North Vietnamese from captivity, Jon was flown to Clarke AFB in the Philippines, then immediately to Travis Air Force Base for transport to Letterman Army Hospital, The Presidio, San Francisco, California for evaluation, treatment, and recovery.

Jon required many surgeries due to his wounds. He was also struggling with PTSD. He fought through his nightmares, but they recurred almost daily. His treatment at Letterman was lengthy. Physically, it took almost six months for him to relearn how to walk and swing his arms just so that he could function, much less, march. Psychological healing would take longer.

Jon Cavaiani was one of the multitudes of Vietnam Veterans who struggled with and coped with Post Traumatic Stress Disorder. The term Post Traumatic Stress Disorder (PTSD was coined in 1980), on the heels of 'Battle Fatigue' from WW2, where some of our military carried their emotional, psychological, and mental demons from the horrors of combat for the rest of their lives.

Cavaiani was a classic case for this disorder. It was while he was at Letterman that Jon heard about and read about anti-war protests occurring on the campus of The University of California, Berkeley. Jon had been away from news reports and general information about the political climate in the U. S. for almost two years. Being in close proximity, Jon decided to drive over in hopes of finding out why his fellow Americans were spewing such negative words toward him and his fellow servicemen and women.

Jon drove to the UC Berkeley campus thinking that he might confront some protestors, but as he arrived at Sproul Plaza he saw a North Vietnamese flag painted on the pavement. This set Jon off big-time, and he began driving the car in a way to do donuts right on top of the flag and spinning the tires as he did so. He blackened the flag, looked at it and then went back to add more marks to obscure the symbol of oppression. The Campus police arrived in short order and pulled Jon to a halt.

Because of his treatment status, Jon had been given a letter by Letterman Army Hospital explaining his special status and treatment. The letter instructed the reader to call the Letterman Army Hospital if a problem was encountered.

Jon handed over his driver's license, military ID, and the letter to the police. An officer looked the documents over. He went to his car to check the license information and told his partner to call Letterman and check out the validity of the letter. The officer called the number provided in the letter and after a few minutes returned and told the other officers, *"This guy is just back from 'Nam and he is going to receive the Medal of Honor!"*

The police officer then turned to Jon and asked, *"Do you want to do it again - some more donuts on that flag? We will keep folks back if you want."*

Jon responded, *"No, thank you. I got it out of my system."*

After the officers shook his hand, he was released to return to Letterman.[70]

---

[70] Shields, James in interview with Mike Evers June 8 2022

What is Post Traumatic Stress? For those who have served in combat it is undying ghosts that haunt each day. The concept has acquired several names over the years. From Soldiers Heart (Civil War), to Shell shock (WWI), to battle fatigue (WWII), and to post-traumatic stress disorder (Vietnam and Gulf Wars), our men and women have been handcuffed with the emotional trauma of war. PTSD/PTS clings to our warriors like an invisible suit. Both men and women of the Vietnam War deserved more than America was willing to give.[71]

And many who returned from Vietnam were dismissed by society as baby-killers, war mongers, or worse – even the greatest generation dismissed these warriors and denied them any opportunity to be hailed as heroes. They were refugees in their own country. Our own citizens are culpable for instilling this atmosphere. The loneliness and despair that comes from not being acknowledged is a form of PTSD. As stated by a friend who prefers anonymity in a conversation with co-author John Siegfried; *"In their minds, some of our guys never came home."*[72] Being members of the Marine Corps – Law Enforcement Foundation Board, these two frequently converse.

Returning to the U. S. where an ungrateful, but boisterous, few created so much harm and hurt to those who had served was challenging for many, and perhaps even more so for Jon. He had suffered so much for his chosen country, yet Jon soldiered on and helped so many

---

[71] Burkett, B. G. and Glenna Whitley; Stolen Valor; Verity Press; Dallas; 1998

[72] In conversation with John Siegfried

overcome the effects of PTS even as he himself was suffering.

It was while at the Presidio that Jon learned that he had been awarded the Medal of Honor for the valorous efforts taken at Hickory Hill. On December 12, 1974, Jon stood with President Gerald Ford. Jon recounted in a Pritzker Military Museum interview that the President had spent three hours with him and his family. He was humbled by the President's careful attention to himself and his family. The citation recounting his bravery was read and he was awarded the Medal of Honor. After the ceremony the President invited Jon to remain with him in the oval office. They talked for more than one hour. Some say that the President spent time encouraging Jon to forgive the "Ducks" and forget their "treason under pressure."

Once cleared for duty by Letterman Army Hospital for full duty, Jon was assigned to the same location from whence he had departed prior to his duty in Vietnam – Fort Bragg, North Carolina. There, he served in the Training Group as an instructor of the next generation of Green Beret candidates. He did his best to help make each soldier in the Special Forces Training Group better than they believed they could be. He also tried to make changes in the curriculum, based upon his experiences, and his hard-charging attempts to do so, pissed off some of his senior NCOs. In addition, the nightmares persisted, and Jon needed further help fighting his PTSD.

After only one year, Jon was reassigned back to The Presidio in California. At the Presidio, Jon could receive further treatment for his PTSD, while providing a valuable service to the Army's readiness effort.

His Commander at that assignment was Col. Vladimir

Sobichevsky. The Colonel and Jon had some things in common. Vladimir was an émigré, he grew up without a birth father present in his life, he had served as an enlisted soldier and NCO, and he had served in combat with SOG. Colonel Sobichevsky took an interest in Jon's recovery from the trauma of war that was exhibiting itself as PTSD.

Sobichevsky, the grandson of a Czarist Army General, was born in Kiev (currently in Ukraine), Union Soviet Socialist Republic (USSR) in 1937. In 1943, his mother escaped the USSR with her son. They Traveled the emigrants' hard road westward through Poland, Czechoslovakia and at the end of the war ending up in Germany. In 1945, they witnessed the victorious entry of the US Army.

In 1956, he joined the U.S. Army Special Forces and six years later, was promoted to Sergeant First Class. He served nine years with the workhorse of Special Forces, the Operational "A" Detachments. In 1965, he graduated from the Infantry Officer Candidate School as a 2nd Lieutenant of Infantry. He served as a Captain with the Studies and Observation Group (MACV-SOG) in Vietnam.

After serving as operations director for the Special Operations Command, Pacific, Colonel Sobichevsky was transferred to the Defense Language Institute (DLI). Jon was to be assigned to the DLI, but he fought that because of his passion for being with the troops.

As part of the effort to assist Jon in his recovery, Colonel Vladimir Sobichevsky initially wanted to assign Jon to the Defense Language School, Presidio Monterey. However, Jon proved to have no interest in the assignment and requested assignment to a more operational unit. His request was honored, and he was assigned to Readiness Region IX as Advisor to 3rd Battalion, 12th Special Forces

Group

Jon was not the perfect soldier. Colonel Sobichevsky was well aware of this. The Colonel worked with Jon and ensured that he was present for every treatment session at Letterman Army Hospital and other facilities that provided services that Jon needed. There were times when Jon was just another grunt soldier who needed guidance and direction. On one such occasion Sergeant First Class Cavaiani traveled with Major Blair to China Lake in Southern California as part of an active-duty cadre who would provide training to reserve units.

Upon arrival, Jon reported to the Sergeant Major of the training team, SGM Jake Jacobson, who looked at him and immediately directed: *"Sergeant Cavaiani, get your ass to the barber shop right now and get rid of those locks. You are not in San Francisco; you are in my camp!"* Jon did, as directed.[73]

Jon took his duties as an advisor seriously. He loved being in the field with soldiers. It seemed to relieve the stress of his nightmares, the trauma of past abuse, memories that refused to abate, and other aspects of post-traumatic stress. The position of advisor enabled him to apply what Ugo Cavaiani had taught him, that is, to make others better.

Jim Shields shared a story of Jon's willingness to help soldiers and teach soldiers. On one occasion, Jon was working with a reserve unit and advising them on their training. The unit was moving on foot in the China Lake area of California. Jon noticed a young soldier struggling with his PRC-77, a back-packed radio that added weight to the normal load of equipment. The young soldier, while wrestling and

---

[73] Jacobson, Harold "Jake" in interview with Mike Evers 21 May 2022

losing to the piece of equipment, was trying to read his radio manual, adjust various knobs, while talking and walking - all at the same time.

"Jon walked up to me, and like a coach, began teaching the me how to adjust the load for more a comfortable load bearing carry. He then patiently began to teach me how to become a radio operator. He showed me how to preset the radio for rapid frequency change, and how to abbreviate communication into terse, but understandable, phrases. Jon continued to work with me throughout the training period to help hone my commo skills. I learned in that few miles of walking and the follow-on training with Jon Cavaiani all that I needed to know about radio communication ... except, I guess, Morse Code."[74]

"Later in that training cycle some of us were complaining about the conditions at China Lake. Jon asked those of us in training to touch our elbows together. We all did so by putting our arms forward with elbows and forearms in front of our chest. 'No, I mean behind your back!' Some of us tried but found it to be impossible. He then said: 'What you think is impossible is not the extent of the possible! Under certain conditions you can do it, and you can survive it!' He then told us about some of his overcoming the 'impossible' as a POW. Becoming the master of your mind is critical to sanity and survival!"

During that same training cycle Jon was assigned to teach

---

[74] Op Cit; Shields

soldiers how to fire a M72 LAW (Light Antitank Weapon). Being the exacting individual that he was he had laid the LAWs out in a precise order so that the trainees could move quickly and safely to their stations. He had set up a plywood training aid that depicted the nomenclature of the weapon; the arming, aiming, and firing processes; as well as a proper sight alignment.

Jon went through the lecture portion of the training and then worked the young soldiers through the process of arming, aiming, and firing using inert LAW devices that were used as training aids.

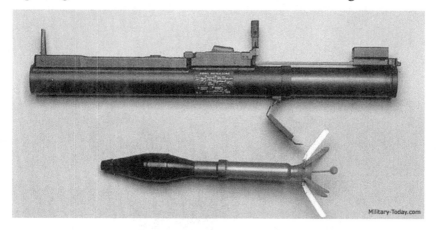

Using his Methods of Instruction (MOI) skills developed at Fort Bragg during his Special Forces qualification training Jon gave a brief but thorough lecture and hands-on walk-through training on the weapon. Following the layout that appeared on the plywood sheet he stressed safety, the nomenclature of the weapon; arming, sighting, aiming, and firing processes. He then had each trainee go-though a dry run exercise with an inert LAW.

Finally, it was time to actually fire live LAWs. The first person to fire stepped forward. Jon pointed at an old D3 Caterpillar tractor that had been placed down range. Following the instruction that he received the soldier armed, aimed, and fired. The rocket flew down range and hit the engine block of the tractor dead-on.

The smoke and dust were settling when a loud "thunk" was heard. Jon, still standing by the plywood sheet glanced to his right and at eye level saw a glow plug protruding from the training aid less than a foot from his right eye. Without losing a beat he said, *"Nice shot! Next man!"*

Toward the end of that training cycle Jon and another NCO had gotten into an argument. No one seems to know for sure what the argument was about, but "the talk" is that the other NCO had felt that Jon had shown him up and made him look bad. The other NCO was one who would give a training lecture and then go drink a beer while the trainees went through their paces.   The other NCO, out of spite, had taken the only jeep available to return to the cantonment area and left Jon in the desert to walk back. When the Sergeant Major saw the other NCO return without Jon he asked about Jon the NCO shrugged and said, "Let him walk." The Sergeant Major jumped into the jeep and hauled ass for the training area. He found Jon walking back toward the cantonment area and asked him what had happened. *"Just a disagreement"* was his response. *"Well, he should not have left you out here!"* exclaimed the Sergeant Major. *"No problem, I have walked farther under worse conditions,"* said Jon, and then refused to say anything more about the situation.[75]

Following that training cycle, Jon returned to duties at The Presidio only to find that his Medal of Honor medallion and ribbon had been stolen. As soon as Colonel Sobichevsky learned of the incident, the entire facility was shut down and a room-to-room search ensued. The Medal was indeed found in a fellow NCO's room, and the individual assigned to that room began shouting that he deserved the Medal more than Jon. *"I deserve this Medal more than him."* It happened to be the same NCO who had left Jon stranded in the desert. PTSD among returnees from Vietnam was not uncommon, and for

---

[75] Op Cit; Jacobson

some, it was indeed severe. War is traumatic and can create fantasies. And those fantasies may give rise to false hopes of escaping the trauma. Jon was hardly the only service member suffering such traumatic impacts.

In an interview with Pritzker Military Museum, Jon said that PTS is a devious thing and that on occasion he would wake up with a gun in his mouth. He also recalled 'living chemically' on prescribed drugs and alcohol to help him cope. He knew firsthand the deviousness of the demons of PTS and realized that others had similar battles within.

Subsequently, Jon took a position with the Berlin Brigade in 1977. The Berlin Wall, erected by the Soviet Powers and East Germany during the cold war, still stood. Jon was an Operations and Training NCO in the center of the besieged city. Much of the effort of operations and training was a show of force on the part of the U. S., but there was a significant psychological effort to influence, in a negative way, any Soviet attempt to move against the quadripartite unity of the U.S., British, French, and free Germany cohesion.

The Berlin Brigade and Special Forces Detachment A were under close scrutiny of Soviet and East German military units. Working with British and French military personnel, Jon helped design training and operations that would deter any thoughts on the part of the Soviets to engage in any military action to take control of West Berlin. This included scheduling and monitoring guard functions and changing of the guard at Spandau Prison. A World War II war criminal was still housed in Spandau Prison. The four nations (US, England, France, and the Soviet Union), on a rotational basis, provided the military guards to the prison.

Convoys of U. S. military vehicles, loaded with soldiers and equipment passed through East Germany on an almost daily basis. The trip between Checkpoint Alpha (near Helmstedt) to Checkpoint Bravo, at West Berlin's perimeter, was monitored by Soviet Forces to observe any flaw or error of the traversing units. U. S. military convoy commanders were required to maintain radio contact with Brigade Operations for the duration of each convoy's travels.

One particular convoy returning from West Germany after an extended training period had a problem that raised some concern. The left center tire of a Gamma Goat (a six wheeled vehicle with multiple universal joints) sheared at the wheel bolts and began traversing the autobahn of East Germany on its own. It traveled past the convoy commander, into the center divider and towards on-coming high-speed traffic. An international incident was in the making.

Fortunately, the tire veered back into the east bound lanes and came to rest next to the convoy commander's vehicle. The convoy commander had pulled the convoy of twenty-four vehicles to the side of the highway.

Immediately soldiers jumped out and retrieved the tire and determined that it was unrepairable. An expedient fix would have to be utilized. The convoy commander radioed into headquarters and described the problem. He was told to move out within ten minutes and if the vehicle was not drivable, then abandon the vehicle.

A young Specialist Four had been assessing the problem and came up with what was essentially a "duct tape" solution whereby a particular universal joint would be locked into place. As long as the vehicle's four-wheeled steering mechanisms could move, generally in a straightforward motion and make wide turns then it should be able to limp back into West Berlin.

The convoy commander said, *"Do it!"* and in short order the convoy was back on the road. As the convoy pulled into Checkpoint Bravo and stopped, the East German soldiers noticed that there was a five wheeled vehicle in the midst. A Russian Colonel was called to come out and inspect the anomaly. Photos were taken and apparently calls were made from the Soviet Checkpoint building to a higher authority.

After a long delay the convoy commander, a young First Lieutenant, offered the Colonel a Marlboro. The Colonel accepted the cigarette and the flame that lit it and then told the checkpoint guards to let the convoy pass.

At Allied headquarters in Berlin Jon had monitored the events, When the convoy commander reported that all vehicles had cleared Checkpoint Bravo it is said that Jon Cavaiani retorted, *"Let 'em eat that goat."* It is likely that the Russians spent several months analyzing the *"new"* U. S. five wheeled vehicle and trying to figure out its capabilities.

For those who went through Special Forces qualification course during the sixties and seventies, "eating goat" brings back special memories.[76]

In Berlin, many training events, physical training sessions, and

---

[76] Evers, Mike; first hand knowledge personal experience.

ceremonies were purposefully conducted in full view of East German and Soviet forces. And the free entry of uniformed allied forces into East Germany was maintained. Because of the close scrutiny by potential enemies, every detail of training, operation, or function and communication had to be both detailed and precise. Jon was just the man for that duty.

The focus of training in Berlin was "combat in cities" or what is more appropriately termed, Military Operations in Urban Terrain (MOUT). Such training was necessary considering the fact that units in West Berlin were surrounded by Soviet Bloc nations. It was a besieged city. The tactics, strategies, planning, and execution were carried- out continuously by units stationed there.

On one occasion Jon was evaluating the training of a rifle company going through a MOUT exercise. A platoon of the Royal Green Jackets, a British Regiment, was engaged with 3rd Battalion, 6th Infantry soldiers in the training. As nature demands of all, Jon had a need to visit the latrine (toilet). Latrines at the MOUT training facility were port-a-potties. After his visit to the toilets Jon came back to the evaluators' station site and looked at a young Operations and Training Captain who was Officer in Charge (OIC) of the training and asked, *"Sir, can we get an SST out here immediately?"* The captain looked at Jon thoughtfully, walked toward the PRC 77 radio that linked the evaluators back to Headquarters on Clay Allee, and then stopped. Turning around, the captain walked back to Cavaiani and asked in a whisper so that the Brit evaluators could not hear, *"Sergeant Cavaiani, what is an SST? Do we have an emergency? Is it a medivac?"*

Jon smiled and whispered back *"Sir, an SST is a shit-sucking-*

truck! Every one of those toilets is overflowing! Field hygiene out here sucks! No pun intended!!" Jon knew firsthand the importance of hygiene after his hygiene deprived experiences as a POW. He also knew how to lead (and prod) a young officer into a learning experience.[77]

After his assignments in Berlin, Jon was reassigned to 10th Special Forces Group, Fort Devens, Massachusetts. Despite his being fully qualified as a Green Beret, this was Jon's first Special Forces Unit assignment. (MACV-SOG was not a Special Forces Command). He was unfamiliar with the structure and functions of an A Team, B Team, C Team concept except from his training back at Fort Bragg, several years previous.

Jon, by then a Sergeant First Class, went to work as NCOIC of combined exercises and training. He worked with Captain Bob Chadwick. In spite of Jon's lack of Special Forces unit experience, he was bull-headed enough to press forward to be the best he could be. He and Captain Chadwick developed a lasting friendship and respect for one another.[78]

Bob recalls the frequent calls to Jon Cavaiani from numerous commands and organizations that sought to have the Medal of Honor recipient be present at a particular ceremony or memorial event was a bit disruptive. Jon was frustrated by these calls asking him to *"be a presence and help serve drinks to dignitaries."* Jon would have preferred to just do his job and not be part of the Pomp and Circumstance of the military and politics. The burden of the MOH was

---

[77] Ibid

[78] Chadwick, Bob in interview with Mike Evers June 2022

sometimes very heavy and onerous.

It was while Bob was at Fort Bragg on a TDY assignment that Bob's wife, who was still in Massachusetts, went into labor and delivered a child. It was Jon who transported the mother-to-be to the hospital while Jon's wife Marty (Jon had remarried) stayed with Bob's two-year-old daughter to care for her while the parents were otherwise engaged. Jon and Marty remained with Bob's family to care for the mother and the baby, a boy, throughout the duration of Bob's TDY stint. Jon Cavaiani became the Godfather of the child.

"Bob Chadwick recalls that at that point in Jon's life, he didn't have any contact with his own children or his relatives. He knew that he and Marty were never going to have children. Most of Jon's contact with kids were with mine, and after having been there for the birth of my son, he knew that he would be in my life and Mike's (my son) going forward. At one point, he wanted to adopt him so Mike could go to West Point on the CMOH golden ticket. As it turned out this was not something that Michael wanted even though Jon offered to do it."[79]

Bob became well aware of Jon's PTSD and some other aspects of Jon's life (such as the period of youth when he was *"Just an orphan."* According to Bob:

"Jon's mental and / or related conditions manifested as

---

[79] Ibid

somewhat of a 'my way or the highway' attitude. He had very-strong convictions. When he felt that he was right he would go the boss or the bosses' boss to tell them they were wrong. He was not afraid to put his job or his personal relationships in peril to prove his point. To a fault, he might not back down when faced with the reality that he was wrong. The four marriages that went wrong, the financial decisions that went awry, and his family relations in California could be examples of the results of his internal struggles. These, along with burning some bridges in the military with people who had once cared for him took a toll. Jon was the only POW/CMOH in Special Forces, however he was never asked to speak at any JFK event or teach or speak at the Special Forces Survival Evasion Resistance and Escape School. Jon said that the snub was because he had told some of the Special Warfare Center and School (SWCS) Sergeant Major and Command Sergeant Major's that they didn't know what they were talking about. That had created bad blood among them continued from Special Operations Group (SOG) through his retirement and after he retired.

Jon coped with situations by having something to do at work. He would throw himself into with another project-some new way to do something or a novel way to perfect something we were already doing. Jon coped with his challenges through work, perhaps with drinking too much on occasion, and a steady regime of prescribed medications from the doctors and psychiatrists that he had seen in the past and continued to see."[80]

---

[80] Ibid

While at Fort Devens Jon had observed numerous Veterans in the area were homeless and or without jobs. He attended group sessions with some and listened to their stories. It was then that he challenged the VA leadership in the region with: *"What are you doing for these men? Why aren't your programs working!?"* He then helped set up several programs in the New England area and as his efforts became known he was invited to help set up and/or reinforce programs in New York.

Before Jon's retirement and while he was serving at Ft. Eustis, Bob and his girlfriend went to the outer banks of North Carolina for a vacation with Jon. Bob's brother, Bill, who just returned to the USA after a year in El Salvador as a Brigade Combat Advisor, joined them for a long weekend. It was a time spent hearing of Jon's and Bill's stories of working with a foreign military as advisors and in many cases leaders during combat operations. It was a great relaxing period of reminiscence.

Bob and Jon remained friends for the rest of Jon's life, visiting one another as opportunity permitted. Jon was present at Bob's second wedding and Jon continued to be a presence in the children's lives. That included, on another occasion, Bob's promotion to LTC in 1995.

Bob's brother Bill, a West Point graduate and also a friend to Cavaiani, saw to it that Jon and his wife Barbara (Jon's fifth wife) were flown out from California (after Jon's retirement} to join them for the promotion celebrations. As Jon walked into the house, he greeted all with a big smile and declared that he was ready to cook for them. Then he began telling people what items he needed to prepare the meals that he had planned for them. He was very precise without thought of offense to anyone. Bob knew of Jon's take-charge personality and smiled, but Bob's wife, Karen, was taken aback. Jon could be so domineering in his desire to cook for his friends that he assumed that that was to be his job for the duration of the visit. Jon was not even aware that he may have offended anyone. Everyone acquiesced to Jon's becoming their chef. He prepared the meal, loving every moment of being able to do so, and almost immediately began telling them what he needed to prepare for the next meal. Bob's wife took a liking to Jon and his cooking skills.

> *"Jon could at times be so affected by his PTSD, that he became domineering in his effort to accomplish what he perceived to be his mission, but he was part of my life, and I loved and respected the guy so much. He was a true friend,"*[81] said Bob Chadwick during an interview on 28 May 2022.

Bob's brother, Bill, also served with Jon and offers the following:

> *"My brother Bob and I completed the Special Forces Qualification Course in 1979. I was assigned to 7th Special Forces Group at Fort Bragg and Bob to 10th Special Forces Group at Fort Devens, Massachusetts. It was Bob who met Jon Cavaiani first while with 10th Group. Bob was a plans officer in the G-3 Section along with Ken Getty and Dick Potter. Jon Cavaiani was the Plans Non-Commissioned Officer-In-Charge (NCOIC). Bob and Jon traveled together often to training events, conferences, and various plans development meetings. They became very close friends.*

---

[81] Ibid

However, later in our careers our paths, that of Jon and I, would come together at Fort Eustis and Little Creek Virginia. I was the Research and Development (R&D) Officer for some unique innovations being applied in Delta Force. Jon was the Squadron Sergeant Major of the unit.

It was during that time that my brother Bob took leave to the Outer Banks of North Carolina with his fiancée. Jon and I decided to join them there. Marty, Jon's wife at the time who happened to be a Lieutenant Colonel in the Adjutant General Branch of the Army, was there as well.

As I recall, Jon walked in the door and began to give directions as to what he needed to prepare meals for the duration of the week. Bob's fiancée was taken aback but soon acquiesced because Jon was so domineering in his ownership of the kitchen.

Jon was an exacting chef. He measured every ingredient, selected only the best meats, produce, and ingredients and et every item to a precise heat and time for cooking. I am not a doctor, so I do not diagnose OCD or PTSD or their potential impacts, but I can say that Jon was exacting and precise. I very pleasantly stood back, with drink in hand, while this fine chef did his work. He prepared every meal for the crew during that week and every meal was a feast.

As an aside I want to note that Jon and Marty purchased a phenomenal collection of Vietnamese art that was displayed in San Francisco. I do not know where the beautiful artwork went, but it seemed to reflect Jon's great love and appreciation of those with whom he had served in the early 1970s. Jon, as hard and muleheaded as he could be, had a soft spot for those with whom he chose to adopt. [Perhaps Marty retained them at their divorce.]

After his time with Delta Force, Jon was assigned to a great job as a ROTC instructor at University of California in Davis. He had a way with students. I think that it was his absolute honesty and openness about life in the military. It was while Jon was at UC Davis that he met Barbara who he would marry. She was a great addition to our lives. Jon told us how they met. It seems that Jon had finished a speaking engagement on campus and was in his dress uniform that day. After giving the speech he went to his favorite bar to have a drink and a bite to eat. That was when a friend of his introduced him to Barbara who looked at Jon and said, 'Well, I didn't know that there was a Halloween costume party here tonight.!' In a short span of time, almost immediately, Jon knew that he was defenseless to her charm and that he had met someone who could handle his personality and do it in a caring manner.

Then, as fate would have it, I was assigned as Group Commander of 3rd Special Forces Group at Fort Bragg just prior to Jon's retirement ceremony there. Jon had requested that he be permitted to retire at Fort Bragg and the request was granted. I had the great good fortune of being the Commander of Troops at Jon's retirement ceremony. That is indeed a great honor that I treasure. And the gala parties that occurred as part of the event are memorable! After his retirement I was able to go to Columbia, California and visit Jon and Barbara. We rekindled the old acquaintance, and again Jon insisted on cooking.

When he retired and went home to Columbia, California he attempted to obtain his adoptive father's farm in Ballico – going into significant debt trying to do so – and failed. He also failed in making in-roads into the remaining family who eschewed his attempts to establish familial relationships – he was an orphan, adopted.

Later in life, I think it was the year 2001{it was 2000}, the Commandant of the Marine Corps, General James L. Jones, named Jon as an Honorary Marine at the Marine Corps Gala for MC-LEF in Atlantic City, NJ, and called on Jon for support in promoting military service (Marine Corps focused of course). Jon accompanied the Commandant to numerous events to include races at the Sonoma Raceway where Army and Marine Corps sponsored cars raced around the track.

In addition to his other activities of supporting the Congressional Medal of Honor Society, The Special Forces Association, The Marine Corps Law Enforcement Foundation, etc... Jon added the Semper Fi Foundation at the request of General Jones. I had the great honor of joining them at the raceway near Sears Point and other Bay Area events. In fact, I am just honored to have known Jon Cavaiani and to have been a small part of his significant life."[82]

---

[82] Ibid

While still in the Army Jon became instrumental in developing treatment for PTSD for those who suffer from the effects of combat and other stress related events. On one occasion, he related how during and immediately after Vietnam no one could talk about the impact of trauma; to do so was seen as a weakness, a negative trait. It wasn't *"macho"* to show emotion or true feelings. It is human instinct to seek contact, so he sought out those who were struggling with PTS and by doing so he fulfilled an inner need and ay the same time assisted folks everywhere with his gravitas, sincere concern, and benevolence.

He pushed the military hierarchy to confront the issue. He challenged the Veterans Administration to fulfill its duties. He became a catalyst for finding means and methods to assist those suffering as he suffered.

Jon said on several occasions: *"PTSD is a devious thing. You have got to realize and admit that you have a problem. You (those who suffer PTSD) must be an active participant in your recovery. Drugs and chemicals will not magically dissipate the stress and angst. And suicide does no one any good."*[83]

Jon at one point informed a friend, George Schnarre, that The Medal of Honor was not just a blessing for him - it was also a burden. He said that it was a constant reminder of what he wanted to forget. But he was forthright in his attempts to tell the public about Post traumatic stress, prescription medications, lasting battles with psychological problems and the label of hero. He used the platform to try to bring light to the situation for returning warriors. For his untiring

---

[83] Op Cit; Pritzker

determined effort, he became a legend in Philadelphia and the Tri-State area. One way Jon dealt with his demons was to help anyone who shared his trauma. This became The Sergeant Major's life mission.

The *"car wash"* of bullets and bombs he, his special operators, and *"little people"* experienced on Hickory Hill along with his captivity wrought an internal war of neurosis later in life, but he found ways to *"busy"* the memories into the background.

Jon was aware of his inner struggles with Post-Traumatic Stress Disorder. Because of this he tried to become a catalyst in getting the military, Veterans Affairs, and other organizations to take significant and meaningful action to help those affected by this type of handicap. *"The physical wounds versus the mental ones can be very different depending on the person."*[84]

Due to the effort of Jon and others, the military services began to help treat people suffering from PTSD and encourage them to open-up and talk about their feelings and to seek help. This assistance for PTSD was extended to family members of Veterans. Jon was instrumental in assisting not only Vietnam Veterans, but those who served in Iraq and Afghanistan as well.

Jon helped establish five outreach and resource centers to provide in-house care for those with severe PTSD. His openness about his own experiences and how they impacted him resonated at the highest levels. The military services began to establish outreach and resource centers for active-duty servicemen and women and their families. The

---

[84] Fluck, Michael in interview with John Siegfried

Veterans Administration (VA) began assistance, counseling, and aid for PTSD. This type of work by Jon with PTSD sufferers continued after Jon retired and continues today.

CHAPTER TEN

Retiring To New Missions and Recovery

"Keep your face to the sunshine and you cannot see a shadow." - **Helen Keller**

Eventually it came time for Jon to retire from the military and seek the solace of a well-deserved rest. The shadows of the past still haunted Jon, and he knew it was time for a change and a new way to live. Though he loved serving in the Army, he knew it was time to search for brighter and more positive ways to serve.

Early morning 31 May 1990 Jon Cavaiani awoke and saw that it was reminiscently haunting as a fog hugged the ground. Foggy mornings always took him back to Hickory Hill. He looked skyward, and as if challenging all of nature he smiled. His expression was as if to say, *"Not today, Mama Nature, not today."*

The soft rain had given way to a morning sun creating a muggy morning in late May. The rain had washed the dirt away from the plaza of the John F. Kennedy Special Operations Center (JFKSOC) at Fort Bragg, North Carolina. A host of Green Beret soldiers, other soldiers and Veterans of other services, and civilians gathered to honor Sergeant Major Jon Robert Cavaiani. 3rd Special Forces Group Soldiers were formed on the granite slabs that covered the ground in front of the John F. Kennedy Special Operations Center main headquarters. A huge gleaming statue of a Green Beret, fondly called *"Big Bruce"* stood watch over the event as it occurred in the JFKSOC plaza.

As fate would have it, a dear friend of Jon's who had recently been assigned to Fort Bragg to reactivate 3rd Special Forces Group and take command of that Group was at the fore. That close personal friend who stood in front of the formation of troops was William Chadwick. It was Bill's duty to serve as Commander of Troops for a very meaningful ceremony. But to Bill it was not a duty, it was an absolute honor! It was a highlight of his career, one that he would remember for the rest of his life.

After some preliminary ceremonial commands and responses, Major Chadwick gave the command *of "Parade rest,"* and the soldiers responded instantly with an audible *"snap."* He then did an about face and then ordered himself and his staff, located directly behind him, to assume the same position. They did so.

The dais was surrounded by friends and fellow soldiers of Jon. The guest speaker at the ceremony was Brigadier General Joe Stringham (Ret), a United States Military Academy Graduate Class of 1961. BG Stringham was an Airborne Ranger Infantryman who, as a Green Beret, organized, trained, and led in combat the first MIKE Force unit (an indigenous rapid-reaction force unit) in Vietnam. In his more than thirty-two years of military service, Stringham commanded at every echelon from rifle platoon through brigade. This included command of the 75th Ranger Regiment; three US Army Infantry Battalions, including the 1st Ranger Battalion; and the US Military Group in El Salvador at a pivotal point in the war in that country. General Stringham was well aware of Jon's heroics and the kind of man that Jon was – one who exhibited the behavior of a true warrior who stood valiantly and steadfastly with his soldiers.

At the ceremony Jon was hailed as a hero. Accolades for the honoree – the reason for the ceremony – were read. The honoree's Medal of Honor Citation was read. Then the honoree himself spoke – briefly, but forcefully.

Statue of a Green Beret, fondly called "Big Bruce" at Fort Bragg, NC

Bill Chadwick, standing at the front of the formation of soldiers wanted to retain what his friend said, but his thoughts were overcome by his awe at this person's aura. The speaker, retiring Sergeant Major Jon Cavaiani, was expressing great gratitude and appreciation to soldiers and as he did so he was not speaking to the *"brass"* assembled around the podium, it was to the soldiers standing in the sun before him. He was thanking them as proxies to those with whom he had served over the years. At the same time, he was encouraging those before him to do more than they thought capable. He tried to instill in them that their perception of the impossible was not the extent of the possible.

Jon loved soldiers! Hard working soldiers, and he wanted to, one last time, express his great appreciation to *"the little people"* who are the bearers of victory when victory is won. He wanted to honor and hold forth the bravery of the grunt, the dog-faced soldier, and the tribal spirit of the Montagnard among us. Jon loved soldiers who soldiered.

He retired that day in a ceremony on Fort Bragg. After the ceremony Jon was asked what he was going to do in retirement? He responded humbly that he would retire to his 294-acre farm in central California, where he would grow peaches. *"I'm just a farm boy,"* he said.

Those in attendance at the ceremony then moved to Moon Hall to toast the Sergeant Major and wish him well. Rank was set aside as hugs and handshakes replaced salutes as friends and comrades wished Jon well. In that welcoming spot, the tavern at Moon Hall, rounds of drinks and words well wishes were shared. Toasts were offered and a hero honored.

That evening in Major Bill Chadwick's back yard in a military housing area near the MATA mile on Fort Bragg, North Carolina, more than sixty people gathered to again celebrate the heroism and leadership of the Wolf from Livingstone High School; the farmer from Ballico, the soldier who refused to leave his warriors behind. They celebrated Jon Cavaiani.

It was 31 May 1990 that Jon hung up his boots. He told friends that all he wanted to do was retire to his adoptive father's farm and bring it back to what Ugo had once made it -a vibrant and productive land that served the local community and beyond. While Jon was in the service, the land had gone fallow.

However, as it turned out he found himself becoming engaged in the Medal of Honor Society, The Special Forces Association, Veterans' affairs as an advocate for improved service especially for homeless Veterans, and support for Veterans with PTSD, pharma-abuse, and job placement difficulties. He also became quite engaged in car racing events.

While trying to regain the land in Ballico, Jon met Barbara Elf, who Jon described as the love of his life. In fact, Jon credited her with saving his life. It was as if she were his sunshine in his new life episode. Barb had a calming effect on Jon and played a huge role in his managing the effects of PTSD. Jon and his wife Barb moved to a nice cozy nest in Columbia, California.

The Northern California climate suited his physical ailments as well as his attitude. He loved relaxing on his patio with a glass of Jack Daniels and just being with Barbara. With Barb's encouragement and support Jon enrolled in, and completed with honors, a culinary arts program.

The culinary arts program at Columbia College provided Jon an opportunity to improve on skills that he had learned while growing up, and permitted him with an outlet to take his mind off of the haunting memories. Creating a fine meal, to Jon, was equivalent to an artist painting a beautiful picture of nature – the only problem was that his picture disappeared as part of the participants appreciation, so he would have to do it again.

Jon loved to cook and especially enjoyed cooking for and treating guests. Cooking had a calming effect on him as it helped take his mind off his life's past nightmare–like, but all too real experiences. There were times when Jon prepared meals for and served more than eighty people on his patio.

But he, restless as ever, continued to be active in the Medal of Honor Society, Special Forces Association, and various activities to include advising law enforcement and emergency response teams on security issues. He was deeply concerned about other Veterans who were suffering from the effects of war and struggling to regain meaning in their lives.

On one occasion Jon spoke at a Memorial Day Ceremony in San Bernardino, California. He had graciously agreed to do so. Jon was not aware that he was about to meet an *"old salt,"* who he had trained at Dam Neck Virginia a few years earlier.

"Upon arrival Jon met me, Police Commissioner George Schnarre. I looked Jon in the eye and said, 'Sergeant Major, you may not remember me, but in 1983 I was in the Navy and a member of a search/salvage/rescue team and was on temporary assigned duty (TAD) in support of Operation Urgent Fury in Grenada. Our group was to receive specialized close quarter hand-to-hand combat training in preparation for mission support. We were told by our Master Chief 'that a good friend of his, who was an Army Sergeant and Medal of Honor recipient, was going to try to teach us.' And that was you!" We laughed.

The training had taken place at Dam Neck / Naval Air

Station Oceana, near Virginia Beach. *"I recall you walking into the mat room and after a brief introduction and explanation of what we could expect to gain from the training you asked for a volunteer. I was 20 years old and arrogant enough and sufficiently dumb enough to volunteer!*

You asked that I try to take you down, so I charged straight at you. In an instant I was on my back, looking at the rafters, trying to reclaim the wind that you had knocked out of my body. I have never forgotten that day!

Jon smiled with that twinkle in his eye and said, *"Well, Navy: I've knocked the wind out of a lot of men in training, I see it worked!"*[85]

George invited Jon to dinner at his home that night where Jon met Melinda, George's wife. They hit it off so well that soon George and Melinda began visiting Jon and Barb in Columbia. It became a close relationship that lasted for Jon and Barb's remaining years. Every Saturday during the college football season George and Jon would be laughing and giggling like the little boys in men's bodies that they were! The Army / Navy Football Game was a special time too.

Later, in 2002, in the aftermath of the 9/11 attacks, George asked Jon, who was the Police Commissioner in San Bernardino, to provide his professional assessment of law enforcement practices and procedures and assistance with upgrading the area's tactics and structural fortification of public buildings. Jon willingly accepted the offer and drove frequently from Columbia to San Bernardino sometimes

---

[85] Schnarre, George; email to Mike Evers May 2022

bringing Barb with him so that she could visit with Melinda.

George recalls how Jon jumped right in, in his usual professional but casual manner to assess the operations of the law enforcement and emergency response departments, their training and their procedures. He was easy to talk with and it was easy to understand his reasoning for any recommended changes. He aided in the programs to fortify public structures whose vulnerabilities had become a great concern after 9/11/2001.

Jon often stayed at the Schnarres' home during each of his on-site visits. They became such good friends that Jon kept a bottle of Jack Daniels at their home. George's wife Melinda insured that only Jon touched the bottle. The Schnarres' continued visiting the Cavaiani's in Columbia and the friendship grew. Thanksgiving, Christmas, or just a quiet weekend. The trust and friendship grew strong, and George and Melinda remained supporters of Barb upon Jon's demise, which happened earlier than any ever wanted.

> *"I treasure the Medallion of Valor that he gave me. It was an honor to have known and spent those years with Jon. It was an honor to refer to him as Sergeant Major, and an even greater honor to introduce him as a Medal of Honor recipient. I am forever blessed to be able to have called him friend. He was like a brother to me and even today I still love him."*[86]

Jon attended many Special Forces Association and SOG Reunions. He was also a sought after as a guest speaker for many events.

---

[86] Schnarre; ibid.

On one such occasion he was asked to be guest speaker at a Special Forces Chapter Mardi Gras event in New Orleans. After the formal portion of the event, a Cajun styled hamburger / hotdog feast ensued. Jon insisted on manning the grill to cook and serve the meats. While serving those going through the line Jon saw a General Officer, who had joined late, but in time to eat, moving through the line. Jon served the General a burger, as had been requested, and turned to the next individual in line.

As the General Officer moved to a table, one of the attendees asked, *"General, do you know who just served you?"* The General hesitated, then looked back toward Jon, and said, *"No, who is he?"*

"Sir, that is Medal of Honor recipient, Jon Cavaiani."

The General set his plate down and went to the back of the serving line. As his turn came to be served a second time he stepped in front of Jon, came to attention, and saluted. Jon was a bit surprised but instinctively began to raise his right arm. It was a bit awkward because Jon still held a spatula in his right hand. Transferring the flipper to his left hand, Jon returned the salute in a snappy manner. The two then smiled and laughed a bit and Jon said, *"Thank you, Sir."* To which the General responded, *"No! Thank you!"* When Jon finished his tour of duty at the grill he and the General sat together, chatted; and became very good friends.

Retirement allowed Jon to become more engaged in motorcycling and car racing. In fact, he loved car racing. Much of Jon's outreach to fellow Veterans came through motorcycle rallies and car racing events. The SgtMaj was named Veterans Ambassador to the National Hot Rod Association, and he was named starter for Chicago

Land Speedway in 2011 as noted below:

CAVAIANI THE VETERANS' CAR RACING AMBASSADOR

Medal of Honor recipient Cavaiani named Honorary Starter of GEICO 400: Medal of Honor recipient Jon Cavaiani has been named the Honorary Starter for Sunday's GEICO 400 at Chicagoland Speedway. As the Honorary Starter, Cavaiani will wave the green flag, to officially kick off the 10-race Chase for the NASCAR Sprint Cup. Cavaiani, a retired United States Army Special Force's Staff Sergeant, is one of only 83 living Medal of Honor recipients. The Medal of Honor is the military's highest honor.[87]

And he was honored at Daytona Internal Speedway on July 4 of that same year as revealed below as appeared in an article of Fan's View:

Fan's View: NASCAR Honoring the 2011 Medal of Honor Recipients

4 July 2011 By <u>Front stretch Staff</u>

"Happy 235th Birthday to America! I hope all of you enjoyed a Happy 4th of July full of delicious food, the company of loyal friends and your family. But not everybody was able to spend the holiday with those they love. Thousands of men and

---

[87] GEICO 9-16-2011

(https://promo.espn.com/news/tracks/archive/story?page=chicagoland-speedway-news-archive) *women serving our country are stationed far away from home, fighting against terrorism and enemies of the freedom we hold so dear.*

Each week when I turn on the race, I am proud of the way NASCAR celebrates our country and honors those that serve in the military. Cameras often pan over uniformed individuals during the presentation of the flag and the singing of the Star-Spangled Banner. It's a small thank you for their service. Very small, when all is considered."

When Daytona International Speedway (DIS) once again honored four Congressional Medal of Honor recipients and the cameras showed us their aged faces for a few seconds, I felt it behooves all of us to think on their sacrifices a bit longer than a wide shot between the opening ceremonies and *"Gentlemen, start your engines!"*

Sure, the four recipients were treated by DIS over the weekend to VIP access, a special luncheon and even participated in an autograph session in the Fan Zone. But considering the sacrifice they give for our country; I can't help but feel a little more recognition of these heroes should have been made by TNT. So, in an effort to correct that lack of publicity the following is a brief description of the actions that earned Staff Sergeant Jon R. Cavaiani, Captain Harold A. Fritz, Staff Sergeant Don J. Jenkins, and Lieutenant Leo K. Thorsness the highest award for valor for those serving in our armed forces.

"All tales of bravery, self-sacrifice, and a commitment to those who stand with them in a fight, the recipients of the

Congressional Medal of Honor demonstrated the very best in all of us at a time when they were most needed. In these uncertain times, there are soldiers of a new generation who must make these kinds of decisions, too.

As the U.S. continues at war, the roster for the CMOH continues to grow each day; we are just rarely told the stories, as many times we'd rather pretend we live in a world far more innocent than it is. There were no Hollywood actors, timed explosions or even a happy ever after for the experiences listed above; in fact, two of the men were captured, suffering as POWs.

Yes, we just celebrated Independence Day. But we should always remember that freedom was not something that America was entitled. We fought for it. And the men and women who serve our country in the Armed Forces even now continue to fight, putting their lives on the line when circumstances demand it, preserving our freedom still.

"I thank them, the Veterans of wars past and present and the active-duty personnel. Thank you for everything you do for me."[88]

And a tribute to Jon by Frank Hawley was printed in Drag Illustrated in the August 2014 edition. Frank Hawley (born 1954 in London, Ontario, Canada) is a two-time World champion drag racing driver. He won seven National Hot Rod Association (NHRA) Top Fuel

---

[88] https://www.frontstretch.com/2011/07/04/nascar-honors-2011-medal-of-honor/

Funny Car and two Top Fuel Dragster national events during his 10-year drag racing career that included the 1982 and 1983 NHRA Funny Car World Championship. Frank Hawley is an NHRA World Champion driver, author, and a motivational speaker. His school is the most respected and visited school of its kind in the world. For close to three decades the Hawley School has been the leader in racing instruction and entertainment. From teaching today's professionals to providing customers with the thrilling experience of speed and acceleration, Hawley's programs deliver.

Additionally, the news articles below, provide a glimpse into Jon's involvement in racing and the reasoning behind that involvement. For one thing, Jon was into car racing. He especially like the individual precision with which each member had to perform in order to gain a team victory. But an even more important mission for Jon was that racing drew numerous Veterans who he knew needed support and care. Being at the track enabled Jon to reach out to a slew of Veterans and encourage them to keep fighting to improve themselves and society. He encouraged them to band together as brothers and sisters and uplift one another. Jon used racing as a platform from which he could reach a number of people who would have been left to suffer alone with PTSD and other war scars.

NEWS

Hawley Tribute to MOH Veteran Jon Cavaiani

By

Drag Illustrated

Published

August 7, 2014

By Frank Hawley

"There are thousands of people far more qualified to write this than am I. I never served in the Armed Services, although I have tremendous admiration for those that currently serve and those that have. I did not know Jon Cavaiani his entire life story; but was fortunate enough to meet him several years ago and got to learn what an amazing man he was. And I'd like to remind the racing community that this past week our country lost a true hero.

I was introduced to Jon by Roger Burgess a number of years ago. Roger, also a Vet, served with Jon for several years and the two had become close friends. Roger had also been a big supporter of the Medal of Honor Society of which Jon was a member. When I was first introduced to Jon, I must admit I was a little nervous however Jon made it instantly apparent he did not see himself as an important person. He was welcoming and not the least bit intimidating. His voice was raspy from a battle injury, his walk was stiff from another battle injury, his smile was huge, and his handshakes and hugs were bigger. He laughed all the time.

I was working with R2B2 Racing at the time and Roger would host several Vietnam Vets at each race. Jon would fly in for these get togethers to meet and spend time with each of the Vets. If you took time to stand back and watch the interaction between Jon and the Vets, it was amazing. They, of course, had the utmost respect for him. but he also did for them. He was so giving of his time. He would talk to them about drag racing or their family or their time in the service or anything else. It was on these weekends that I also got to spend time with Jon.

I might guess that you don't know the details of Jon's story, his time as a POW, or why he was selected to receive the Medal of Honor (MOH). I think you should. You should buy a book about all of the MOH heroes, or at the least search the Internet and read about some of their stories, especially Jon's.

One important point I'd like to share about the MOH members. They didn't 'win' the Medal of Honor. It wasn't a contest. It wasn't a lottery. They didn't do what they did to earn the MOH. Not one of them was seeking this prestigious award. What they did was demonstrate incredible courage to protect and save the lives of others while placing their own lives at risk. It was a selfless act. Jon pointed out to me once that there were definitely many, many more acts of selfless courage that never got reported simply because no one survived to tell the story. {John Siegfried: Drew Dix, another MOH, stated the same thing}.

The last time I was with Jon was in Washington DC. A friend of ours, Bob Pence, hosted a 'Christmas Concert for the Troops' at the Kennedy Center. My wife Lana and I were told we could bring a guest. We immediately thought of Jon. I was not sure if he would make the trip across the country for one night, but I called to ask. He said that if it was a tribute to the 'troops,' he'd be there.

That night at the Kennedy Center I saw, among many others, a U.S. Army General wait in line to shake Jon's hand. I sat next to Jon while he was introduced to the audience of thousands which gave him a standing ovation and when the evening was over, I watched him slowly descend a flight of stairs carefully holding the railing. I asked him if he was hurting tonight? He laughed out loud and said he was always hurting! Jon was a man who gave everything and asked for nothing in return. I remember being at a race with Jon. We'd lost first round and exploded a motor. I was sitting in the pits more than a little dejected. Jon walked over and asked what was wrong. I told him we'd had a bad day. He smiled kindly, put his hand on my back and said, 'Frank, I've seen bad days...this isn't one of them.' If you never got to meet Jon, I wish you had. He would have added something to your life. Last week there were 80 living Medal of Honor recipients. This week there are 79 {**Authors:** *As of this writing, there are 65*)

To Sergeant Major Jon Cavaiani, a man who lived in the arena...thanks for your kindness and service. We already miss you."

Further, Roger Burgess, a veteran of the Vietnam war, a good friend of Jon Cavaiani, and well-respected member of the National Hot Rod Association was interviewed and provided more detail on Jon's significance to NHRA drivers, crew, and fans. The article below appeared at **http://competitionplus.com/drag-racing/news/6469-burgess-honors-Veterans** and expresses a great deal about the respect given to Jon and the humility with which he accepted that respect.

By the way, Roger considered Jon a member of his team and had him in the pits with his teams often. Jon told Roger about how impressed he was with the teamwork that went into competing in and winning a race. With each crew member having precise and specific duties to carry out, the was little room for error and hardly any time to correct an error or shortfall. Everything had to occur in sequence and on time. Jon lauded the pit crews and considered them (the little people) as the real reason for victory, as equal to any driver or owner.

BURGESS HONORS VETERANS
Thursday 2008-05-15 14:30
Team owner chartering jet to send drivers to Congressional Medal of Honor function

While many of the NHRA POWERADE teams are preparing for competition at this weekend's NHRA Thunder Valley Dragway in Bristol, Tenn., at least one team will put racing aside long enough to honor those heroes who have disregarded their personal safety for valor on the battlefield.

Roger Burgess, co-owner of Gotham City Racing, has arranged for a private jet to fly the team's drivers Melanie Troxel, Frank Hawley and Mike Ashley as well as Kenny Bernstein Racing's Tommy Johnson Jr. from Bristol, Tenn. to Atlanta, Ga., on Thursday evening for the In the Company of

Heroes dinner. This gala function is presented by The Congressional Medal of Honor Foundation.

Burgess feels this event is one the team can learn from and apply to their everyday actions.

"I wanted the people on our team to be there because the things these guys stand for, we want those qualities within our team. I feel we have a lot of those qualities on our team, but the environment is a lot different. Our team isn't in combat and sacrificing their lives, but it takes an awful lot of teamwork helping one another and that's what the Medal of Honor folks are all about. " **Roger Burgess**

Roger Burgess, co-owner of Gotham City Racing, has arranged for a private jet to fly the team's drivers Melanie Troxel, Frank Hawley and Mike Ashley as well as Kenny Bernstein Racing's Tommy Johnson Jr. from Bristol, Tenn. to Atlanta, Ga., on Thursday evening for the In the Company of Heroes dinner. This gala function is presented by The Congressional Medal of Honor Foundation.

"The concept is to honor true American heroes," Burgess said. *"We will have the opportunity to learn a bit more about them and the things they did and what made them*

perpetuate these values of sacrifice and service and loyalty.

Johnson, whose wife Melanie has worked with Veterans and the POW-MIA program for the last two seasons, looks forward to attending the event.

"It is quite an honor to have an opportunity to attend this dinner," said Johnson. *"I'm looking forward to being in the company of some of our country's real heroes."*

Burgess said attendance at this event was something that he feels will leave a lasting impression on the team.

FOR AN IN-HOUSE MEDAL OF HONOR RECIPIENT – Burgess doesn't have to search far for a Medal of Honor example to present to his team.

Jon Cavaiani, a close friend, and special guest of Gotham City Racing co-owner Roger Burgess, will entertain the Veterans in 2008 as part of the Gotham City Racing veteran's outreach program. He is a Medal of Honor recipient and former POW. (Roger Burgess).

As a member of the Gotham City Racing team, Cavaiani works with the team's outreach for Veterans program as part of their POW-MIA/ Vietnam Veterans mantra. Each Saturday at 10 AM at NHRA POWERADE events, Cavaiani is assisted by team manager Angelo Angelico and veteran drag racing journalist Bobby Bennett in welcoming Veterans to the race track and thanking them for their service.

He will attend as many as sixteen NHRA national events

this year in support of the program.

"We have the MIA car and anything I can do to support the Veterans and the families of the missing, I just do whatever I can to fill in," Cavaiani said. *"I'll be interacting with the Veterans of all wars, it's important they know we all appreciate their service."*

Cavaiani served with Burgess in the U.S. Military and over the years they remained in communication. For Burgess, Cavaiani's appointment to the program had nothing to do with friendship and everything to do with qualification.

Just having Jon at the gatherings brings something special for the Veterans to relate to," Burgess said. *"He's great in working with them."*

Cavaiani expects to reach the Vets afflicted with Post Traumatic Stress Disorder [PTSD] and *"provide a place to just sit down and talk."* PTSD is described as an anxiety disorder that can occur after someone who has been through a traumatic event. A traumatic event is described as something horrible and scary that the individual sees or that happened to them. During this type of event, the person's life or others' lives are in danger. A person with PTSD may relive this experience over and over in their mind and feel the same fear as when the incident took place.

Many of the Veterans attending the gatherings on Saturday mornings have been diagnosed with PTSD. The experience of attending the drag races and interacting with fellow Veterans serves as a healing experience.

"I think the program is vitally important," Cavaiani said. *"I think this program should extend into other sports, not just drag racing. I think there needs to be a greater veteran awareness through this country."*

Cavaiani is thankful for the Congressional Medal of Honor award bestowed upon him but feels his actions were that of a soldier. The situation presented itself, and as he puts it, *"I reacted."*

He wants to be known as much more than just a Congressional Medal of Honor award recipient.

"If that's my sole contribution to America then that's a sad commentary," Cavaiani said. *"I've done a lot more things since then that I'm very proud of. Working with the Veterans and those currently deployed is what it's all about. It's about supporting all of those brave men and women serving our country domestic and abroad."[89]*

Jon was also into motorcycles and those who enjoyed a good motorcycle outing. He rode as often as he could and joined others in doing so. One such occasion follows:

MCGUIRE AIR FORCE BASE, N.J. -- -- Sponsors of the second annual Armed Forces Freedom Ride expect up to 1,000 motorcyclists to participate in the event that takes place May 18 and starts in West Collingswood, passes through historic Mount

---

[89] http://competitionplus.com/drag-racing/news/6469-burgess-honors-Veterans

Holly and then down a runway here, ending at Fort Dix.

The Burlington County Military Affairs Committee, Marine Corps Law Enforcement Foundation, and Barb's Harley-Davidson sponsored the ride and raised $25,000 last year. Over 750 people and 600 motorcycles took part in that inaugural ride.

Barbara Borowiec, owner of Barb's Harley-Davidson and member of the BCMAC, was happy at the money raised in last year's ride, but she was also pleased with something else.

"They (military) saw all the support from the community," said Borowiec. *"That was one of my main goals, to show the men and women at Fort Dix, McGuire Air Force Base and Lakehurst Naval Air Engineering Station, that we know you're here. You're right here in our backyard and we support you and we love you."*

This year's ride will be led by Jon Cavaiani. Accompanying Cavaiani will be Philadelphia Eagles offensive tackle Jon Runyan, former Philadelphia Flyers Bob Kelly and Brian Propp and former Philadelphia Phantom Frank Bialowas.

The approximately 40-mile route starts at Barb's Harley-Davidson at 926 Black Horse Pike in West Collingswood Heights at 10 a.m., follows Interstate-295 north, through Mount Holly and on to McGuire Air Force base, concluding down a runway and to Fort Dix.

"We're hoping this year when we ride through Mount Holly we can have some people come out of their houses and cheer the riders on," said Mary Duffy, an organizer and employee at Barb's Harley-Davidson.

Duffy said there was a large crowd of spectators outside the dealership when the ride started last year and Cavaiani was a highlight of the event.

"People were in tears last year shaking his hand," she said.

"I am thankful we have civic organizations that recognize our freedom and want to help those who help ensure that freedom," said Col James L. Kerr, commander of the 514th Air Mobility Wing.

"This event encompasses an American pastime, motorcycle riding, something I personally enjoy," said Colonel Kerr, who plans to participate in the Freedom Ride.

"It's a good thing when like minds rally together and pay tribute the heritage of sacrifice, as well as the present sacrifice, for freedom," said Colonel Kerr. *"This is a joint base and joint community event and the 514th is a valuable part of the team. I highly encourage participation."*[90]

Jon engaged himself in so many endeavors that would lift people's spirits. He attempted to give hope to all he met whether at reunions, the racetrack, a motorcycle rally/ride, or just a down-home meet, greet, and eat. Jon was always just himself with no pretense. All he wanted to give was encouragement and hope.

Through his altruistic and philanthropic endeavors Jon the orphan had become brother to many; Jon the Wolf had become a

---

[90] Retrieved from: Annual Freedom Ride open to all motorcyclists; Published April 23, 2008; by Staff Sgt. Monica Dalberg; 514th Air Mobility Wing; https://www.514amw.afrc.af.mil/News/Articles/Article/194427/annual-freedom-ride-open-to-all-motorcyclists/

Shepherd to the wandering; Jon the warrior had become an ambassador for the battle weary; and Jon the high school chaplain had become minister to many who were helpless and hopeless. Yet he still had another mission to complete.

There remained, for Jon, one meaningful operation that needed to be brought to closure. The body of Sergeant John R. Jones, his Special Forces brother at Hickory Hill, had never been recovered. A veteran who had worked in ASA, and became a noted historian and writer about the Vietnam War and he had educated himself about the assault on hill 950 and the persons who had fought there.

> *"I mentioned to Mr. X that it would be good to see if we could get those who had fought on Hickory to attend a reunion at one of our Special Operations Association Reunions (SOAR). He agreed. We decided to see if we could get them to attend the 2010 SOAR. Mr. X sent out invitations to all. I personally extended one to Jon Cavaiani when I was at his home in California getting him to sign the SOG Medal of Honor print. Jon promised me he would attend – and he did. The reunion in Las Vegas was a huge success. None of the Hickory survivors had seen or communicated with each other after they left Vietnam. As part of their History Project, the SOA filmed the recollections of the participants of the battle and the history of the research outlined by Mr. X. One of the central topics was JPAC's on-going search for the remains of SF/SOG SGT John R. Jones. At the SOAR, Steve Thompson of JPAC told Mr. X that the bunker identified by Jon Cavaiani had just been discovered! The word passed quickly to the Hickory survivors. The mission was not over.*

JPAC's 'Recovery Team' would still have to carefully excavate the area of the bunker, discover the remains, return them to their labs at Hickam AFB in Hawaii, and (if possible) confirm the identification."[91]

"Four decades after the battle on Hickory Hill, Sgt. Maj. Cavaiani returned to Vietnam to help Defense Department officials locate the remains of Jones, the sergeant who had remained behind with him and whose body had not been recovered."

"Sgt. Maj. Cavaiani remembered and precisely identified the bunker where he and Jones had taken refuge, recalled Page, who also returned to Vietnam to assist in the effort. Jones' remains were located, and, in 2012, he was buried at Arlington National Cemetery."

"I think you can never repay that debt," Jones' brother, James D. Jones, said in an interview. *"We say; we leave no one behind. In this case, they did not."*[92]

After Forty years Jon returned with two battle buddies searching for the remains of Sgt. John R. Jones. The Vietnamese had assisted the American JPAC teams for years trying to unearth remains. Jon was able to pinpoint the area of the bunker. With this some sense of closure to one nagging nightmare was addressed and it brought some relief to Jon Cavaiani.

When John Robert Jones' remains were laid to rest in Arlington

---

[91] http://www.macvsog.cc/attack_of_hickory_hill.htm

[92] Langer, Op Cit

National Cemetery Jon Cavaiani was there to render a salute and a farewell to his brother. He was accompanied by Lieutenant General Charles T. Cleveland, Commander of the United States Army Special Operations Command.

After the graveside ceremony, an informal reception was held at the Arlington Court Suites (near the ANC) hosted by Special Forces veteran Terry English, President of the Board, and representative of the Special Forces Charitable Trust. During the reception, Medal of Honor recipient, Jon Cavaiani, presented James and Sammie Jones with plaques from the Special Operations Association (SOA). The participants at the memorial service, grave site ceremony, and reception, included several of the soldiers who defended or participated in the defense of Hill 950 during the assault of June 4-5, 1971 -- Roger Hill, Larry Page, Jon Cavaiani, Skip Holland, and Horace Boner.

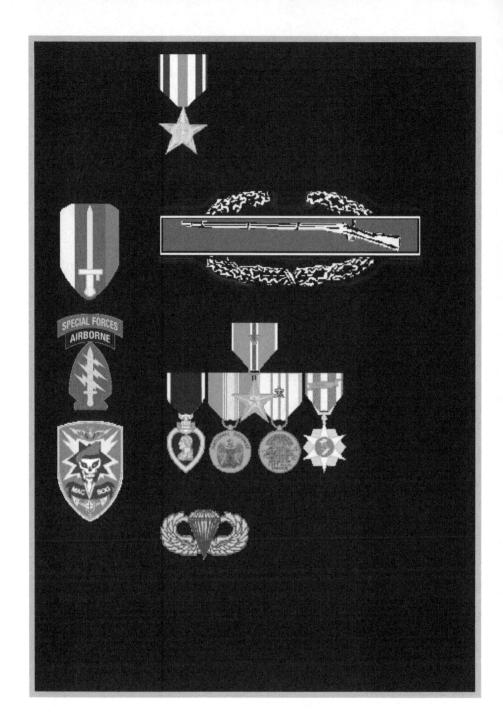

HONOR BOARD OF SGT. JOHN JONES

This is the last known history of Sgt. John Robert Jones, U.S. Army Special Forces:

Status (in 1973): Presumed Dead, (at age 22).

SYNOPSIS: In 1971, MACV-SOG's Command and Control North, Central and South were redesignated as Task Force Advisory Elements 1, 2 and 3 respectively. These titular changes had little initial impact on actual activities. Their missions were still quite sensitive and highly classified. Each task force was composed of 244 Special Forces and 780 indigenous commandos, and their reconnaissance teams remained actively engaged in cross-border intelligence collection and interdiction operations. The USARV TAG (Training Advisory Group) supported the USARV Special Missions Advisory Group and was composed of U.S. Army Special Forces and MACV advisors. SMAG formed at Nha Trang from former personnel from B-53, the MACV Recondo School cadre, CCN and CCS to train the South Vietnamese Special Missions Force teams drawn from LLDB and Ranger units.

Task Force 1 Advisory Element was forced from its Hickory Hill radio relay site at Dong Tri in early June 1971. The Hickory Hill post had existed on strategic Hill 953, in northwest Quang Tri Province at the edge of the DMZ, since June 1968. On June 3, heavy North Vietnamese artillery began battering the bunkered Hickory Hill defenses.

On June 4, five wounded Special Forces and ten indigenous commandos were medically evacuated, leaving SSgt. Jon R. Cavaiani and Sgt. John R. Jones with 23 commandos defending the mountaintop. At about 0400 hours on June 5, Jones and Cavaiani were in a bunker when a hand grenade was dropped through the air vent, wounding Sgt. Jones in the leg. Jones left the bunker and was seen shot in the chest by an NVA soldier.

An NVA battalion stormed the summit and captured Hickory Hill on June 5 in adverse weather which prevented air support. In the bunker, Cavaiani played dead as NVA soldiers came in looking for survivors. As his bunker was set on fire, Cavaiani ran, burned, to another bunker. He spotted a helicopter and attempted to signal it, serving only to alert the enemy to his position. Cavaiani was captured as the last positions fell.

Later searches failed to turn up any sign of John R. Jones, dead or alive. He was among nearly 2500 Americans still missing in Southeast Asia. There can be little question that the enemy knows his fate, yet the Vietnamese deny knowledge of him. Evidence mounts that hundreds of these men are still alive, captive, waiting for their country to bring them home. One of them could be John R. Jones.

In 2011, Remains were found. After 3 months, it was determined through family DNA that they were, in fact, Sgt Jones. He was repatriated, and buried at Arlington.

Sgt. Jon R. Cavaiani was released by the Provisional Government of Vietnam on March 27, 1973. He was awarded the Congressional Medal of Honor for his attempt to defend Hickory Hill.

Taken from the
POW Network

Jon Cavaiani and Lieutenant General Charles T. Cleveland Awaiting Interment of John R. Jones at Arlington National Cemetery

Jon was also a frequent guest speaker to groups of ROTC cadets at universities and high schools throughout California. Cadets were in awe of him, and it is said that ROTC enrollments increased during Jon's service to the program. It was as Jon was speaking at an ROTC gathering in 2013 that Jon suddenly began bleeding as he stood at the podium and had to be taken for emergency treatment. This was the last speaking engagement that Jon would be able to attend.

CHAPTER ELEVEN

Jon's Service To, and Impact On, Philadelphia / The Tri-State Area / and Others

"For those of us who know Jon, the smile of victory that shines from Jon's face is imbedded in our minds. Whether with or without a beard, with or without glasses, in or out of uniform, Jon's smile after a good meal, a good joke, a warm hug, or a moment of love and friendship lights up a room."

George Schnarre: Excerpt from *A Birthday Letter to Jon* August 2014

Philadelphia and its surrounding communities in the Tri-State Area have long been proud of its patriotic fervor. Philly's history is rich. Philadelphians have possessed an *"attitude"* since the early days of the militia. Through immigration from Europe and elsewhere, they were destined to become a blue-collar union town. It was The Capital of the country initially and a town loaded with law firms, but possessed its fair share of marketing, industry, and manufacturing. The inner-city consists of mixed neighborhoods. Philly folks are tough. It is known that significant numbers of Philadelphians have served in capacities of first responder, law enforcement, and the military. During Vietnam, more people volunteered for military service than were drafted.

The Marine Corps Law Enforcement Foundation chapter in Philadelphia illuminates the patriotic support of service to country. Thanks to its generous donors, MC-LEF currently establishes a $35,000 educational account for every child who loses a parent serving on active duty in the United States Marine Corps, Navy Corpsman or as a Federal Law Enforcement Agent. Since its founding in 1995, MC-LEF has awarded over $90 million in educational accounts and other humanitarian assistance to over 4700 recipients. The foundation has only one paid employee and, therefore, the vast majority of its efforts are performed by a dedicated group of volunteers who run various events. Additionally, all officers and board members are unpaid. As a team, they are extremely efficient in running the organization so that donor funds are predominantly used to accomplish its mission of Educating the Children of Those Who Sacrificed All.[93]

When MCLEF began its benevolent work, it turned to the Congressional Medal of Honor Society (CMOHS) to ask for assistance and support. Jon Cavaiani had already established an excellent reputation among community leaders in the area. Because of his work with active duty and veteran support in New York and New England, especially in and around Boston while still on active duty, the MC-LEF Philadelphia and the Tri-State Area was a good fit.

When Jon first arrived in Philly in the early nineties, his presence was immediately felt by all who met him. His humor and winning smile made it easy to approach him. His openly honest assessments of his environment and events were refreshing. Many of the people who

---

[93] Marine Corps Law Enforcement Foundation: Mission Statement; https://www.mc-lef.org/

worked with him to enhance the post war condition of Veterans and scholarship opportunities for Veterans' survivors became life-long friends. His benevolence - perhaps enhanced by his experiences as an orphan, as a combat veteran, his treatment by the enemy, and the subsequent years of recovery from inhumane "handling" by his captors - was what enabled him to always project an outward show of strength when speaking to *anyone*. His body was tarnished, but his spirit was strong as he maintained an aura of grace and integrity. The SGM was a beacon of positivity; his bearing and demeanor did not reveal his internal struggles and pains. There was seldom a discouraging word to anyone who crossed his path. But when he saw that things were awry, he spoke bluntly, forcefully, and directly.

On one of the first trips to Philadelphia, upon being picked up and driven to a full-dress event (perhaps to a Congressional Medal of Honor Society event), he suddenly asked that the police escort car be stopped. Jon had seen a few young men standing on the sidewalk in fatigues and field jackets. Jon went and talked with them and after several minutes returned to the car. He then asked, *"What is being done for those guys!!??"* He had been convinced that they were indeed Veterans and that they were homeless. Thus began a unified effort in Philadelphia to support Vietnam Veterans, many of whom had come home to nothing but disdain and despair. Because of Jon's question and his encouragement to take-action, Philadelphia became known for its care of Veterans and its outreach to support and strengthen them.[94]

---

[94] Murphy, Jerry Retired Philly Police Dept, as told to Jim Shields and verified 18 July 2022 to John A. Siegfried

With Jon's help, Philadelphia became a model for Veterans' services and family / survivor support. He helped bring bikers and car racing enthusiasts together to encourage and support one another, He challenged the community leaders to take positive action to engage Veterans in productive work and community activities. And he helped raise significant amounts of financial donations that continue to aid survivors of those who served.

As the stories that follow yield, Jon's initial visit to Philadelphia in the 90's had a profound effect on everyone with whom he rubbed shoulders. Daddy Wags, Mike Wallace, Chief Inspector Tony Boyle, Mike Reilly, Joe Looker, Judge Jimmy Lynn, and Jack Cummings (to name a few), had both individual and group interaction with the SGM.

As time progressed, Jon's visits increased, either by invitation, or as follows…

"Jon never slept well. So, he would get-up late evening/early morning Pacific time, fly red eye to Philly, and arrive at one of our homes. As the door opened, the SGM would buoyantly say, 'I'm here.'"[95] These resultant visits increased in frequency over time, as he loved and respected the guys in Philly, and appreciated how they treated him. These interactions included a plethora of bars and restaurants, and VA facilities that opened their doors to this brave man. These visits secured and broadened lasting bonds of trust and friendship. The collective agreement is that these interactions aided the SGM in his daily

---

[95] Cummings, Jack in interview with John Siegfried prior to his death in May 2013

fight with his invisible wounds. The camaraderie, just as the SGM had said about the Montagnards, *"was reciprocal."*

California was Jon's home and his retreat. Philadelphia, however, became his area of operation and his realm of service. The synergy that was exhibited was formidable. Jon fed off of the activities in and around Philadelphia to help him suppress the nagging residuals of PTS, while those with whom he met in Philadelphia were encouraged to action by his energy.

The ingredients that served to flavor the relationships helped Jon form the *"Philly Connection,"* and was the main reason why he requested, prior to his passing, that his remains be flown to the City of Brotherly Love enroute to Arlington.

The testimonials below along with several photos attest to the close relationships that were formed. The words of Jons' friends appear as they wrote or stated them.

Medal of Honor recipient retired Army Sgt. Maj. Jon Cavaiani kneels to autograph his picture in the program booklet for the Marine Corps Law Enforcement Foundation's 10th Annual Invitational Gala in Atlantic City, NJ on June 12. 2005. Meanwhile, Army Lt. Col. Carl Glenn Ayers, left, military assistant to the Secretary of Defense, chats with two other Vietnam War Medal of Honor recipients, retired Army Command Sgt. Maj. Robert Patterson, center, and former Army 1st Lt. Brian M. Thacker. Photo by Rudi Williams

The Marine Corps-Law Enforcement Foundation Coin

The Marine Corps-Law Enforcement Foundation

Jim Kallstrom, a 'Nam Marine, and a former FBI Assistant Director in Charge of the New York Field Office, created the Foundation in New York City to honor Marines and Federal Law Enforcement killed in the line of duty. The first scholarships were awarded following the Oklahoma City Bombing in '95, amounting to $260,300.00 for families of thirty-two men and women killed that day. At that time, $30,000 was donated to each child of a fallen Marine/Federal Law Enforcement officer.

In 1999, the Philly Chapter was formed. As the years progressed, and interest grew, coupled with the over 7,000 Armed Forces that were killed in action in Iraq and Afghanistan, The New York Office moved the amount per child under 18 to $35,000.

With just one part time employee, the donations received from fundraising efforts direct 98% to the children of the family of our fallen Marines, Federal Law Enforcement, which includes FBI, Secret Service, Border Patrol, US Marshalls, ATF, DEA, and any of the agencies under the Federal umbrella.

In Philadelphia, the MC-LEF also covers the Philly Police Department. Jim passed on 3 July 2021. His legacy lives on through all the volunteers at MC-LEF.

Mike Wallace. Chairman: Philadelphia Marine Corps-Law Enforcement Foundation

"I first met Jon Cavaiani at the Philadelphia Medal of Honor Convention in the mid 90's. Jimmy 'Daddy' Wags (Wagner) and I went over to the Marriott Convention Center and joined about a hundred of the MOHs at the bar. Wags did his thing and next thing I know Wags, Ray La Gioia, and I were taking 20 MOHs to play golf at Melrose Country Club. Among those were Barney [Colonel Barnum], Commandant Lou Wilson, Cavaiani, Jimmy Taylor, Van Barfoot, and a group of others. We then went to a VFW post in Cheltenham for lunch:

Awesome day. Before he left on Monday, Jon and Barbara stopped down at Cookies Tavern (Jimmy Wagner's bar) before his plane left, and we ate Cheese Steaks and assorted goodies, and Jon proceeded to miss two connections, but Barbara learned how to play Morra (Italian fingers game) and we drank Bourbon. He finally left late that night but promised to attend the Port Richmond Memorial Day Parade coming up and never turned us down. He was our guest of Honor at the affair on the Battleship New Jersey for MCLEF which kicked off a series of successful Galas up to his death. I was in San Francisco shortly thereafter and while checking out a menu in a place (where) we had dinner reservations, they rushed out the door and yelled 'Judge- what the hell are you doing here?' This led to a very, very, long day and night, followed by a trip the next day to Sausalito for breakfast, and the beginning of a 20-year friendship, which will never be forgotten.

We played golf together many times, and each outing was a memorable experience."

Mike Wallace and Jon

Obverse side of Challenge coin

Reverse side of Challenge coin given to given to Mike Wallace

Jon, Jacqui Oates, Ralph Race Master Chief US Merchant Marines, and Judge Jimmy Lynn

Testimonial: Judge James Lynn (Ret.)

Judge Lynn (Jimmy), like Mike Wallace, met Jon in the early nineties, before MC-LEF Philly was incorporated. Back then, Medal of Honor challenge coins, which could be given to those who were friends of the MOH recipient, were usually engraved with their name on the back. Jon gave Jimmy his coin, but asked him to write-down the spelling of his name. Time passed, and when they saw each other again, Jon gave the Judge his coin. Upon looking at the inscription, Judge said, *"You spelled my name wrong!"*

Upset, and upon checking the engraving, the meticulous Sergeant Major pulled a note from his pocket. It was the one on which Judge Lynn had written his name prior. Handing the note to the Judge Jon replied, *"YOU spelled your name wrong!"*

Sheepishly, Jimmy spelled his name correctly this time, and Jon had his challenge coin engraved. Again. Correctly!

In 1999, the Marine Corps-Law Enforcement Foundation, Philly Chapter, was started by Daddy Wags, Jack

Cummings, Tom LaMaine, Tim Kelly, and others. Wagner was a Marine who served in Vietnam, and his bar in South Philly, *Cookies*, became **THE Marine Bar** in the United States. Thousands would flock to Cookies on 10 November, the Marine Corps birthday since 1775, and a host of bikers from all over the US as well: Streets blocked- off to accommodate the crowds. My first exposure to this grand event was in 2010. Wags actually staged his own funeral in 1996 at his bar, to see who would attend. MCLEF has the video. This Marine was the persona of a Pisces, born 21 February 1945. Jim got sick, presumably from Agent Orange exposure, but since he never went to the VA, no one will ever know.

At 0317, 2 November 2002, after being diagnosed with a brain tumor, and a subsequent long illness, his wife, and daughters at his side, he passed away. At the EXACT SAME TIME, Judge Lynn was playing pool with Colonel Barney Barnum.

Judge Lynn: *"Wags was the straw that stirred the drink,"* relative to the success of Philly MC-LEF. It is the same line Reggie Jackson coined for himself, relative to the Yankees success while on the team.[96]

---

[96] Jimmy Lynn in interview via phone with John Siegfried; June 2022

Above: Jack Cummings wife, Beth, Jon, and Barb Cavaiani

Below: Dan Jones and The Sergeant Major at The Palm Restaurant on Broad Street in Philly.

Philly Remembrances

Jon R. Cavaiani, my friend
By Dan Jones, May 10, 2022

"Jon suffered from MDS, a blood cancer disorder, that rarely slowed this Hero down but took his life in 2014.

"Jon and I first met when I joined the Philly Committee of MC-LEF.Org circa 2010. I was introduced to Jon by mutual good friends and MC-LEF volunteers, Terry Reilly & Jack Cummings.

We began a tradition of playing golf the day before our annual Gala event in Philly, where Jon and his fellow Medal of Honor Recipients would gather to relax before the heavy lifting began that evening and into the next 48 hours. Jon and his fellow Medal of Honor heroes would help us raise hundreds of thousands annually to help fund $35,000 Education Accounts for the Kids who lost their mom or dad while serving our great country.

My first golf experience with Jon was while we were putting on our golf spikes for the round. He had large hard-plastic stirrups that extended from beneath his heel and up both sides of his calves. They were strapped on, and his shoes were tied snuggly. I awkwardly inquired the source of his injuries requiring him to strap on medical shackles.

Jon didn't like to talk about his 22 months as a POW other than describe the damage to his arms and legs from the binding of his ankles and wrists by ropes and then hung from the ceiling of the torture room. Sometimes his 4 points of connection were forward, somedays the guards would tie his limbs in reverse before hoisting him onto the 'meat-hook' at the Hòa Lò Prison, a.k.a. Fiery Furnace, a.k.a. Hell Hole.

Jon would joke that his diet that enabled him to lose 109 lbs. during his POW tenure, which ended at the Hanoi Hilton and was the easy part. Self-Removing over 100 pieces of shrapnel using a sharpened bamboo spike helped pass the time. I recall him talking about some of his escapes and recaptures, but the Jack Daniels imbibed together clouds those details.

Lastly, after Jon died of blood cancer, I was honored in July 2014 when asked to help carry his coffin from the hearse into the funeral home, so his friends and admirers could pay their last respects. Several months later, we tended to Jon again when we delivered his remains to his final resting place at Arlington.

At Mick's Inn in Port Richmond (Philadelphia), PA we gathered that July evening to open a reserved bottle of JACK in celebration of Jon's Life. Some years earlier, when Jon decided that the Reilly Family would take care of his services at life's end, he placed a new bottle of Jack on a high shelf. He taped a $5.00 bill to the bottle to be used as a tip for the bartender. A motley crew opened that libation and toasted our friend and one of our country's true heroes."

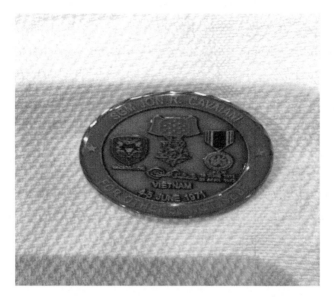

Challenge coin given to Dan Jones

Testimonial: Sgt. Chris Clemens Remembers

**Senior Aviation Pilot for the Philly P.D., Sgt Chris Clemens
with MOH Sergeant Major Jon Cavaiani**

"It was a dusty worn old school watering hole I used to frequent after my tour or mission - the year was on or about 1999. Assigned to the Philly SWAT team we would frequently throw-back beers and decompress at this local pub while lamenting about the woes of the job or the excitement of a protracted barricade or high-risk warrant service we had. One particular evening while 'hot washing' over some suds with the usual suspects on the team I noticed a grey haired and bearded man among the group. Standing alone and dressed in what was his trademark black sport coat and black turtleneck I immediately noticed a pale blue ribbon and medallion around his neck which I immediately recognized as the Medal of Honor. Waiting patiently at the bar for his drink he seemed like a quiet and gentle man. Not knowing who he was, why he would have been there and suspecting he was a poser, I turned to one of my colleagues and inquired, 'who is this kook wearing the Medal?'
"That is Jon Cavaiani and that is the real Medal of Honor" **he** **replied**. *He then introduced me to him. Jon had been in town for a fundraiser and was having drinks with mutual friends. Upon his introduction, Jon embraced me and as a member of the SWAT team began to convey his profound gratitude for my service. He then insisted on buying me a drink. I politely responded, Sir, I respectfully decline, and it will please me if you do me the honor of letting me buy you a drink*

Never once during our prolonged conversation thereafter did Jon mention or talk about himself, but rather made inquiry about my career, my family, and reiterated his respect and thanks he had for first responders. I was completely at a loss. Here is a man who has done more and sacrificed so much so that we can live under the blanket of freedom he provides is commending me for what, in the grand scheme of things, amounts to peanuts compared to what he did for our country. We immediately hit it off and there we initiated and forged a relationship that would last until his regrettable passing years later. I remember Jon as one of the most outward thinking, selfless, funny, engaging men I have ever met. He, like the other MOH recipients are Angels on Earth.

Sometime later, I transferred to the Helicopter Air Support Unit (Aviation) as a pilot. Jon wasted no time in coming up for a flight. As he and Jack Cummings, another great American, warrior and man who left us too soon, boarded the helicopter his face, plastered with a smile that went from ear to ear. He was so excited to go punch holes in the sky over Philadelphia. It was one of the most important flights I ever executed, and he had fun, making phone calls from the helicopter to his family and friends giving a play by play of the patrol flight we were on. He loved being up there.

Jon eventually got sick but that did not stop him from engaging in events and visits. True to fashion, and always in 5th gear, Jon showed up at a dinner at the Palm just shortly before he died. He came directly from the hospital still bearing his patient bracelet and an IV port coming from his arm. It was the last time we saw each other. I miss him, his raspy voice, his sense of humor and mostly his kind and gentle nature, always putting *others before himself. I do cherish the memories of the time we had together. And only wish he were to guide me today through my challenges. We will meet again one day, and I only hope I have lived a life worthy of the great reward because I can guarantee Jon went right to the top and did not pass go."*

Testimonial: Sam Minutola USMC Delaware Connection

"Jon, me, fellow Marines Joe Barnes and Rich Robichaud, and a friend were in a bar in Delaware. He (Jon) visited our post regularly in Delaware. "

"Some time passed in the bar, and this guy walks in. As he approaches, then sits down next to us, a discussion transpires, during which he explained that he was being awarded the Medal of Honor. Jon, being the president of the Medal of Honor Society at that time, stood up and asked him his name. While doing so, he (Jon) casually removed his Medal from underneath his shirt, exposing it: Jon didn't like the notoriety all the time. So, he wore it underneath his clothing in my presence a lot.

The man's face showed 'Holy Shit, I better get out of here,' and began to exit the bar. My one friend darted after him, expletives not included here! He never caught-up with him, but this was one of many situations where our Vets caught someone mimicking that they served. 'Stolen Valor' at its best."

**Four Medal of Honor Recipients at MCLEF Gala
PHILADELPHIA. L-R. Brian Thacker USA, CSM Bob Patterson,
Jon Cavaiani, and Colonel Barney Barnum, USMC**

**Jon with Sue Quinn Morris. New Jerseyite. (Web Designer for
Philly MC-LEF's website. mclefphila.org.) and Jack Cummings.**

Jon, Sue, and Jack Cummings. American Legion Post 372. Cherry Hill, NJ

Sue's Remembrance

Sunday Feb 26th, 2012 – *"Surprise Visit from MOH Recipient and former POW, Jon Cavaiani, MCLEF President Jack Cummings and MCLEF member Brit Henderson. It was a great surprise when Jack and Brit brought Jon over to the American Legion Post 372 – I do recall Brit texting me to see if I was going to be at the Legion and not really responding when I said yes and asked why. Shortly afterwards, Brit, Jon, and Jack walked in. To say it was an honor for all our members at the American Legion to meet Jon is an understatement – Brit had called some of his brothers from the Nam Knights (motorcycle organization) as well, so they all came over to see Jon as well. I suppose one of the things that always stuck out to me about Jon was just how down to earth he was and very funny. And when you put Jon alongside Jack, well the*

2 of them were a trip. On this particular day, after all the greetings and photos everyone took with Jon, and things settled down, it was time for a shuffleboard game according to Jon and Jack – and they were going to teach me since I had only played maybe once or twice many years ago. Between all the carrying on and shenanigans I'm not even sure who won!"

My Story on Sergeant Major Jon Cavaiani: John Siegfried

"Within three months of intense research on Six Degrees of the Bracelet: Vietnam's Continuing Grip, Edward Murphy's Book Vietnam Medal of Honor Heroes *landed in my lap from a friend. Another book that listed all 247 MOH's from 'Nam (as of December 2009) was read cover to cover. After many phone calls, a SEAL provided Jon's address/phone number in California in March 2010. After a brief discussion with Jon, knowing that he would be in Atlantic City for a MC-LEF Gala, we met the following 10 June. That day, Colonel Joe Marm, Medal of Honor recipient from the Battle of Ia Drang Valley 14-17 November 1965, introduced himself as he had already confirmed an interview, via phone, for my Six Degrees book at his home 28 June 2010. After the interview, Colonel Marm wanted to introduce me to MOH David Dolby, but the SF operator passed early August of 2010. Invited to the memorial service in Phoenixville, it was the first time I met US Army Medal of Honor Recipient Brian Thacker.*

Complements of my Uncle Carl Hessinger, who possessed the largest cache of pre-Castro cigars in the country; my cousin bequeathed to me a box of Romeo and Juliet's. Always lifting my spirits to give rather than receive, I handed the SGM one that 10 June day. As it was the end of the event, and after enjoying himself with his favorite libations, for many hours, he summarily dropped it!

*Fast forward October 2010, we met again at the Philly Gala for the Marine Corps-Law Enforcement Foundation (picture listed). It was not until that following January 2011 that a three-hour chat, complements of an invite for dinner at The Vesper Club from Jack Cummings, a co-founder of MC-LEF Philly in 1999, came to pass at the bar. The SGM told me he thought I was part of the smear-campaign that was obfuscated by a SF Major who wrote Traitors Pact. Upon vetting me thru channels, knowing that was not the case, and that Traitors Pact was an exercise in futility (confirmed by many POW's), we had a wonderful conversation: Not about him, as was always the case if self-directed, but about my life. He chose not to be interviewed for Six Degrees. To be sure, after a discussion with the POW Historian Captain Mike McGrath (Prisoner of War: Six Years in Hanoi), the Captain assured me 9 May 2022 the rumors were totally unfounded about Jon and the 'Peace Movement,' and that Jon inserted himself **within** the Peace Movement in the Hanoi Hilton to **dislodge, discredit, and to break-up the seditionists for early release.***

After seeing him at countless Philly Gathering of Heroes (our bi-annual event where many of Jon's MOH compatriots attended) and Annual Marine Corps-Law Enforcement Foundation Gala's in both Jersey and PA, his subsequent exposure to Agent Orange reared its fateful head. I always called him on 2 August to wish him Happy Birthday, and in 2011 he called me back, stating that, through the efforts of The Defense POW/MIA Accounting Agency, his prayer was to find the remains of his friend, Sgt. John R. Jones. The SGM said, emphatically, that if found, he would sleep peacefully for the first time in 40 years.

I saw him for the last time in 2013 at Atlantic City Country Club. Mimicking his Budweiser, Jack Daniels, and Marlboro's, as we had for four years; it was the last time I saw Jon with us. This, during the period when diagnosed with his rare cancer, and having the University of Pennsylvania administer his treatment when in the Philly area.

As his sickness progressed, with no DNA available due to being an orphan, and after a long struggle, Jon succumbed 29 July 2014. His viewing was in his beloved city, Philadelphia. My daily prayers include him from July 2014 to this day.

My belief is that the SGM willed, through Mike Evers, Jim Shields, Dick James, all who touched his life, served with him, his wife Barb (who passed April 2021), and me, this Legacy to him."

SGM Cavaiani, Barb, and John Siegfried: MCLEF Gala October 2010 Philly

Signed/Framed portrait of Jon at the Memorial Day Parade he attended in Philly 2004. Currently hanging at the Philadelphia Vietnam Veterans Memorial Society (The Hooch) Hall in Bridesburg, Philadelphia

Testimonial: Jerry Murphy Philly Police Department - Retired.

"Most of the stories from me, (about) Jon, would be (about) the (security) escorts that the Philadelphia P.D. (provided) when the Medal of Honor guys were in town. (These were) Mostly done by Philadelphia Highway Patrol. Jon loved coming to Philly; he loved the escorts, and especially loved the men and women in blue. But I think the best escort I did was with the Chief (Chief Inspector Tony Boyle), taking Jon to his final resting place amongst his warrior buddies at Arlington. I still haven't seen or heard of an escort topping that one yet.

Also, when the Medal of Honor guys were in town, many of us would stay out well into the night. Our wives would be mad as hell when they came into town. But, when our ladies finally met them, they thought they were the best. My wife would get 'mad' at me for keeping them out."

Testimonial: Sue Manual New Jersey

"I still have his Mass Card on my Bureau. Jon cooked a five-course dinner at Barb Borowiecs' home around 2009. And I think it was his true passion. What a handsome man he was…"

Sue Manuel at Barb's Harley Davidson's Freedom Run with Jon May 2009.

Sergeant Major Jon Cavaiani saluting the Flag at Barb Borowiecs' Annual Harley Davidson's Freedom ride from Barb's dealership in Collingdale, NJ to McGuire Joint Base New Jersey 2009

Testimonial: Joe Looker USMC Vietnam

"(I) *first met Jon when he was still active in the Army at the Trump Plaza with Patty McGahn in the VIP room. We went on the balcony; I asked Jon, and being a Vietnam Vet myself, I asked him if he had any animosity toward the people who held him captive and tortured him. He told me he had none, which surprised the hell out of me with that answer, and I knew then what a special guy he was. A TRUE AMERICAN HERO!"*

Right: Medal of Honor Recipient Brian Thacker, U.S. Marine Joe Looker, and Jon

Left: Joe looker, Dino White, Jon, and Jim Nangle.

Right: Barb, Jon, Terry & Joe Looker

Left: Jon, Patty McGahn, and Joe Looker

Testimonial: Example of Law Enforcement Connection In California

What Jon Cavaiani left the people of San Bernardino California is a letter written by his friend and former Police Commissioner, George Schnarre, shortly after Jon's death:

> The letter could be entitled, "The Security Strategy of Sergeant Major Jon Cavaiani MOH, USA". **(Aug 02, 1943 - Jul 29, 2014)**

> *"In early 2002, our Police Commission took steps to update our city's security plan. 9-11-2001 was a real wake-up call for everyone but as a Police Commissioner for the City of*

San Bernardino, we had a significant realization given the strategic impact that disruption of our area assets could have on the entire United States economy.

San Bernardino has Interstate 10 and Interstate 15 running through it. It has key rail lines, natural gas lines, fuel lines, and critical water infrastructure used by millions of people. As a result of so many important economic assets converging in one area, it was incumbent upon us to ensure our safety and security plan was robust so as to avoid disruption of any of these services.

As I look back now, I can see it was divine intervention that discussions for the area security plan update were occurring around Memorial Day 2002. As I participated in the local Memorial Day Ceremony at Mt. View Cemetery, San Bernardino, I became engaged in a conversation with Sergeant Major Jon Cavaiani MOH, USA, who was the keynote speaker of the event that day. That conversation became the backbone of a security plan which revolutionized strategic planning for areas with key economic attributes to protect.

I brought Jon down to our Police Department Headquarters and showed him the city's current security plan which we were looking to update. After careful review of the plan he said, 'As long as it's the Cub Scouts attacking the city, you'll be fine. If any military trained or terrorist organizations focus on disrupting the San Bernardino area, you're screwed.'"

Sergeant Major Jon Cavaiani went on to show us how all of our electrical infrastructure was vulnerable, how our *natural gas lines could be used against us, how our sewage treatment facility could cause mass disruption, and how easily fireworks or ammonium nitrate could be used to devastate commercial trucking and rail lines. Our whole security strategy was exposed as being a deterrent to ensure good people didn't do bad things rather than having a strong offense in place to defeat an aggressive enemy whose intent is to strike fear in the citizenry.*

Sergeant Major Jon Cavaiani also began the educational process which trained us in the art of open space use and how different parks, parking lots, fields and sports venues could be used as staging areas for rapid response coordination for crises. In October 2003, all of this training would be put to use as the Waterman Canyon Fire would become a major catastrophe which actually would have been worse had Jon not already provided us with his wisdom and experience in crisis response security strategies.

The San Bernardino Police Department owes a tremendous amount of gratitude to Sergeant Major Jon Cavaiani for his time, patience, and training that he provided to our community in the Summer of 2002."

May he rest in peace. Respectively submitted by George Schnarre

From Some Special Forces Soldiers Not Previously Quoted Who Served With / Knew of Jon

Retired Master Sgt. **Jeff Hinton** said he never served

with Cavaiani, but knew him by reputation. Cavaiani was presented with a Yarborough knife -- the kind of blade given to every graduate of the Green Beret Qualification Course by Hinton's business interest which operates the website **Professionalsoldiers.com**. *"He's a great guy,"* said Hinton.

"Jon was a very quiet, soft-spoken soldier whose humility masked his great heroism and courageous fighting spirit from many of us that served in Special Forces with him," **recalled former Staff Sgt. Craig Rutherford**, who served with Cavaiani in the early 1980s, B Co., 2nd Bn., 10th Special Forces Group (A) at Fort Devens, Mass.

Rutherford said Cavaiani was always the professional soldier, but also very modest. He said he had known him more than a year before he learned Cavaiani received the Medal of Honor. He learned it after they and others went out to breakfast following a funeral detail. A junior communications officer noticed the Medal of Honor ribbon among the others on Cavaiani's Class A Uniform.

"When he asked Jon how he had received the Medal of Honor, Jon meekly replied, 'I was in the wrong place at the wrong time,' and nothing else was said," Rutherford explained. *"He never spoke of his exploits but did quietly give guidance to his subordinates and superiors alike."*

That part of his character was also revealed to **Gary W. Ferrera**, who also remembered Cavaiani from 10th Special Forces Group. At the time, Ferrera said he was an 18–19-year-old assigned to the unit as an intelligence analyst and had not even attended the Special Forces Qualification Course.

"He (Sergeant Major Cavaiani) was very humble, and I only actually saw him wear his Medal Of Honor once, which was when he was asked to come speak to a class at a local college," Ferrera wrote. *"I corrected a second lieutenant from the Intelligence School at Fort Devens for not saluting Jon when he walked past us that day as he was wearing his ribbon, and then Jon quietly corrected me for bringing attention to him -- I felt like crap after that. Lesson learned!"*

Ferrera said that Cavaiani set an example for him by his attention to detail and ability to put in long, arduous hours to prepare troops for deployment.[97]

Richard Whitman related to Mike Evers (while at a Special Forces Association Convention) that his team had been on standby ready to go to Hickory Hill to reinforce or extract Jon and his men who were under attack. *"For some reason, we were told to stand down. When we got word of the fall of Hickory, and the destruction that had been seen, we assumed Jon to be dead. Later in life I learned that Jon was alive, and I cried tears of joy. Then when I saw him at a gathering of Green Berets I hugged him and cried again. Jon and I shared, over the years, many good times, good tales, and good libation! Jon was a professional soldier of the highest order, a great and principled human being, and a true friend. There is one word to describe Jon Cavaiani and that is 'fabulous!'"*

Cliff Newman also spoke with Mike Evers about Jon

---

[97] Ferrera, Gary in interview with John Siegfried via phone; June 2022).

while at a Special Forces Association Convention. *"There were many who, in Vietnam, did extraordinary things. Some were awarded, some were not. What Jon did (on Hickory Hill) was beyond extraordinary. What he did after Vietnam and after active duty was likewise extraordinary. Jon was a driven man who served those with whom he served."*

Alex Quade, whose web site appears at **https://alexquade.com**, is a War Reporter who covers U.S. Special Operations Forces on combat missions. She is the only reporter, male or female, ever embedded *long-term* with these elite, secretive units downrange. She is the recipient of two national RTDNA *Edward R. Murrow Awards*, as well as the Congressional Medal Of Honor Society's *"Tex McCrary Award For Excellence In Journalism"* for her war reportage. Alex informed Mike Evers that she *"had last seen Sergeant Major Jon Cavaiani at a SOAR (Special Operations Assoc. Reunion) wearing a Harley Davidson t-shirt, drink in hand. He always gave me a huge smile and a hug."* She acknowledged that Jon loved motorcycles and race cars, and Jack Daniels, but *"I think that he truly just loved people. He was always so genuine and warm, no pretense. I think that he was a model that others should try to emulate."*

Below is an autographed page from the massive MEDAL OF HONOR book that was presented to Alex by the CMOH Society at the Reagan Presidential Library. Alex was called home from Afghanistan to receive the book as a measure of appreciation for her work.

The photograph on the left shows Jon's signature in the MOH book presented to Alex Quade; the photograph on the right was taken by Alex, Memorial Day Weekend 2021.

Jim Shorten: Jon's instructor at 0-1 Recon school and Jon in Philadelphia.
The memories and friendship lasted well beyond their experiences in Vietnam

CHAPTER TWELVE

The Final Struggle

"Once when Marshall Ney was going into battle, looking down at his knees which were smiting together, he said to his troops, 'You may well shake; you would shake worse yet if you knew where I am going to take you.' Napoleon was so much impressed with the courage and resources of Marshall Ney he said, 'I have two hundred million in my coffers, and I would give up them all for Ney."

Orison Swett Marden

It is unlikely that anyone wants to be told that they are terminally ill. While we all know in the back of our minds that death is the final step of life, we have difficulty facing it. However, Jon had already faced death, more than once, over the span of his illustrious life. He knew where *"he was going."*

As if the God's of Challenge and Struggle wanted test to Jon one more time, Jon was, in 2012 diagnosed with bone marrow cancer. When Jon was informed of his bone marrow cancer, he nodded. He seemed to take it in stride. He had been ill for a while and had tried to combat it with over-the counter medicines and sheer determination, relying on local doctors and pharmacists to keep him going.

All he wanted to do at this point in his life was return to

Columbia, take care of his garden, cook a bit, and be with the love of his life Barbara. Several friends told him to seek medical help, but his reply was: *"No, I will let the Lord decide."*[98]

He and Barbara had returned to their humble dwelling in Columbia, California, to spend their time together enjoying one another. But calls continued to come in asking for his support for various worthwhile events. He was determined to keep going as long as he could. He chose to return to Philadelphia, to continue the work he had done with the Marine Corps Law Enforcement Foundation regarding educational scholarships, improving the plight of homeless Veterans in the area, and encouraging people to be better than they think they can be.

He planned to be an ongoing ambassador to Veterans at racing events. He planned to also attend the Special Forces Conventions as he had done for so many years, and he was going to play a more active role in the Congressional Medal of Honor Society. Also, he wanted to support his friends in the Northern California Special Forces Association Chapter (Chapter 23 – The Golden Gate Chapter).

He was going to do these things for as long as he could and when his time was up, he was going to rest in peace.

Jon had fought for as long as he could, having received treatment in Sonora, California Veterans Clinics in California, and even at the University of Pennsylvania Hospital when he went there to fulfill his missions for Veterans and the Marine Corps Law Enforcement Foundation.

---

[98] Op Cit; Shields

Columbia is a small town with a small-town drug store. One day shortly after the diagnosis, Jon was at the drug store discussing with the pharmacist the drugs that had been prescribed to help treat his condition and/or comfort the struggle that was ahead. That conversation was overheard and within hours the news of Jon's condition had spread beyond Columbia to fellow Special Forces alumnae. In fact, it was a SFA Chapter 23 member who had overheard the conversation at the local pharmacy in Sonora and reported it to Chapter 23.

With the degree of suffering increasing, and at Barbara's encouraging plea, Jon had already chosen to commence treatment at Stanford University, and was preparing to begin his treatment, but not until he fulfilled a promised to speak to ROTC students at Cal Poly San Luis Obispo.

It was while speaking in San Luis Obispo to ROTC Cadets that Jon collapsed. He was rushed to a hospital there and again diagnosed with MDS (myelodysplastic syndrome) a form of leukemia.

Prior to his collapse, Jon had received medical consultation, treatment, blood transfusions, and chemotherapy from various hospitals to include Sonora (California) Hospital, University of Pennsylvania Hospital (while valiantly trying to continue to fulfill his desires to continue his work in Philadelphia and the surrounding areas) , and San Francisco Veterans Hospital.

The communication between these various entities was phenomenal. Jon refused to stop serving people that he loved, and he continued to go to numerous events for as long as he could. This required the VA, Stanford University Medical Center and The University of Pennsylvania to communicate on almost a daily basis in order to provide treatment. It was not unusual for Jon to appear at an event immediately after receiving treatment. That is how determined Jon was to press on with his mission of service.

The medical memo below indicates the communications involved between treatment providers on Jon's behalf and serves only as one example of many such communications.

█████████████, MD, PhD – Blood and Bone Marrow Transplantation

████████████████ – Contact Nurse

Jon is considered High Risk (Moderate Risk by old evaluation system) MDS. Median survival is 1.5 years. Chemotherapy drugs (Azacitidine) have been shown to extend this. Jon had a bone marrow biopsy done at Sonora Regional on July 15, 2013. Test results run at Stanford show that the blasts are now between 5-10%, a decreased amount, showing that the chemo is helping Jon. Only 50% of the population responds to this chemo. Jon was given instructions to continue on chemotherapy while the transplantation testing and waiting process takes place. Transplant is the only "cure." Tests to occur will include lung and liver function, as well as x-rays. They wanted Jon to get x-rays done at Stanford, but his blood levels were too low and he was not strong enough to wait the extra time required. We need to make sure these tests are scheduled and hopefully performed here in Sonora. The transplant Jon will hopefully undergo is called non-myeloablative – "TLI-ATG". His immune system will first be suppressed – total lymphoid irradiation (TLI) – 9 days. Anti-thymocyte globulin –(ATG) – 5 days. This will occur in the hospital. Transplant from donor (which on average takes 2-3 months to find a match), will occur on about the 12th day. Once they determine the transplant went well, Jon can become an outpatient, with regular visits to Stanford as determined. Patient told to relocate near the hospital for a minimum of 100 days.

Calendar –Jon undergoes tests to determine if he is a good candidate. Blood samples were drawn at Stanford, some of which will be sent to the Donor Registry. X-ray(s) required, which were not done at Stanford. These need to be ordered. Coordination between Sonora Regional Oncology and ███████████████, RN, Stanford, needs to occur to ensure all of the proper testing takes place.

The search for the donor begins. Takes 2-3 months.
3 classes must be attended by Jon and Barb prior to transplant
Chemotherapy continues throughout the waiting period

As fate would have it, the young soldier, Jim Shields, who had learned from Jon at China Lake on how to prepare and use the PRC 77 was now an active member of Special Forces Association Chapter 23 – The Golden Gate Chapter. Jim immediately jumped into action.

Also, the Chapter members quickly contacted their former Battalion Surgeon. When Jon was an advisor at the Presidio, he had met a young orthopedic surgeon named David G. Mohler. "Doc Mohler" as he was fondly called, was the Battalion Surgeon for 3rd Battalion, 12th Special Forces Group. By the time that Jon was diagnosed with cancer, Doctor Mohler was working as Chief of Orthopedic Oncology of the Stanford University Medical Center in Palo Alto. Doc Mohler immediately acted on Jon's behalf. As soon as could be arranged, Jon was admitted for treatment, but the frequent drives from Columbia to Palo Alto was going to be too much of an undertaking. Never-the-less, Jon was happy to see the familiar face of a Special Forces Doctor who he trusted.

Jon was told that he would need to find dust and pollen accommodations near Stanford Medical Center. However, due to a massive construction project at Stanford there were no dust-free accommodations nearby.

Again, Jim Shields and Chapter 23 took-action by calling various veteran and military facilities. They were able to, but not without having to get an active-duty Admiral involved, find new dust and pollen-free housing for Jon and Barb at NAS Moffett Field. It seems that an Army Major (Major Gerdys) who was in charge of housing had overruled local regulations and circumvented policy and protocol by allowing a retired Army NCO to live in the quarters. Reserve Officers and other retired personnel heard of this and complained up the Chain of Command. Some people demanded that the Major be relieved of his position and Cavaiani removed from the facility. In response, the Admiral awarded the Major with a Letter of Commendation for his compassionate act and assured the quarters would remain available to the Cavaiani family.

In short order the Northern California chapter of Special Forces members (Chapter 23) took steps to begin raising funds to help support Jon and Barb in their latest challenge. Word spread to other organizations across the U.S. – and not just Special Forces brothers, but to other organizations that had come to love and respect Jon. These included the CMOHS and the MCLEF. Special Forces Chapter 23 also they helped with the move to Moffett Field so that Jon could be near the cancer center at Stanford University Hospital. They also provided transportation to and from treatment facilities.

Dick James of SFA Chapter 23 presents a check to Jon and Barbara in support of Jon's fight against leukemia.

Below is a copy of the plan that was developed for the move. Two important points of the plan were getting Jon and Barbara's concurrence and the next to the last bullet point, that of Jon wanting his grill and it had to be set up in accordance with his specifications. Yes, Jon loved to cook, and he was precise in his culinary artistry.

```
┌─────────────────────────────────────────────────────────────────┐
│                                                                   │
│            PLAN FOR MOVING JON AND BARB TO MOFFETT                │
│                                                                   │
│ SEPT 9 2013 – House is vacated.                                   │
│ House is inspected and, prior to cleaning, bug bombs set off in   │
│ each room with A/C operating. House is left overnight             │
│  SEPT 10, 2013                                                    │
│ Professional Duct Cleaner is given access and all ducting and     │
│ furnace interior is cleaned and dusted.  High flow air filters    │
│ are installed to remove any particles in the system.              │
│ SEPT 11 2013                                                      │
│ Chapter 23 Cleaning Team will clean EACH room in preparation      │
│ for carpet cleaning contractor. Walls are to be washed but NOT    │
│ repainted due to vapors from fresh paint.                         │
│ SEPT 12 2013                                                      │
│ Carpets are washed and vacuumed by cleaning contractor.           │
│ SEPT 13 2013                                                      │
│ Final Inspection and walk through                                 │
│ SEPT 14 2013                                                      │
│ Furniture Rental Company Delivery Chapter 23 team at Columbia     │
│ to move needed items to Moffett                                   │
│ TV CABLE INSTALLED                                                │
│ **Barbeque delivered to Jon's specs**                            │
│ SEPT 15, 2013                                                     │
│ Property is able to receive Jon and Barb.                         │
│                                                                   │
│ This plan was submitted for approval by Jon and Barb – Then the   │
│ assignments of team members were posted and distributed --        │
│                                                                   │
└─────────────────────────────────────────────────────────────────┘
```

The actions of Special Forces Association Chapter 23 became known to others. The following notes from MCLEF archives attest to the valiant efforts of Chapter 23.

> *"Jon and Barb have been advised to find a place to stay near enough to Stanford to assure them ready access to the medical center whenever Jon's condition demands. Finding a "clean" house is a major challenge.*
>
> *Because his immune system will be compromised, the house has*

to be extra clean to avoid contributing to sicknesses when Jon is vulnerable during treatments. It's perhaps easy to gloss over these efforts as just securing a temporary residence. Consequently, this update amplifies the volunteer efforts by the members of Jon's Special Forces Association (Chapter 23) to provide a safe, temporary home.

There are a lot of complicated but still necessary details to pay attention to, but Jon's SFA has made significant progress. Here is the amazing campaign SFA Chapter 23 has put together:

- Researched numerous housing opportunities near Stanford

- Selected a property with wheelchair access near other military families who will provide support to Jon and Barb during his treatment at Stanford.

- Ensured access to local markets which can provide local organic foods that Jon will require.

- Established communication with all Chapter 23 members who live nearby and can provide any specialized support Jon or Barb may need.

- Coordinated with Stanford Hospital for recommended safe cleaning chemicals and recommendations for air filters.

- Began organic pest extermination.

- Cleaned all the home HVAC ducting to remove all dust and dander. The contractor is an expert on home filtration and will recommend appropriate additional HEPA filters for each room.

- On Sept 14 a Chapter 23 Team will clean each room; washing all walls twice prior to a professional carpet cleaning.

- The next day, a thorough professional carpet cleaning will be

performed.

- The Wounded Warriors Project will provide the necessary rental furniture and Cable TV. Rental furniture was reviewed with hospital experts to ensure the furniture can remain clean and free of dust and pollen.

- Provide and install a BBQ so Jon (a world class chef) can direct all culinary activities allowed by Stanford Medical.

- Dust and pollen sensors are being installed to ensure the environment remains clean.

- Weed and upgrade the home garden to minimize pollen.

- The American Legion has volunteered to Coordinate and provide small kitchen appliances, silverware, and dishes.

- Another Chapter 23 team will help Jon and Barb unload personal items from Columbia and help them get settled.

- A final inspection by Stanford medical experts is planned before moving in to ensure all issues have been addressed.

If anything isn't on Chapter 23's list, it hasn't been invented yet."

The severity of the disease could not be overstated. The need for support, especially blood transfusions and bone marrow transplants, were critical. Perhaps an article that appeared in *Military* Magazine says it best.

"A Vietnam War Medal of Honor recipient is in a different kind of fight today as he battles a blood disease that has already required chemotherapy and blood transfusions.

Retired Army Sgt. Maj. John Cavaiani, 69, needs a bone marrow transplant and family and friends are reaching out for support.

"Tons and tons of people are calling," said Debby Lemmons Fowler, Cavaiani's cousin. "He's probably had too many visitors. He's pretty worn down, I understand ... but he's doing well at home considering he's taking it day by day."

Cavaiani suffers from myelodysplastic syndrome, or MDS, a disease of the blood and bone marrow once known as preleukemia. Since February, he has undergone consultations, blood transfusions and chemotherapy at the San Francisco Veterans Hospital, Hospital of the University of Pennsylvania and Sonora Regional Medical Center, Calif.

Once a marrow donor is located the procedure will be done at Stanford University Hospital. For that reason, family and friends also are trying to raise $50,000 to cover the costs of living in Stanford for a little more than three months after the transfusion.

Fowler said that doctors want him to remain in the area for monitoring during that time. Though the VA and private insurance are likely to cover most if not all medical expenses, the cost of a hotel room alone there for three months will be about $17,000, she said. *As of Aug. 6, supporters had raised nearly $38,000 toward the goal through the crowd funding charity website Give Forward. The $50K goal was hit shortly thereafter."*

Fowler said there was a noticeable spike in contributions last month during the Veterans of Foreign Wars convention in Louisville, Ky., where officials put out the word about Jon's health issues.

"It's very important to get the word out there to do and blood donation," she said. *"Jon is all about paying it forward. He has used so much blood [from transfusions] and he wants to make sure there is not a shortage because of that."*[99]

Almost as immediately calls went out across the United States to organizations with which Jon had been closely engaged establishing means from which to obtain and provide funds to help support the high costs of treatment and the relocation for treatment. Significant funds were raised in the Bay Area and Philadelphia as well as from other locations.

On or about 24 November 2013 Jon received the bone marrow transplant that he needed. A ten-point donor had stepped forward and Jon was now in recovery – or so it was hoped.

Below are some email message exchanges between Barb and members of Special Forces Chapter 23 that recount the efforts made toward that recovery. The emails are unedited except for the removal of some identities.

Jan 4, 2014

Dick & Jim,

"Thanks for the phone call today and your continued tireless efforts on our medical behalf.

Jon has reached his 57th day since transplant.

---

[99] Jordan, Bryant; Military; (Military.com); 7 Aug 2013

Throughout these days, he has had very few that were not filled with some sort of side effect, some worse than others. He is currently struggling with a lot of pain due to his second reaction to the rabbit protein pretreatment that occurred prior to transplant. His connective tissue around his rib cage is inflamed causing pain throughout his upper torso. Consequently, they have increased his Prednisone once again.

He is also struggling with extreme shaking of his limbs and stomach, so they reduced some of his immune suppressant drugs.

This being said, his spirits remain decent. As his favorite Nurse Practitioner said, 'you know this is a mental game.' Well, I am not totally certain about that, but I do know what she means.

If in the beginning I didn't quite understand why we needed to move near Stanford for 100 days after transplant, I sure do now. Some weeks we spend 15+ hours at the Cancer Center.

As I have mentioned before, the quality of care that Stanford Cancer Center provides I believe is unparalleled. And by the way, the entire staff of Doctors, Nurses and support staff all of [have} one of Jon's Medal of Honor coins, so if you ever find yourself at Stanford and they realize you know Jon, you will probably be coined. They joke about having a separate white board for who owes who a beer as they have fun coining each other.

I know I speak for Jon in saying we can't wait to get out

of medical isolation and into the real world again so that we can look each of you in the face and say Thank You in person."

From: Jon Cavaiani
To:
Sent: Monday, 20 January 2014 12:05 PM
Subject: Re: Deposit

Dick,

"Thanks so much for your email and your continued assistance for us. Prayers are working. Jon has not had any major setbacks in over two weeks. Hoping for blood numbers to start improving, as they took him off of an anti-viral drug last Friday that has a tendency to suppress these counts.

We are now under the 30-day mark for going home. We won't have the final approval for another couple weeks. He still has to go through 3rd test that shows % healthy cells that have grafted into him as well as a bone marrow biopsy.

We are both so home sick.

I can relate to the feeling of knowing the roads to/from medical facilities like the back of your hand!

Take care and thanks so much,"

Barb

Dick and Jim

"Sorry for delay in getting back to you, but [I] have been at Stanford all day. Jon [is] receiving blood transfusion as we speak.

His blood numbers are slow in recovering, something that they are not alarmed to see, but they just do what needs to be done.

Jon had a bone marrow biopsy this morning. I watched this long screw/needle going into his lower back. They did get a good sample and also took a sample of his bones. I know he is glad that is over, although this is his fourth bone marrow biopsy. One tough cookie he is.

We also got our medical release to move home on 2/15/14 today from his Doctor. Once home, he will be monitored one week at Sonora Oncology, next week at Stanford, 3rd week home, 4th week at Stanford.

We are terribly excited to get back to God's country.

Jon and I are truly humbled at the outpouring of financial and emotional assistance we have received from the Special Forces Community. This last donation was really something.

I do hope you can convey to the proper people that we simply could not have gone through this without all of their help. Please let them know that they helped save a Medal of Honor Recipient's life, no small feat.

Thank you, Dick, for all your continued work on our behalf. You guys are beyond the best.

Take care,

Off to Stanford to pick-up Jon. I took a little break to clean house while he is being transfused."

Barb

----

4 FEB 2014

Dick,

"Please let them know that they helped save a Medal of Honor Recipient's life, no small feat.

Thank you, Dick, for all your continued work on our behalf. You guys are beyond the best."

Barb

----

6 FEB 2014

[From Dick James to the SF Chapter Members and others]

*"Jon received his release from Stanford yesterday. While this is information that warrants celebration, I need to remind all that Jon is not going back to his normal social life in the mountains. He is starting a **long program** of careful reintroduction to his environment. That means that while his blood numbers are low, he will not be able to host visitors.*

On February 15, a team from SFA Chapter 23 and a load of ruffians from the mountains will gather in Mountain View to assist Jon with all the tasks relating to his move back home. Jon is still extremely tired and will need plenty of rest as a result of the move.

Oh yeah... those "Ruffians" will also be keeping things quiet around Jon and Barb's home."

Dick

----

25 FEB 2014

([From Dick James])

An email from Jon's wife, Barb. Jon definitely needs our prayers

"Things are not looking up for Jon at this point. Hemoglobin 7.9, needs transfusion, but Sonora doesn't have specs for requested blood and even if they did, they have to order blood from Stockton, so transfusion could not take place until tomorrow.

Stanford couldn't provide specs in a timely manner, so we will be going to Stanford Wed., not Thurs.

White blood count also tanked, so getting daily neupogen (sic) shots today, tomorrow and Wed at Stanford (?).

His skin rash due to graft vs host is returning in an ugly way, which means they will probably put him back on prednisone, which slows grafting process.

His eyes are having issues and hurting him, so have eye appt. tomorrow to make sure there is no infection.

He remains in bed and is not drinking required liquids, so will require hydration while at Stanford."

----

3 MAR 2014

(Sent by Jim Shields)

"We have been informed that Jon will be needing blood transfusions at Stanford over the next few months to keep the grafting process going. We are working on the details of a blood drive in the Western Region so Jon can benefit from blood donations.

You will be receiving this information over the next few days.

Just a note for all of us 'old guys.' The protocols for giving blood have changed radically over the past 10 years. The program we intend to establish to assist in Jon's case will be planned to meet the new requirements and will be coordinated with the good folks at Stanford Medical."

Thanks again for all your continued donations. Dick James remains the primary POC for all these donations. In the event you wish to send some funds, your check should be made out to Jon Cavaiani and addressed to:

Dick James

P.O. Box ▮▮

Arnold, CA 95223-3076

A sent by Jim Shields:

This from Barb:

"Hey guys,

Just realized my phone was on mute since last Dr. appts. Obviously not my priority right now.

Yes, been busy with Jon, but am tentatively happy to report no new side effects for a few days. Nausea and diarrhea have subsided, but rash still there. I am applying topical steroids on Jon's skin to keep it from becoming really inflamed.

There is still lots of nursing to do. Food is quite a challenge, as he seems to want something and then he can't or doesn't eat it.

Jon's immune system is not yet 5 months old. He can be likened to a five-month-old baby with cancer.

They are hoping they can kill the balance of cancer cells and allow his donor to take over with her healthy cells. This remains to be seen.

All of his blood levels, white, red and platelet counts have really tanked. He is still requiring red blood cell transfusions, platelet transfusions and daily shots of neupogen (sic) to boost his white blood cell count. As a result of this, he is still under medical isolation. This because his risk of infection is extremely high

Jon remains in bed all of the time unless we have to go to Oncology Dept. which has been daily over the past few weeks.

I can't leave him except to quick trip to store of pharmacy, as he is very weak and dizzy when he is up.

I wish I had better news to report to you all, but we are just taking this one day at a time.

All of your thoughts and prayers help."

Love, Barb

I [Jim] would like to also ask that you forward this information to all of your contacts who might be considering visiting or calling Jon.

1. Jon cannot have visitors as he is still in medical isolation.

2. Jon is too tired to even answer the phone. The message box is full, and they are both too tired to deal with the messages.

3. If someone calls – all that happens is that it wakes Jon up.

4. Stanford is working on Jon's blood problems.

5. Stanford is still working on follow - up bone marrow issues.

6. Barb and Jon wish to express their appreciation for all the well-wishes

7. Dick James is still the local POC for Jon and is handling all donations made to Jon and Barb.

8. The messages of cheer for Jon on St. Patrick's Day gave Jon a great lift. He appreciated all of the kind thoughts.

9. The medical Staff at Jon's local hospital are in daily communication with the Doctors and staff at Stanford. There is good communication and both medical staffs are working closely together for Jon's benefit.

Barb said she would let us know if there is any chance of him safely having visitors or receiving phone calls.

Jim

----

2 APRIL

(From Barb)

"Jon's lab results from yesterday were very disappointing.

His platelets dropped from 53 to 18, hemoglobin from 10.5 to 9.4, and white blood count from 9.4 to 1.5.

All this from Monday to yesterday. He finished his 7th day of chemo today

It has been so difficult on him this time.

Mitch will drive us tomorrow to Palo Alto for Thurs. am appt.

I am without words!"

Barb

----

9 APR 2014

(From Barb)

"Jon has had it very rough lately. All his counts are still very low. He required two units of blood locally in Sonora yesterday. He had a reaction to second unit, so it took a total of 7 hours to finish up after multiple drugs to stop reaction.

Still also requiring daily shots of neupogen (sic) to boost white blood count.

We are on our way to Stanford now for an unexpected transfusion of two units of platelets.

They are unable to do this in Sonora, as Jon has to have platelets with plasma removed due to allergic reactions in the past."

Barb

----

22 APR 2014

(From Barb)

Hello All,

"Sorry for delay in update, but unfortunately Jon is not doing very well over the past few weeks and consequently, at cancer center every day

He is in second round of chemo since being home and it is really taking it's (sic) toll on him. Just had to delay today's appt. due to nausea.

None of his blood numbers are holding. He is requiring platelet and red blood transfusions every few days. Almost daily shots to boost his white blood counts to prevent infection. Cancer seems to be in charge now.

There is a bone marrow biopsy scheduled at Stanford on May 1 and discussions of transplanting more donor cells into him. With this I am sure will be another entire round of side effects and graft vs. host disease.

I know his is very weary and tired of all if this, as I am.

Thank you for continued thoughts and prayers."

Barb

----

25 APR 2014

Message from Barb (forwarded).

"They are at Stanford Med now.

They have halted Jon's chemo, as his platelets are dropping to dangerously low levels. Off to Stanford again tomorrow for platelet transfusion. He will be seen by a Dr. due to very painful recent side effects. MRI set up for his brain next week."

Barb

----

30 APR 2014

(From Barb)

"Things are not any better with Jon.

2 bags of platelets at Stanford on Fri., and level only at 27, way too low.

Hemoglobin at 9.2 yesterday, ready for red blood transfusion.

White blood count tanked very rapidly to Almost (sic) nothing.

Daily trips to Oncology. Stanford Thurs. for Dr. And bone marrow biopsy.

Jon remains in bed, except medical trips.

Take care,"

Barb

----

4 MAY 2014 (From Jim Shields)

"Jon is currently in serious condition at Stanford medical center. He is currently receiving specially processed blood products due to his adverse reaction to blood plasma.

The docs at Stanford are working closely with Jon's local

hospital and have arranged for Jon to receive this special blood component.

The blood donation department at Stanford has assured me that they have a sufficient supply of the blood type that has been matched to Jon's changing requirements.

On the subject of visits. Please understand that Jon is very tired and whenever he can, he sleeps. Receiving visitors is extremely stressful on him and his wife.

Also, he is still in medical isolation.

This means that he cannot be in any type of contact with anyone but his wife.

We would appreciate you getting the word out to anyone who may not have gotten the word.

Please let me know if you have any questions. Also let me know if you want to be added to the information net."

Jim Shields USASF-RET

----

10 MAY 2014 (from Jim Shields)

"One thing that cheers Jon up is your notes of encouragement (and old war stories). When he is awake, Barb reads them to him.

I will start collecting your notes and put them in one email for the month of May.

I have been getting a lot of requests for Jon's blood type. Jon has developed a sensitivity to blood plasma. This means that whole blood donations cannot be used. Stanford and the surrounding area blood banks are producing special blood products for Jon due to his specific needs.

I have confirmed with Stanford blood bank that they have sufficient supplies of the blood products he requires.

Please be assured that if Jon has any needs, I will get the word out to you all.

Here is the latest from Barb. "

> *"Jon's platelets were down to 18 on Wed., so am anticipating having to go to Stanford for transfusion this weekend.*
>
> *Will have results by early afternoon, which will determine our next course of action.*
>
> *White blood count down to almost nothing, so daily Neupogen shots once again.*
>
> *Hoping his hemoglobin will hold above 9.0; will have to schedule red blood cell transfusion also."*
>
> **Barb**

---

14 MAY 2014

"Mitch Wilson is helping Jon by driving him to all his doctor's appointments from Sonora. This allows Barb to care for Jon during these arduous trips. (Mitch has learned to scrub thoroughly and wear his mask for all contact with Jon).

On Saturday, Chapter 23 is holding a Barbeque and will recognize Mitch for all the good work he is doing for Jon.

Barbs message encompasses all of the "Old Guys" in the SOA as well as the SFA who have given so much to assist Jon."

----

30 MAY 2014

(From Barb)

"As of now, Jon is still not able to sit at a computer and compose messages to his friends and well-wishers. The immune suppressant drugs have really taken a toll on him

We are at the local cancer center at least 4, if not 5 days week to get Jon's Neupogen shots. All of the more delicate blood issues are being handled directly (sic) by the folks at Stanford.

During yesterdays (sic) visit at Stanford, the Stanford Doctor reported the results of Jon's last bone marrow biopsy. He stated that the bone marrow cancer has not changed, for better or worse since prior to transplant. MDS cancer still there, no reduction.

So, we play the waiting game while Jon has to continually receive support in the form of red blood transfusions, platelets, and neupogen (sic) shots for white blood count to prevent infection.

He is in bed all days most days and up in the evenings.

This last week he seemed to feel a little better as his hemoglobin was up a bit. We can only hope that it holds, but we have been her before. The proverbial roller coaster ride. Now I know why I never liked that ride!

He still continues to have various side effects in the form of graft vs. host disease, but nothing as serious as before, although I do know they are not comfortable for him.

His donor T-cells are still strong in him, so as before, it is a matter of whether the new cells can kick cancer out. They want him to continue chemo to help kill off balance of cancer, but his platelet counts are too low at this point.

It is day by day.

Mitch has been so helpful when called upon. An angel dropped from heaven. I am so happy you at Chapter 23 honored him. I wish we could honor all of you for your hard work and dedication.

God bless you and all those that have assisted."

Take care, Barb

Friends from all over the country, having learned of Jon's condition, were sending well wishes to Jon. One such letter was from the Commanding General of Special Operations Lieutenant General Charles T. Cleveland. (Shown next page).

Office of the Commanding General
United States Army Special Operations Command
Fort Bragg, North Carolina 28310-9110

March 3, 2014

Dear Sergeant Major Cavaiani: *Jon,*

Sir, I heard through your remarkable network of friends and supporters that you recently went through a particularly trying round of medical treatments. I'm sorry that you've had to go through so much recently and hope that you are feeling better.

Your career and accomplishments are both an inspiration and a significant source of pride to our Special Forces Regiment. Please accept my heartfelt wishes, on the behalf of the entire Army Special Operations Command. I hope to hear that you are up and around very soon!

Sincerely,

Jon,
Bearly a day goes
by that I don't
think about you
and pray. The
entire command and
your SF Brothers, active and retired
are here for you!

Charles T. Cleveland
Lieutenant General, U.S. Army
Commanding

SGM (Ret) Jon R. Cavaiani
10956 Green St. Unit 230
Columbia, California 95310-9742

As noted above, Jon was placed into isolation in a sterile environment. Visitors were limited to family, mostly Barbara, and necessary assistants. Jon had suffered in isolation as a POW, but this isolation was different. Jon was not just cared for, he was admired and loved.

However, that admiration was not always conducted in a manner that was beneficial to anyone. On one occasion, an individual who had lied numerous times, to include in writing, that he was Special Forces qualified – as it turned out, an absolute lie – entered Jon's room without appropriate personal protective equipment (PPE) so that he could take a selfie-photo of himself with Jon. Jon was not positioned, nor strong enough to stop the intruder. The selfie-photo was taken.

To a number of individuals, the self-serving scumbag who entered Jon's room in an unauthorized manner exacerbated Jon's condition and likely caused Jon's negative response to treatment and thus for his recovery efforts to collapse. That person is rightfully shunned in Special Forces circles.

In spite of his own sufferings, Jon tried to cheer the medical staff who worked with so many ailing patients. From day one he made it a point to give as many challenge coin medallions as he could to other patients and to "his staff of Stanford heroes" who worked diligently to help him recover.

From the onset of his treatment visits to Stanford, Jon took challenge coins to hand out to the staff. He explained to them how to use the challenge coins to "win" drinks from compatriots. From then on the staff enjoyed challenging one another to see if a drink during break could be had at the expense of one who had forgotten their coin. Perhaps they were used as well as to gain libation during happy hour after a long day's work. In any case. The staff was uplifted by Jon's positive spirit.

On one occasion as Jon was arriving for treatment, he was met by the Special Patient's Services Representative. It was she who would be called upon when dignitaries and celebrities were to receive treatment at Stanford. She greeted Jon and assured him that she would ensure the finest treatment that Stanford could provide. Jon reached into his pocket then extended his hand as if to shake hands as he thanked her.

To her surprise Jon had pulled one of his challenge coin medallions from his pocket and placed in the palm of her hand. He explained the challenge coin concept to her. Almost immediately she turned to the awaiting treatment staff and said "challenge!"

Once again she was surprised when every member of the treatment team held up their own coins. "You owe us!" The laughter that ensued brightened the day for Jon and for the Stanford treatment staff.

A staff member would sometimes challenge Jon, and having lost the challenge, would bring him a glass of orange or cranberry juice. On occasion Jon would "forget" to bring his coin and he would buy the entire staff drinks during their breaks the rest of the day. Even in his struggle with cancer Jon attempted to exude a positive spirit that would uplift everyone he met.

Jon's treatment required several teams that provided specialized care and support. Below are photos of three of those teams.

James Shields and Conrad 'Ben' Baker of Special Forces Association Chapter 23 (Jon's home Chapter) present a Certificate of Appreciation to one of the care teams at Stanford University Hospital on behalf of Jon Cavaiani

James Shields and Conrad 'Ben' Baker of Special Forces Association Chapter 23 (Jon's home Chapter) present Certificates of Appreciation to other care teams at Stanford University Hospital on behalf of Jon Cavaiani

Jon wanted so very much to encourage people. He wanted to be out and moving with his friends and comrades who were conducting valuable services for Veterans, especially the homeless and those suffering with PTSD. He wanted to return to Philadelphia and New Jersey to continue the work there.

He wanted to cook for his friends and serve them the finest foods that he could prepare. He wanted to make others happy and encourage them to be better than they thought that they could be.

But his body just would not permit it, so he decided to encourage those who he met and that was primarily his treatment staff.

A 10-point match donor had stepped forward to be a bone marrow transplant donor. Perhaps the transfusion helped prolong Jon's life for a short while, but the toll of years of physical, emotional, and psychological abuse, PTSD, and poisons associated with combat that he encountered during his service to his country finally took their toll.

On about July 25th Jon became unresponsive to those tending to him, and began to pull at his IV needles. He no longer responded to the voice of his beloved Barbara. Jon's hands had to strapped down in order to prevent significant damage.

Barbara was exhausted! A doctor on staff at Stanford called Jim Shields and told him that Barbara was going to precede Jon in death if she did not get some rest and relief. Jim loaded into his vehicle and upon arrival at the hospital, relieved Barbara, allowing Barbara's good friend Anne Marie Persiani to take her to Moffett for a much-needed rest and then back home. Ms. Persiani did so and in fact continued to be, essentially, Barb's caregiver for the rest of her life as well as caring friend.

Jim, dressed in cowl, gown, mask, and gloves, spent the last four days with Jon, holding his hand. The doctor had told him to hold his hand in order to feel any muscle spasms or jerks. If and when he did he was to ring for the nurse who could administer appropriate pain remedies. Jim was holding the hand of his brother when Jon breathed his last.

George Schnarre had kept tabs on Jon's situation and was greatly concerned, At the same time he wanted to cheer and encourage Jon and

Barb. With Jon's 71st birthday approaching, George sat down and wrote a very moving Happy Birthday letter to Jon that he addressed to Barbara in hopes that it might be read to Jon.

A WRITTEN BIRTHDAY CARD FOR JON
Intended for what would have been his 71st Birthday

Hi Barb,

"I know it is touch and go right now. But I hope you might be able to read this to Jon.

I never though this day would come, but here it is: Sergeant Major Jon R. Cavaiani, USA, Retired, turns 71 years old. Against all odds and against those that counted him out at various times along the way; I can only smile knowing that Jon is breathing right now and those who bet against him have once again underestimated the tenacity of Jon Robert Cavaiani.

For those of us who know Jon, the smile of victory that shines from Jon's face is imbedded in our minds. Whether with or without a beard, with or without glasses, in or out of uniform, Jon's smile after a good meal, a good joke, a warm hug, or a moment of love and friendship lights up a room.

Although light years away from the White House Ceremony where President Gerald Ford placed the Medal of Honor around Jon's neck; Betty Ford related the story to me many years later of how 'Impressed Jerry was with Jon.' On December 12, 1974, as Claire Cavaiani, Leslie & Suzanne Cavaiani; Mr. & Mrs. Ugo Cavaiani; Delbert & Dorothy

Hidbon, and Carl Cavaiani all watched Jon Robert Cavaiani receive the United States Army Medal of Honor for distinguishing himself by conspicuous gallantry and intrepidity at the risk of life above and beyond the call of duty in action in the Republic of Vietnam on 4 and 5 June 1971.

The story that Mrs. Ford told me years later was that President Gerald Ford had particularly remembered because the President told Mrs. Ford: 'He shouldn't have made it off that hill and definitely should not have survived as a Prisoner of War, don't ever bet against that guy!' How right you were Mr. President. How right you are!

Every morning when I wake up I see the sunrise and I know that Earth would not exist without this amazing Sun. Every morning I wake up and I also so know that I would not exist without Sergeant Major Jon R. Cavaiani, having touched my life. There are many of us who live today with these simple truths. They are self-evident.

On the occasion of Jon's 71ˢᵗ birthday, I know that thousands of people join me in toasting Jon Robert Cavaiani. Many of us call him friend, many of us call him brother, some call him other names, but we know that it doesn't matter what you call him, just make sure you call him for dinner. A better feast cannot be had than those at which Jon and Barb are present. May each of us who have enjoyed the banquet of life with Jon savor that taste of a 71-year-old wine that was bottled in England, aged on six continents, and enjoyed here in the United States of America

May God bless Jon and Barb, and may God bless the United States of America."

Happy Birthday Brother!

Love, George

George spoke for so many. It was as if he had captured the hearts, thoughts, and prayers of the vast number of people that Jon had befriended.

On July 29, 2014 Jon Cavaiani, the survivor of significant numbers of shrapnel shards (metal, rock, sand, wood, fibers from sandbags), a bullet in the back, torture, and abuse at the hands of heinous captors, and the trauma of memories that accompanied these terrible experiences finally succumbed to an invisible attacker that may well have been brought to him by friendly fire. It is indeed possible that the final attacker that speared Jon Cavaiani's heart was a product of the U. S.'s own creation – the scourge of cancer and other conditions brought on due to exposure to Agent Orange.

It is unlikely that Barbara, having been sent home by the doctors at Stanford for her own health's sake, had the opportunity to read George's letter to Jon. She may not have read it herself until sometime after the letter was delivered and after Jon's death. Barbara was so exhausted from having cared for Jon. She had sacrificed her own health trying to help Jon recover. She needed treatment, and sadly, she did not get what she needed. Again, Special Forces Chapter 23 went to work on her behalf and as part of that effort submitted a letter to her elected representative seeking assistance. Attached to the letter were twenty-one pages of documents that revealed bureaucratic delays by insurance providers, and in some instances, failure to provide needed medical services.

Special Forces Association Northern California Chapter 23

TO: The Honorable Thomas McClintock
2200A Douglas Blvd, Suite 240
Roseville, CA 95661

RE: Medical Assistance for Widow of Medal of Honor Recipient Jon R.   Cavaiani
Sir;

On July 29, 2014, SGM Jon Cavaiani passed away at Stanford University Medical Center fighting the cancer caused by his exposure to agent orange while serving in the Republic of Vietnam.

His wife, Barbara Elf- Cavaiani was by his side throughout his two-year (sic) battle.

She collapsed and was hospitalized for treatment of numerous health issues mostly relating to her exhaustion from caring for her husband.

Upon Jon's death, she was offered a choice of taking care through either the VA Hospital system or TRICARE (Tri-West) insurance. She chose Tri-West.

I have attached documentation presented to me by her long tome (sic) friends and holders of her power of attorney Patrick and

Jessalyn Fitzsimmons of Davis, California. Patrick has been working tirelessly to assist Barbara with her health issues and has had serious issues with the "TRICARE for LIFE" administration that constantly impede the process to assist in her treatment and recovery. The issues listed below have also introduced a significant amount of stress into Barb Cavaiani's life as she also has to assist in caring for her own aged mother. I would appreciate your assistance in looking into the following issues:

> *1. Failure of Tri-West officials to promptly return phone calls concerning care requirements*
>
> *2. Denying coverage for treatment ordered by medical professionals.*
>
> *3. Forcing complex administrative appeals for such denials.*
>
> *4. If the above issues are not resolved, Tri-West will not be in a position to approve her required liver transplant.*

I have spoken with representatives of the Medal of Honor Society and they, after reviewing the circumstances in this case, have stated that " No other widow of a Medal of honor Recipient is having the problems from their health care provider that Mrs. Cavaiani is having".

Jon's Medal of Honor Recipient friends have asked that I assist Patrick Fitzsimmons in resolving these issues through your office.

Points of contact for your ease in understanding these issues:

I thank you for your assistance in this matter

U.S. Army Special Forces (Retired)

Secretary - Chapter 23 U.S. Army Special Forces Association

ATTACHMENTS:

Barbara Elf Cavaiani never regained her health. The vivacious lady who had accompanied Jon on so many occasions to so many places: Philadelphia, New Orleans, Chicago, Las Vegas could no longer be the vibrant energy burst that she had been. She had been an advisor, a cheerleader, a therapist, and a tremendously supportive partner of Jon. She followed Jon in death a few years later and never recovered from her exhaustion enhanced ailments. Physically, she was worn out and likely a victim of ***compassion fatigue***.

CHAPTER THIRTEEN

Arlington

"A True Leader has the confidence to stand alone. The courage to make tough decisions. And the Compassion to listen to the needs of others. He does set out to be a leader. But becomes one by the equality of his actions and the integrity of his intent."
General Douglas McArthur

Few dignitaries receive the farewell that Jon Robert Cavaiani received. His transport and internment after death was indeed a celebration of life!

The staff at Stanford, who were blessed to receive Jon's praise and encouragement as they treated his rapidly failing body, were in tears. He had told them to celebrate upon his death with a toast – he recommended Jack Daniels.

Jon's body was moved from Stanford to San Jose, California, for a small memorial service and in preparation for flight to Philadelphia, where his body would lay at rest in Reilly Funeral Home. Services in the Bay Area and Philadelphia had been pre-arranged, and the two mortuaries serving Jon and Barbara had coordinated a very smooth and honorable transport of Jon's remains.

The memorials services began in California with an intimate gathering on the morning of July 31 at Bay Area mortuary. An Army Honor Guard was present with a few close friends all Veterans and mostly Special Forces comrades. After the memorial, the flag draped coffin bearing Jon's body was then taken for air transport to Philadelphia.

Over the next few weeks numerous memorial services were held in honor of Jon by friends and fellow Veterans. Danville California, Lake Leelanau, Michigan, Fayetteville, North Carolina, just to name a few. The following is brief account of one such memorial.

Testimonial from Judge James Lynn 4 June 2022

Hi John (Siegfried),

"There is a YouTube video of a memorial ceremony held for Jon on 31 July 2014 in Fountain Point Resort, Lake Leelanau, Michigan, 2 days after his death on 29 July 2014.

My wife Barbara and I were at a rowing camp directed by Steve 'Pops' Wagner, a legendary crew coach at Rutgers University.

When we heard the news of Jon's passing, we felt we had to do something to honor him. The pulse beat to do that was more pronounced by the distance we were from his friends and family on both coasts, especially Philadelphia. We were both very sad. We both lost a good friend. He attended our wedding.

The owner of the resort and Coach Wagner were in on doing this. The resort provided the videographer, the brochures, and staff to make it happen.

This was the same day that Jon was flown from Northern

California to Philadelphia.

I told you that a commercial jet flew over the resort during the ceremony and I imagined the plane was carrying Jon to Philly. Hey, it might have been as it was about the time it would have gotten over Michigan, if it did fly that way at all.

Anyway, this was my emotional action taken far away in order to honor a man who called me 'Brother' and whom I loved."

Go to YouTube and type - Jon Cavaiani flag ceremony. It will pop - up.

Cordially,

Jimmy Lynn

Community Chapel Bay Area Mortuary San Jose California July 31, 2014

IN REPOSE AT BAY AREA MORTUARY, SAN JOSE

DEPARTING BAY AREA MORTUARY 31 JULY 2014
Special Forces Chapter 23 Members Attending

Word had gotten out quickly in Philadelphia that Jon was returning "home" to Philly. A large gathering of people awaited his arrival at the airport, and then moved along behind him as his transport moved through the city to the small chapel of the mortuary. Once in Philadelphia, Reilly Mortuary Services – owned by Jon's close friend Michael Reilly – made preparations and arrangements for a ceremony befitting any king, president, dignitary, or common Jon. And just as befitting is that Jon's funeral occurred in the "City of Brotherly Love." The immigrant who served his adoptive family, his adoptive nation, and his adoptive tribe of Hill People, exemplified brotherly love to all with whom he served.

Procession from Philly International 31 July 2-14 to Reilly Funeral Home.

Front-Left to Right: Joe Wolk, Lt. Bill Lynch, and George Soto.

Chief Inspector Tony Boyle (in rear-in black behind Joe Wolk). Jerry Murphy (hidden) on driver's side front fender.

Pic below in front of Reilly Funeral Home. Pall bearers Right Front to back: Jim McNesby, Richie Cray, Joe Waters. Rear. Tom Reilly. Left Front to back: Mike Wallace, Joe O'Hara (3rd from the left-hidden), Dan Jones. Front. Reilly Funeral Director. Andrew Rakowski.

In August 2014, after Jon's body was transported to Philadelphia, a very special event honoring Jon occurred as indicated by the notice below:

Jon Cavaiani Memorial Dinner – MCLEF – Palm Restaurant

Philadelphia

Dear Friends,

As many of you know, our national hero, and dear friend, Medal of Honor Recipient, Jon Cavaiani passed away on Tuesday, July 29, 2014, after a long battle with cancer. Jon was the embodiment of valor and courage, on the battlefield and in life. He leaves behind his remarkable wife Barbara.

Despite the lifelong effects of multiple wounds and injuries, Jon distinguished himself, not only as a combat soldier, POW, Special Forces and Delta Force NCO, but as a tireless champion for military and law enforcement causes. Whenever the Philadelphia committee of The Marine Corps Law Enforcement Foundation (MC-LEF) needed Jon, he was there. Sometimes barely able to walk, or stand, for more than a short time, Jon would tough it out for the "Philly Gang".

After his birth in Ireland and adoption, Jon grew up in

California, entered the Army from, and retired to, California. Despite all his ties to the Golden State, Jon's desire was to be buried from Philadelphia. Such was his love for the folks from Philly.

The last eighteen months may have been Jon's toughest challenge, a challenge he took on with his characteristic strength and humor. Countless three hundred-mile round trips to Stanford Medical Center for exhausting treatments and transfusions, the painful bone marrow transplant, and a hundred days of isolation. Throughout it all Barb stood with Jon, all the while caring for her failing mother. These demands and obligations prevented Barb from working, and Jon's retirement pay was the only source of income. As Barbara prepares to meet new challenges, and to bring Jon to his final place of rest, her need for funds may be greater than ever.

We are unable to lessen the burden of Jon's loss on Barb, but we can lessen the financial burden his illness has created. Jon's Philly family is hosting a special Surf and Turf dinner at the Palm Restaurant, complete with wines and dessert. The Palm and its wine producers have answered the call, allowing us to provide Barb with over 90% of the funds raised. We hope you're able to join us; and ask that you reach out to anyone you know who might be able to attend. Details below.

Jon Cavaiani Memorial Dinner

Wednesday, 27 August 2014 at 6:00 PM

The Palm Restaurant

200 South Broad Street

$1000.00 per person

To confirm attendance, or for more information, please contact:

Tony Boyle,

Brian Grady,

Mike Wallace,

Checks should be made to the Jon Cavaiani Memorial Fund. If you are unable to attend, but would like to make a donation, a special memorial fund has been established through the Philadelphia Federal Credit Union. Donations can be mailed to the Jon Cavaiani Memorial Fund, PO Box 11653, Philadelphia, PA 19116. View a short tribute to our brother Jon at http://www.mclefphila.org/JC/

Sincerely,

MC-LEF, Philadelphia Committee

Semper Fi

Later, an obituary notice was posted informing the people of Philadelphia of Jon's memorial ceremony.

JON CAVAIANI OBITUARY

 *CAVAIANI*

SGM JON R., US ARMY Medal of Honor recipient. Died July 29, 2014. He was the beloved and devoted husband of Barbara Elf Cavaiani. Relatives, friends and members of our Armed Forces are invited to attend his Memorial Gathering Sunday [Nov 2] from 1 P.M. until 4 P.M. **THE REILLY FUNERAL HOME, 2632 E. Allegheny Ave., Phila, PA 19134.** *Interment full military honors will be held in Arlington National Cemetery on Wednesday, Nov. 5, 2014.*

As Published by Philadelphia Inquirer/Philadelphia Daily News from Oct. 29 to Oct. 31, 2014.

Word spread rapidly, and on November 5th a significant number of people came together as they traveled to Philadelphia and then to Arlington, Virginia. Some were dressed in their finest clothing of suit and tie, others were in Military Dress uniform, yet others were in jeans, sporting a do-rag, and motorcyclist's vest. Some were well accomplished persons of society while others were recovered drug addicts still struggling to become the person Jon had encouraged them to become. All were there to honor Jon Cavaiani, an adopted lad who adopted so many who seemed left behind; a farmer-warrior – a Lone Wolf who protected his Pack - who had positively impacted their lives.

The service in Philadelphia was appropriately solemn, it was respectful, and it was honorable. The small chapel, Old Post Chapel, at Arlington overflowed. Siegfried was standing, sandwiched, between two four-star U.S. Army Generals. Jim Shields stood with Col. (Ret) Roger Donlon MOH. The celebration of Jon's life was moving. The accolades were abundant as speakers recalled, not so much his heroism as the "Wolf of Hickory Hill," the Medal Honor recipient, the leader and care giver of soldiers, but rather of his service and inspiration to humanity. Those carrying Jon's coffin from the chapel were stoic, but they could not restrain their tears.

After the services in Philadelphia a convoy of vehicles and motorcycles departed Philadelphia accompanying Jon's body down I-95, around Washington DC, to the Old Post Chapel at Arlington National Cemetery.

The hearse stopped just short of the gate at Arlington National Cemetery directly in front of The Old Post Chapel. The flagged draped coffin bearing Jon's remains were carefully withdrawn from the hearse by an honor guard from the U. S. Army "Old Guard:" 3rd Regiment, and taken into the chapel. There, services were conducted, and words of honor and tribute rendered.

Jim Shields and Col. (Ret) Roger Donlon MOH at Old Post Chapel

Then the 3rd Regiment Honor Guard, escorted by the several Medal of Honor Recipients, carried Jon's casket to the awaiting caisson and laid it carefully onto the deck. Then upon command, six white horses began pulling the caisson forward and into the national cemetery. Accompanying them was a riderless horse, signifying Jon's absence.

"A typical caisson team consists of a minimum of seven horses, matched gray or black, four riders, and a serviceman displaying the colors of the deceased members branch of service. Six of the horses pull the caisson, three of which have riders. The three other horses are riderless. The two horses closest to the caisson are called the wheel horses, and these are the most experienced horses and act as the brakes. The two front

horses are the leads, and they are the second most experienced.
The two middle horses are called the swings, and they are the
least experienced. The seventh horse, which has a rider, is the
guide horse.

The seventh horse is ridden off the team to allow the
section chief to move independently, ensuring that the
designated route is clear, and to coordinate with the marching
troops prior to the funeral service. In battles, the horses on the
right side were used for carrying provisions and replacing a
main horse if needed. Caissons were used to carry the wounded
and deceased from the battlefield as well as hauling
ammunition. The field artillery used a six-horse hitch, and today,
the platoon uses their equipment, tack, techniques, and training
methods laid out in the artillery manual printed by the Army in
1942.

Special funerals have a caparisoned, or 'cap' horse, often
referred to as the 'riderless horse,' in which empty boots are positioned
backward in the stirrups. This horse follows the caisson with the casket
and was led by a single foot soldier. The purpose of a caparisoned
horse originated in the ancient custom of sacrificing a horse at the
burial of a warrior. It symbolized that a soldier had fallen as a warrior
and would ride no more. Eventually that evolved into the horse being
riderless during funeral processions to symbolize the fallen
warrior."[100]

---

[100] Reed, Margaret, PHD; Horses & Hounds: The Horses Of Arlington

Members of the Army band played hymns while the casket was placed on the caisson but then, as the caisson began its movement through the gates and into the cemetery, the band broke into songs of tribute known to many who have served into the military.

The caisson was led by a detachment from the Army Band and the National Colors through the Fort Myer Gate. Two chaplains, one a Green Beret, followed the band. The caisson was drawn smoothly as if the horses knew the significance of the moment. Following the caisson bearing Jon's flag draped coffin were several Medal of Honor recipients. Following that distinguished group were numerous uniformed individuals. Then came the more than one hundred "little people" in civilian clothing of various description who loved Jon because he had loved and cared for them.

At a designated location the caisson stopped, and the 3rd Regiment Honor Guard drew the casket off of the caisson and carried it to the designated final resting place for Jon. As they did so, the Medal

National Cemetery; The New Town Bee; Jan 27, 2019.

of Honor recipients present formed a line and saluted as Jon, resting in his catafalque, passed by.

Once the casket was set in place and family members were seated. A Chaplain gave a few brief words and then the flag that draped Jon's casket was precisely folded and presented to Jon's family members by a Three Star General. As the flag was being folded the band had played *America the Beautiful,* a song that Jon would hum on occasion. It should be noted that Jon's family members still called him "Bobby,' just as Ugo and Ramon and his fellow school mates had done.

Once folded, the flag was presented to Jon's family members and the sound of a military aircraft flyover could be heard. It was as if it was flying in salute to Jon.

Chaplains conducting Jon's memorial service express condolence to Jon's family members.

The hundreds who had gathered took time to greet one another, hug one another, and appreciate one another – just as Jon would have wanted.

One individual, who preferred anonymity, stood holding the flag that had been given to family members but bequeathed to Barb. He was holding it so that Jon's family members could freely shake hands and thank the many who had joined the occasion. As he held the flag he looked toward the center of the National Cemetery and thought to himself: *"Right over there, at the eternal flame...right over there is where Jon stood and saluted John F. Kennedy on the day that he had received his Medal of Honor. Jon had done so as if to say: 'Sir, mission accomplished!'"*

There, near the very place where he once stood and saluted the memory of John F, Kennedy, Jon was laid to rest. The band played, a gun salute was offered, and Jon Robert Cavaiani was finally rid of the trauma, the tragedy, and the pain of unselfish service. It was the classic line from a song by Khoi My and La Thang in Vietnamese: *"Bong Tay.'* **Which means " *Letting go,"*** that may have been one of Jon's last thoughts....

Sergeant Major Jon Robert Cavaiani left us 29 July 2014, just 4 days from his 71st Birthday. Mike Reilly knew Jon as long as anyone in Philly, and he proudly held, at Jon's request, the SGM's viewing shortly afterwards. Jon was interred on a cold, rainy fall-day. There was a massive turnout that included: eight (8) fellow Medal of Honor recipients; Veterans; Special Forces mates who flew-in from all over the country; current serving military; The Old Guard (who always accompany the body of fallen comrade who is to be lain in the sacred grounds of Arlington National Cemetery); several people from California; and busloads of folks from the Tr-State Philly area.

A few of the Medal of Honor recipients at Jon's ceremony: Major General James Livingston USMC, Colonel Barney Barnum USMC, Mike Thornton USN, Brian Thacker USA, Colonel Joe Marm USA, Roger Donlon USA. Not to mention the horde of racing fans and motorcyclists who made the trip that day.

"Following Jon's burial, they bussed us back to Fort Meade, and into The Patton Room. There were at least a few hundred folks there. A few of his Medal of Honor friends spoke, and I remember a member of the Special Forces Association said a few words. I sat with a Special Forces member, Cliff Newman. We spoke about the 'Yards' and Jon for some time. It

wasn't like an Irish funeral: It was more like a solemn get together for a warrior who had passed."[101]

After internment repast with a few of Jon's friends in attendance: Among those at the table: Cliff Newman -Maj Ret John Padgett- Omar Carcamo - Jim Shorten - Jim Shields; and of significance, Anne Marie Persiani –(Friend of Jon and Barb from Sonora, California who supported Jon and Barb during Jon's final year and who took sisterly care of Barb in her last several months of life).

---

[101] Siegfried, John; personal experience statement

The Sergeant Major had finally earned his entry into Avalon, that magical resting place in England. This seemed appropriate, as he spent his formidable early years on that island. May he rest in peace in that **Cemetery of Heroes Section 60, Site 10590**

His captors had mercilessly tried to kill his body, but they could never capture his soul. His mind never forgot what his eyes had seen. A man who everyone trusted, and a man who treated everyone as an equal. The consummate Ambassador of Freedom, and steward of those with whom he served, who now, finally, is with his wife Barb, fallen mates, his "little people" who fought and died serving with him, and his friend, Sgt John R. Jones, who possessed the same middle name.

Medal of Honor Recipients. Date unknown. Standing-L to R: PFC Hector Cafferata; MajGen James Livingston, Captain Thomas Hudner, Jr., Col Wesley L. Fox; Col Van Barfoot; Master Sergeant Nick Oresko. Kneeling: L-R. SgtMaj. Jon R. Cavaiani; Lt. Brian Thacker. and Lt. Mike Thornton.

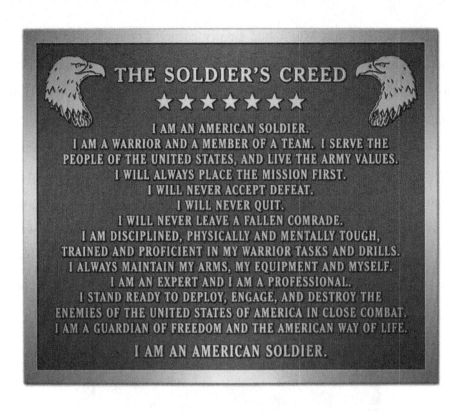

THE SOLDIER'S CREED

★ ★ ★ ★ ★ ★ ★

I AM AN AMERICAN SOLDIER.
I AM A WARRIOR AND A MEMBER OF A TEAM. I SERVE THE
PEOPLE OF THE UNITED STATES, AND LIVE THE ARMY VALUES.
I WILL ALWAYS PLACE THE MISSION FIRST.
I WILL NEVER ACCEPT DEFEAT.
I WILL NEVER QUIT.
I WILL NEVER LEAVE A FALLEN COMRADE.
I AM DISCIPLINED, PHYSICALLY AND MENTALLY TOUGH,
TRAINED AND PROFICIENT IN MY WARRIOR TASKS AND DRILLS.
I ALWAYS MAINTAIN MY ARMS, MY EQUIPMENT AND MYSELF.
I AM AN EXPERT AND I AM A PROFESSIONAL.
I STAND READY TO DEPLOY, ENGAGE, AND DESTROY THE
ENEMIES OF THE UNITED STATES OF AMERICA IN CLOSE COMBAT.
I AM A GUARDIAN OF FREEDOM AND THE AMERICAN WAY OF LIFE.

I AM AN AMERICAN SOLDIER.

Plaque Posted At the 18th century Carversville Inn in Carversville, PA

"Those of us who've never served don't always understand.

The sacrifices that you've made, protecting hearth and land.

We take for granted our freedom and forget to count the cost.

To those who protect that freedom, from war and holocaust.

So, this simple poem is a thank you, to tell you someone cares.

And that you are remembered

In our hearts and in our prayers."

Lt. George M. Jones. USAF 1981-1985

Epilogue

In compiling this moving account about the life of one human being born as Jon Lemmons, and who took on the name, willingly, of Jon Robert "Bobby" Cavaiani, the authors learned that he was not a "superman." Jon Cavaiani was a person of passion who served when allowed to serve and fought when he had to fight. He was a person who hurt and who suffered when others suffered, such as his Bru Montagnards under the iron rule of the Vietnamese. He moaned when his fellow POWs were abused, and he tried to divert the camp guard's attention away from others to himself. He ached when he saw Veterans who felt left behind by an ungrateful society. Finally, he created joy when it was time to party.

Jon was a survivor. Left by parents to a farmer in the San Juaquin Valley of California, electing to stay behind in the heat of battle so that others could flee to safety, and beset with psychological and emotional trauma because of his rejection while a youth, and his abuse as a POW, he proved himself resilient in the face of devastation.

Jon could be domineering in his attempts to control situations and to follow policy and procedure and take care of soldiers and Veterans. He was precise. So much so that he pissed off some of his fellow NCOs who were content *"to go with the flow."*

When Jon saw gaping holes in spirit and action for what he deemed was the correct thing to do for soldiers he persisted stubbornly to correct the deficiencies. It was the same spirit in Jon that enabled him, when told to abandon his Bru Montagnard Brothers to say: "You gotta be frickin' kidding!" and caused him to remain on Hickory Hill with his little soldiers. It was that same attitude that enabled him and caused him to ask of community officials, *"what the hell are you doing for them?"* when he encountered homeless Veterans on the streets of numerous cities. It was that same attitude that enabled him and caused him to ask Veterans Administration leadership, *"what are you doing to help suffering Veterans who are victims of PTSD, neglect, and Agent Orange?"* It was that same spirit that caused him to be precise and particular in cooking for and serving his friends.

Perhaps it was his internal drive to be accurate and precise that led to his being married five times; why he failed financially to bring his adoptive father's farm back to life after it went fallow; and why he continued to use his Medal of Honor credentials to fight for assistance to those who suffered from PTSD, those who were homeless Veterans and in need of one caring person, or those who were in need of financial support for educational endeavors.

Jon Cavaiani did not leave a great financial inheritance. In fact, he and his fifth wife, Barbara, settled into a trailer house in rural Columbia, California living paycheck to paycheck. He did not fulfill his dream of restoring Ugo Cavaiani's farm to greatness. The loan he took to try to do so bankrupted him. He did not win over the devastatingly cruel pain of bone marrow cancer.

What Jon Cavaiani won over, what he defeated, were the ghosts of a traumatic youth, a horrendous military battle, a long period of abuse as a POW, and the effects of PTSD that could have caused him to shut down decades prior to his death. Instead, he chose to continue to serve. And through his service to others, he won the hearts of the many with whom he interacted. His was a legacy, an inheritance, of will, determination, and fortitude to survive, seek happiness, and encourage others to do the same. He was the "Quiet Professional" in every way.

What Jon Cavaiani left in the way of an inheritance for us all was the point that *"it is the heart that matters:"* It is as if he challenges each of us to *"Never give up. Fight for what you know to be right, and when you do, be the alpha wolf that leads the way."*

It is a well-deserved rest for you Jon, yet you still whisper to us over time – *"Never give up, never give in."* Your spirit stirs us on to be better than we think we can be. We are encouraged by the farmer from Ballico, the "Wolf" of Livingston High School, to be the Wolf that cares for the least of the pack – for the forgotten, the forsaken, for "the little people."

Thomas A. Edison once said: *"Our greatest weakness lies in giving up. The most certain way to succeed is to always to try just one more time."* As stated by some unknown, but very wise, sage, to Siegfried in May of 2022, *"Father Time is undefeated."* The youngster from the Emerald Isle never quit. John died exactly 70 years after his brother's birth: Jon was 70 when he passed away on 29 July 2014, four days prior to his 71st birthday.

Sergeant Major Jon Robert Cavaiani was a prophetic testament of those words. It was his doctrine. RIP, from all of us, who were honored to be your compatriots, acquaintances, and friends. The "Little People" will never forget you through the ages. You will always be extant in our hearts, minds, and souls.

Gettysburg Cemetery

SGM Jon R. Cavaiani MOH

August 2, 1943 - July 29, 2014

ADDENDA

Addendum 1
Brief History of Special Forces

The "quiet warrior" founder of Special Forces, Colonel Aaron Bank, served in the OSS during World War II and was instrumental in establishing the CIA. He formed a rough concept of Special Forces type of actions which he derived from the 1st Special Service Force, a combined Canadian American regiment during World War II. The force was constituted 5 July 1942, in the U.S. Army, as Headquarters and Headquarters Detachment, 1st Battalion, 3rd Regiment, 1st Special Service Force.

Activated 9 July 1942, the unit trained at Fort William Henry Harrison, Montana. The force participated in the Italian Campaign and saw action in southern France before being deactivated 6 Feb 1945.

In the mid to late 50's, about 13,000 "advisors" were embedded in the South Vietnamese Army (ARVN) and were under the operational control of the CIA, which was incorporated in 1947. Originally called the OSS (Office of Strategic Services during WW2), these folks trained the indigent Viet Minh (called "the people from the south" by the Chinese) on weapons and tactics. Combined with the 1st Special Forces Group, this training went on until the early 60's, when MACV-SOG took over. The Military Assistance Command/Vietnam had direct jurisdiction over the Studies and Observation Group (SOG), which included the 5th Special Forces Group when it was refocused from the

Middle East and South Asia to Vietnam.

Jon Cavaiani was, in his initial assignment after earning the Green Beret, assigned to be a member of the 5^{tth} Special Forces Group, Vietnam.

U. S. Army Special Forces continue to serve in numerous countries and environments around the world providing unconventional and guerrilla warfare capabilities in support of United States vital interests. Most operations continue to require Green Berets to work closely with the indigenous people in their areas of operations.

Addendum 2
Special Forces Specialties

Special Forces Detachment Officer

Selected and trained officers conduct the critical branch tasks and competencies required to perform the duties of a detachment commander of a Special Forces ODA.

Weapons Sergeant

Weapons sergeants have a working knowledge with weapons systems found throughout the world, and extensive knowledge about various types of small arms, submachine guns, machine guns, grenade launchers, indirect-fire weapons (mortars and artillery) forward-observer procedures, and anti-tank missiles, They know the capabilities and characteristics of U.S. and foreign air defense and anti-tank weapons systems, tactical training, and range fire as well as how to teach marksmanship and the employment of weapons to others.

Engineer Sergeant

Engineer Sergeants are experts in employing offensive and defensive combat engineer capabilities, including demolitions, landmines, explosives, improvised munitions, and home-made explosives. They also are experts in rigging and ropework; construction and field sanitation to include water supplies; reconnaissance; and target analysis.

Medical Sergeant

Medical sergeants specialize in trauma management, infectious diseases, cardiac life support, and surgical procedures, with a basic understanding of veterinary and dental medicine. General healthcare and emergency healthcare are stressed. Medical sergeants provide emergency, routine, and long-term medical care for detachment members and associated allied members and host-nation personnel. They establish field medical facilities to support unconventional-warfare operations. They provide veterinary care. They prepare the medical portion of area studies, brief-backs, and operation plans and orders.

Communications Sergeant

The Special Forces communications sergeant learns U.S. communication systems as well as those systems globally. He incorporates this information and technology into his communications planning and teaches it to the other members of his ODA. Communications sergeants have a thorough grounding in communication basics, communications procedures, computer technology, assembly, and systems applications.

Addendum 3

POW Camps Of North Vietnam

Below is an outline of known prisons and treatments administered upon POWs by their captors as revealed by former POWs.

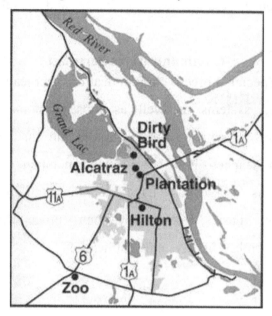

By Honor Bound, **Naval Institute Press**

(Ministry of National Defense) List and Description of NVA POW ENCAMPMENTS

Alcatraz

Perhaps the worst of the North's prisons, this facility was built to house POWs the North Vietnamese wanted to isolate. It was more of a dungeon than a prison. It may have been the cruelest of the many sites in the North. The tiny cells were sunk underground with the only ventilation coming from pencil-sized holes above each door and recessed space below them.   Located in north central Hanoi, Alcatraz was used to detain 11 particularly defiant American prisoners known as the Alcatraz Gang, including Jeremiah Denton, future U.S. Senator from Alabama, Sam Johnson, future U.S. Representative from Texas and James Stockdale, later a Vice Admiral and recipient of the Medal of Honor.

Zoo

This prison was opened in September 1965 just southwest of Hanoi. The Zoo had all the windows in the cells bricked up shortly after opening. The rooms were padlocked but had a slight give that allowed prisoners to peek out. This feature also allowed guards, or livestock at the prison, to look in, a feature that earned the prison the name "Zoo." Located in the suburbs of Hanoi, the Zoo remained operational until December 1970, when all U.S. prisoners were transferred to Hỏa Lò prison.

Dirty Bird (Power Plant)

This Hanoi prison opened in October 1967 in the vicinity of the Yen Phu thermal power plant in northern Hanoi. The North Vietnamese publicized the location of the prisoners, in what many believe was an attempt to discourage U.S. bombing of the plant and the area. Prisoners called the place "dirty bird" in honor of the camp's black dust, debris, and general filthiness. Beginning in June 1967, several locations in the immediate vicinity of the Hanoi Thermal Power Plant were used to house POWs. Approximately 30 Americans were held at the Dirty Bird Camp. In October 1967, all prisoners held in Dirty Bird were removed to regular POW camps.

Plantation (Citadel)

Hanoi's Citadel, the North Vietnamese "showcase" prison, had once been the home of the colonial mayor of the city. Part of the facility was converted to a village of clean cells, garden patches, and scrubbed corridors where captives were photographed and shown to delegations to convince visitors that the North Vietnamese treated prisoners humanely. Located in northeast Hanoi, the Plantation opened in June 1967. It was a Potemkin village-style camp run by the North Vietnamese as a propaganda showplace for foreign visitors to see and as a preparation camp for prisoners about to be released. Physical mistreatment of prisoners was rarer than in other camps, but did occur to some Plantation prisoners. The camp operated until July 1970, when a major consolidation of U.S. POWs occurred.

Hanoi Hilton (Hoa Lo).

American POWs gave Hoa Lo, perhaps the best known of all the North's prison camps, the ironic tag of "Hanoi Hilton." The French occupiers of Vietnam had built it at the turn of the century. Speaking about the prison's rusted shackles and ever-present rats, Lt. Ronald Bliss reflected: *"You could look at this place and . . . just hear the screams of about fifty years, because it was -- it is -- a hard place."* Some of the most brutal torture of Americans took place here in specially equipped rooms also known as the Hanoi Hilton was Located in downtown Hanoi. Hỏa Lò prison was first used by the French colonists to hold political prisoners in what was then French Indochina. The prison became operational during the Vietnam War when it was used to house Everett Alvarez, Jr. The prison was used without interruption until the repatriation of U.S. POWs in 1973.

Briarpatch (Xom Ap Lo)

Located about 35 miles west of Hanoi, this prison was opened in the late summer of 1965 to accommodate the overcrowding at Hoa Lo ("Hanoi Hilton"). The prison had no running water or electricity, and the diet was so severe that prisoners kept here for long periods inevitably suffered from malnutrition. The Briarpatch camp, intermittently held U.S. prisoners between 1965 and 1971. Conditions at the Briarpatch were notoriously grim, even by the standards of North Vietnamese prisons. Multiple POWs contracted beriberi at the camp due to severe malnutrition.

Camp Hope (Son Tay)

Located 20 miles northwest of Hanoi, this prison opened in May 1968 to alleviate overcrowding in Hanoi's prisons. American prisoners were also removed from Hoa Lo to undermine POW camaraderie there. The camp was filthy, and the cells had little ventilation. Rats ran rampant. Yet, many occupants here were spared the more brutal torture routine at other camps. Also known as Sơn Tây, Camp Hope was operational between 1968 and 1970, holding 55 POWs. The camp emptied just prior to the Sơn Tây Raid and closed following The Raid

Faith (Dan Hoi)

The Dan Hoi prison, just northwest of Hanoi, was actually six compounds in one that imprisoned 220 prisoners at its peak. Treatment here was generally more humane than at the other POW camps. Many of the prisoners transferred from other facilities found the freedom to congregate, which was permitted at Faith, exhilarating. Located 9 miles (14 km) west of Hanoi, Camp Faith became operational in July 1970, when a major consolidation of U.S. prisoners began. Three days after the Sơn Tây Raid, Camp Faith POWs moved to Hỏa Lò prison in Hanoi.

Farnsworth (Duong Ke)
This facility opened south of Hanoi in the summer of 1968. Farnsworth guards' treatment of officers in the U.S. armed forces was especially brutal. American officers occupied small, windowless rooms painted black and were seldom allowed outside. The North Vietnamese treated the enlisted men better, keeping them in larger groups and giving them regular exercise and recreation after 1970.

Located 18 miles (29 km) southwest of Hanoi, Farnsworth became operational in August 1968, when 28 U.S. POWs captured outside North Vietnam were moved to this location. Over the next two years, several groups of POWs captured outside of North Vietnam were brought to the camp. Following the Sơn Tây Raid, Farnsworth's prisoner population was transferred to the Plantation Camp in Hanoi

Skid Row (Ban Liet)
The Skid Row camp, located six miles (9.7 km) southwest of Hanoi, became operational as a U.S. POW detention facility in July 1968, when U.S. civilian and military prisoners captured outside North Vietnam were moved there. Prisoners named this prison for its filth and poor condition. After 1971 the prison became a place of banishment for

POWs who did not cooperate at Hoa Lo prison.

Dogpatch (Loung Lang)

Located in the northeast corner of North Vietnam, Dogpatch was colder, damper, and darker than Hoa Lo. Its cells had small slits for windows, thick walls, and ceilings, and were crammed with up to 20 prisoners. One prisoner there recalled that the camp had *"about all the qualities of a dungeon except that it was not underground."* The Dogpatch camp, located 105 miles (169 km) northeast of Hanoi, opened in May 1972, when 220 POWs were transferred there from Hỏa Lò prison. The camp ceased operation in early 1973, when the POWs were transferred to Hanoi for repatriation to the United States

Mountain Camp (K-49)

The name given this camp reflected its location in rugged mountain terrain just north of Hanoi. Although prisoners were isolated from one another, the basic conditions were better than in many other camps. Each room had a table, stool, and toilet and, a rarity in almost all POW camps, a straw mattress bed. The Mountain Camp, located 40 miles (64 km) northwest of Hanoi, became operational in December 1971, when one prisoner from Hỏa Lò and eight prisoners from Skid row were moved to this location. This camp was used until January 1973 when its POW population was permanently moved to Hanoi for repatriation.

Rockpile (Noi Coc)

Despite its grim name, this prison, located 30 miles south of Hanoi, was comfortable compared to other facilities. The sleeping quarters were larger than most, and prisoners were given a dining room, a separate latrine and even a bathing area. Prisoners were allowed to move around the camp and mingle, a freedom almost never granted elsewhere. The Rockpile camp, located 32 miles (51 km) south of Hanoi, became operational in June 1971 when 14 Americans and foreign POWs captured outside North Vietnam were moved from Skid Row, to the Rockpile. The camp was closed in February 1973, when its POWs were moved to Hanoi for repatriation.

Addendum 4

Notes on AGENT ORANGE: THE SLOW KILLER

Because Jon Cavaiani was likely exposed to agent orange, and may well have been affected by its detrimental effects on those who were exposed, we offer the following information.

According to www.history.com millions of those who served in Vietnam (there were approximately 2.6 million stationed in Vietnam, with 3.4 million throughout all of Southeast Asia, including Laos, Cambodia, and Thailand) survived the combat, the accidents, and diseases like malaria, only to come home to suffer a slow agonizing decline into sicknesses and death. When our Armed Forces personnel were exposed to the various "Agents" sprayed to kill the foliage, trees, and enemy crops in Vietnam, many times, the children, spouses, and partners were/are affected. We know that these Agents, complements of Operation Ranch Hand (1962-1971), were sprayed from C-123's, helicopters, and various other aircraft. They also used trucks, hand sprayers, while spraying in the brown waters from boats. Almost 20 MILLION gallons of agent orange were sprayed in Vietnam, Laos, and Cambodia. I (John Siegfried) know a Colonel (USA Ret.), who co-wrote the Foreword on my manuscript *The New Agent Orange,* who was a Captain on these C-123's, who directionally ordered what areas to be hit. Many of these crew members are sick or dead to their exposure. Agent Orange has always been the agent referred to in Vietnam, because its potency was greater than all the others (White, Blue, Purple), and made, complements of Monsanto (now Baer Pharmaceuticals) and Dow Chemical. Agent Orange was sprayed nearly 60% of the time within those 9 years. It was outlawed in the US in 1970.

The following, taken from Veterans Administration web site at https://www.publichealth.va.gov/exposures/agentorange/condition s/ informs us that the VA assumes that certain diseases can be related to a Veteran's qualifying military service. We call these "presumptive diseases."

The VA has recognized certain cancers and other health problems as presumptive diseases associated with exposure to Agent Orange or other herbicides during military service. Veterans and their survivors may be eligible for benefits for these diseases.

- **AL Amyloidosis**

  A rare disease caused when an abnormal protein, amyloid, enters tissues or organs

- **Bladder Cancer**

  A type of cancer that affects the bladder where urine is stored before it leaves the body

- **Chronic B-cell Leukemias**

  A type of cancer which affects white blood cells

- **Chloracne (or similar acneiform disease)**

  A skin condition that occurs soon after exposure to chemicals and looks like common forms of acne seen in teenagers. Under VA's rating regulations, it must be at least 10 percent disabling within one year of exposure to herbicides.

- **Diabetes Mellitus Type 2**

  A disease characterized by high blood sugar levels resulting from the body's inability to respond properly to the hormone insulin

- **Hodgkin's Disease**

  A malignant lymphoma (cancer) characterized by progressive enlargement of the lymph nodes, liver, and spleen, and by progressive anemia

- **Hypothyroidism**

  A condition that causes the thyroid gland to not produce enough of certain important hormones

- **Ischemic Heart Disease**

  A disease characterized by a reduced supply of blood to the

heart, that leads to chest pain

- **Multiple Myeloma**

  A cancer of plasma cells, a type of white blood cell in bone marrow

- **Non-Hodgkin's Lymphoma**

  A group of cancers that affect the lymph glands and other lymphatic tissue

- **Parkinsonism_**

  Any condition that causes a combination of abnormal movements. These include slow movements, trouble speaking, stiff muscles, or tremors.

- **Parkinson's Disease**

  A progressive disorder of the nervous system that affects muscle movement

- **Peripheral Neuropathy, Early-Onset**

  A nervous system condition that causes numbness, tingling, and motor weakness. Under VA's rating regulations, it must be at least 10 percent disabling within one year of herbicide exposure.

- **Porphyria Cutanea Tarda**

  A disorder characterized by liver dysfunction and by thinning and blistering of the skin in sun-exposed areas. Under VA's rating regulations, it must be at least 10 percent disabling within one year of exposure to herbicides.

- **Prostate Cancer**

  Cancer of the prostate; one of the most common cancers among men

- **Respiratory Cancers (includes lung cancer)**
  Cancers of the lung, larynx, trachea, and bronchus
- **Soft Tissue Sarcomas (other than osteosarcoma, chondrosarcoma, Kaposi's sarcoma, or mesothelioma)**
  A group of different types of cancers in body tissues such as muscle, fat, blood and lymph vessels, and connective tissues

As of 2019, the VA has broadened the scope of which Veterans may qualify for Agent Orange connected ailments to Blue Water Navy Veterans. Blue Water Navy Veterans as those who served on open sea ships off the shore of Vietnam during the Vietnam War. There are estimated to be 50,000 to 90,000 such Veterans still alive. In 2021 The V.A. has increased the "presumptive" diseases to almost 30.

"Unfortunately, the health effects of Agent Orange use continue to affect unknown millions of people. The World Health Organization, in their latest fact sheet on dioxin, related the continuous exposure to humans through the food chain. Because the chemical doesn't degrade naturally, it tends to accumulate in the fatty tissues of animals. Most countries monitor their food supply for dioxin, and it has been found throughout the world and throughout the animal food supply. Unfortunately, the chemical compound is still being produced, used, and accidentally released into the environment by industries around

the world.[102]

Agent Orange exposure does not end with the Veteran; it may also contribute to birth defects and disorders in Veterans' children. Studies have indicated that Agent Orange exposure has led to increased rates of stillbirths and birth defects in the children of Veterans exposed to Agent Orange.

---

[102] VETERANS LAW GROUP https://www.Veteranslaw.com/long-term-effects-of-agent-orange-exposure/

Addendum 5

Comments on PTSD

"If you are willing to send your boys off to fight Wars, then be ready to help them fight their demons when they return home."

Unknown origin

Dr. Roger Pitman, a world-class psychiatrist from Harvard Medical and Mass General in Boston; following his endorsement of "Six Degrees," told John Siegfried that PTSD was an injury to the brain. First *coined "Post Traumatic Psychic Injury"* by a Dr. Oppenheim in the late 19th century, the world psychiatric community agreed with Oppenheim's premise, on the heels of what they called *"Soldiers Heart"* after the Civil War. Unfortunately, it got lost in the shuffle in wars in the late 1800's/early 1900's. Following WW1, with over 400 MILLION artillery rounds fired in just 4 years, the condition during/after battle was called *"Shell Shock."*[103]

As a spin-off of *PTS* is a condition referred to as *Operator Syndrome,* Health issues from *Operator Syndrome* include functional impairments, endocrine dysfunction, sleep disturbance, obstructive sleep apnea, chronic pain, chronic headaches, orthopedic problems, headaches, substance abuse, depression and suicide, marital and family dysfunction, problems with sexual health and intimacy, hypervigilance,

---

[103] Pitman, Roger, MD; in interview with Jhn Siegfried June 2010

memory, vision, and cognitive impairment.

The impact of *PTS* and *Operator Syndrome* can have significant impact on family and friends of the affected person. It is not unusual for family and friends of a *PTS* or *Operator Syndrome* affected person to suffer Compassion Fatigue.

Compassion fatigue is defined as emotional and physical exhaustion leading to a diminished ability to empathize or feel compassion for others. It is often described as the "negative cost of caring" or referred to as secondary traumatic stress (STS).

Almost inevitably, symptoms such as lack of empathy, detachment, depression, anxiety, and physical and mental fatigue are the result. The human support system is overloaded and overwhelmed. Physiological changes occur in the brain creating a real need to address both the cause and the symptom. These factors surely contribute to heightened family tension, as well as the higher-than-average divorce rate we see in the SOCOM community.

Jon continued for as long as he could to serve his fellow servicemen, women, and Veterans. Even in death, Jon speaks to us via technologies that allow him to continue to speak to us. Jon's message to Veterans is transcribed below:

> *"Hi there, Thank you for your service to this great nation. I am so proud of you. I know firsthand the challenges of war. I am Jon Cavaiani and I was privileged to serve with Special Forces during the Vietnam war. Let me tell you, post-Vietnam they did not have the services, resources and tools that are available today to support service members and their families to stay*

mentally strong and to deal with the challenges of adjusting after deployment. I wish they had; it would have alleviated a lot of the problems that I later had. The tools and resources to help you are available now. Make use of them. I did much later, and it continues to help me stay strong. We cannot allow the enemy to defeat you at home."[104]

[104] MEDAL OF HONOR -SPEAK OUT;

https://www.youtube.com/watch?v=-1JdH2WRyiU (Cavaiani

presentation to Veterans)

Addendum 6

Foundations

Save The Montagnards

100% Unpaid Volunteer Organization

Mission

Although the STMP was founded to provide assistance to Montagnard immigrants, we can also assist non Montagnard refugees from Indochina of a U.S. Special Operations affinity.

Additionally, our role has expanded to include improving the chances of survival for their vanishing culture in Vietnam. Their distinct ethnogeny as the aborigines of southeast Indochina dating to 200 BC, is nearly dead. Following the North Vietnamese victory in 1975, the communists instituted Cultural Leveling (long term ethnic cleansing) to eradicate all ethnic minority cultures.

STMP assistance may take the form of advocacy with the U.S. and foreign governments and providing refugee resettlement and educational funds, goods, and services.

Located on 100 acres in Asheboro NC, the New Central Highlands is the epicenter of US Montagnard activity. There is a Rhade longhouse has been built, a Montagnard cemetery has been established, a pavilion built for events and on any given weekend, hundreds of Montagnards gather to work the land and to network with their countrymen. Plans for a cultural center and additional tribal structures are in place and work is underway to expand.

Overview

STMP is an IRS 501c3 non-profit charity founded by Vietnam Veterans in 1986. Many of us were U.S. Army Special Forces soldiers ("Green Berets") who lived with and led the Montagnard hill tribes against the communists during the Vietnam War. Other members fought with Cambodian, Cham, Vietnamese, Chinese Nung, and/or the Hmong hill tribe of the "Secret Army" in Laos. We also have vet members who served in conventional US units during the Vietnam and other wars, and many non-Vets who have come to admire the Christian ideals and unparalleled work ethic of the 3,000 US Montagnard refugees. **www.montagnards.org**

Save the Montagnard People, Inc. | The New Central Highlands...
9005 Erect Rd
Seagrove , NC 27341
United States
stmpmontagnards@yahoo.com

SGM JON CAVAIANI MOH MEMORIAL SCHOLARSHIP FUND

The Jon R. Cavaiani (MOH) Memorial Scholarship Program has, since 2015, awarded scholarships in Jon's honor to young wolf-pups of Livingstone High School in hopes they will inherit his spirit of compassion, perseverance, and service.

Today, in honor of Jon's memory, Special Forces Chapter 23, The Golden Gate Chapter, is the SGM Jon R. Cavaiani MOH Memorial Chapter and funds the Jon Cavaiani Memorial Scholarship Program for students from Jon's high school; and keeps the memory of Jon alive among the wolfpack students and alumni. Special Forces Chapter 23 established a scholarship fund in 2015 and awards deserving graduates of Jon's high school alma mater with funds to be used as needed to further their education.

This program, on an annual basis, funds financial scholarship support to selected graduates of Jon Cavaiani's high school alma mater. 100% of funds received go to scholarship recipients. Funds are managed and administered by Special Forces Association Chapter 23 – The Jon Cavaiani MOH Memorial Chapter.

Donations can be made to:

https://www.paypal.com/donate?hosted_button_id=9QX3HW7NX YW3E

Since 2015 (through 2022) there have been eighteen WOLFPACK

student recipients of funds to assist them in their educational endeavors.

Bibliography

Baldi, Bob; **THE SAGA OF BOXIE (sic) JON by Sp4 Bob Baldi; (SOLDIERS: Vol 40., No. 4; April 1985**

Bay Area Mortuary:

https://www.facebook.com/BayAreaMortuaryServices/phot os/?tab=album&album_id=822467357777341

Blackburn, Gary B. and Long, Lonnie M.; *Unlikely Warriors: The Vietnam Security Agency's Secret War In Vietnam: 1961 – 1973*; Universe Publishing, Bloomington, Indiana; 2013

Burgess, Roger: **http://competitionplus.com/drag-racing/news/6469-burgess-honors-Veterans**

Burkett, B. G. and Whitley, Glenna; *Stolen Valor: How The Vietnam Generation Was Robbed Of Its Heroes and Its History*; Verity Press; Dallas; 1998

Celaya, Ray and Janous, William; *Montagnard Uprising Christmas Day 1969, Camp   A233 – Trang Phuc: The Clash of Cultures: The Sit-Rep, Vol 30 Ed 3 May 2021*

Celaya, Ray; *Interviews and e-mails with Mike Evers in June and July 2022*

Chadwick, Bill; *Interviews and e-mails with Mike Evers in April-June 2022*

Chadwick, Bob; *Interviews and e-mails with Mike Evers June and July 2022*

Cleveau, Victor; There are Medals and There are Medals...Profile on Columbia Medal of Honor   Recipient, Jon Cavaiani~

https://docs.google.com/document/d/1p87EO9SBO3rTNj6r-

g3yjlOeNvdjbFOB/edit#; Posted by: Kim Hamilton on 02/01/2009 11:14 PM

Updated by: Kim Hamilton on 02/03/2009 09:12 AM

Couch, Dick, Tom Norris and Mike Thornton; *By Honor Bound Intro*; Page xxi, McMillan, New York; 2016

Crowell, Bob, **Northern Nevada Business Weekly, May 2, 2018**

DROP, The (SFA periodical) *"The Assault on Hickory Hill – June 1971."* ; pages 42, 43, 44 & 47; Fall 2013; Fayetteville, NC; based on Chapter 25, "The Explorer Saga", "Unlikely Warriors: The Army Security Agency's Secret War in Vietnam 1961 – 1973", by Lonnie M. Long and Gary B. Blackburn, Universe; 2013

Daly, James A.; *Black Prisoner Of War, A Conscientious Objector's Vietnam Memoir*; 1975; University Press of Kansas; Lawrence, KS

Dufner, Frank; *interview with John Siegfried; 2013*

Fan's View: **NASCAR Honoring the 2011 Medal of Honor Recipients**

4 July 2011 By Front stretch Staff

Farrell, John Aloysius **"A Refining Experience"; The Boston Globe;** (008-01-23

Fluck, Michael; conversations with John Siegfried

Frontstretch Staff; **https://www.frontstretch.com/2011/07/04/nascar-honors-2011-medal-of-honor/** 4 July 2011

Galati, Ralph; **Interview with John Siegfried;** 7 July 2022.

GEICO (9-16-2011)

(https://promo.espn.com/news/tracks/archive/story?page=c

hicagoland-speedway-news-archive)

Harris, Carlyle "Smitty" and Sara W. Berry; **TAP CODE;**
https://www.zondervan.com/p/tap-code-epic-survival-tale-
vietnam-pow-secret-code-changed-everything/

Hawley, Frank: *Drag Illustrated*: *Hawley Tribute to MOH Veteran
Jon Cavaiani* - **Drag Illustrated | Drag Racing News,
Opinion, Interviews, Photos, Videos and More;** August 2014

Jacobson, Jake; telephone *interview with Mike Evers; 21 May 2022*

James, Dick; telephone interviews with Mike Evers; 06 May and 12
May 2022

James, Dick; *Slurp Sends! On Becoming a Green Beret: Book 1*;
self-published; Arnold, CA; 2019

James, Dick; *Slurp Sends! Experiences of an A-Team Green Beret:
Book 2*; self-published; Arnold, CA; 2020

James, Dick; *Slurp Sends! Experiences of a Green Beret Vietnam
Veteran: Book 3*; self-published; Arnold, CA; 2020

James, Dick; *Slurp Sends! Green Beret's Vietnam Experiences:
Book 4*; self-published; Arnold, CA; 2020

Jones, R. A.; *The Swamp: Rangers and Insurgents in the Mekong
Delta*; no-date; self-published; no place given

Jordan, Bryant; **Military.com 7 Aug 2013**

Knuboff, "Doc" Steven; numerous communications with John Siegfried

Langer, Emily; *Washington Post 2 August 2014;*
**https://www.washingtonpost.com/national/jon-r-cavaiani-
dies-at-70-medal-of-honor-recipient-from-vietnam-
war/2014/08/02/bcd24e5a-18bf-11e4-85b6-
c1451e622637_story.html**

Laurence, Pete; written compilation of research and numerous
  interviews by Laurence with Jon Cavaiani over several years
  and provided to Mike Evers that described the events of June
  1971 at and near Hickory Hill.

Leovy, Jill; Jon Cavaiani dies at 70; desperate stand in '71 led to
  Medal of Honor; LA Times, August 2, 2014

Library of Congress; ***BOARD OF INQUIRY: SGT CAVAIANI, JON
  R., JONES, JOHN R., WITNESS STATEMENTS*** (e-location
  at - https://www.loc.gov/item/powmia/pwmaster_76566/

*Living History of Medal of Honor Recipient Jon Cavaiani; interview
  at: https://youtube.com/watch?v=4SeTr-itHkc&feature=share*

Wolves, 1959; Yearbook of Livingston High School, Livingstone,
  California.

Livingstonian, 1960; Yearbook of Livingston High School,
  Livingstone, California.

Livingstonian, 1961; Yearbook of Livingston High School,
  Livingstone, California.

Livingstonian, 1962; Yearbook of Livingston High School,
  Livingstone, California.

Lodge, Henry Cabot. Ambassador; This Day in History
  https://thisdayinusmilhist.wordpress.com/2014/11/06/novembe
  r-6/

Lyles, Gary; ***My Story, Vietnam 1968, 196th Light Infantry Brigade***;
  Publisher, E BOOKTIME LLC; 2014

Mac's Facts no. 47; **Annals of War: The Prisoner *(Jim Thompson—
  Longest Held POW)***; New Yorker, Pg. 52, April 2, 2001

Mac's Facts no. 48.... ***Hanoi Taxi, Operation Homecoming 1973.***

January 9, 2020 (**Note: there are 50 pages to this document**)

McCain, John S. III, Lieutenant Commander United States Navy (1973-05-14) (reposted under title :\ **"John McCain, Prisoner of War: A First Person Account", 2008-01-28**)

McKim, Keith; *Vietnam: Green Beret SOG Medal of Honor Recipients*; Yucca Creek Records, 2015

Medal of Honor recipients – Vietnam (A-L)".
United States Army Center of Military History0
https://www.youtube.com/watch?v=4SeTr-ithkc&authuser=0

Mercando, Elena; interview with Mike Evers; August 16, 2022

National Museum, The; **https://www.thenmusa.org/biographies/jon-r-cavaiani/**

Noe, Robert L,; *Jon Cavaiani's Experience As A Prisoner Of War And "Member" Of The "Peace Committee" Debunked*; http://www.macvsog.cc/jon_cavaiani's_pow_&_peace_committee_experience.htm

Noe, Robert L.;
https://www.flickr.com/photos/13476480@N07/27669207725

Palmer, Laura; Shrapnel in the Heart: Letters and Remembrances from the Vietnam Veterans Memorial; Vintage; New York; 1988

Plaster, John; **#macvsog#macvsogteam**

Pritzker Military Museum and Library; Pritzker Military Presents with special guest MOH SGM Jon Cavaiani
https://www.pritzkermilitary.org/whats_on/medal-honor/medal-honor-recipient-jon-cavaiani-interview

Quade, Alex; several telephone and electronic messaging means; July

– August 2022

Roberts, Surry; *Montagnards: NCPedia;* edited by William S, Powell; UNC Press; Chapel Hill, NC; 2006

Rochester, Stuart I.; and Kiley, Frederick; *HONOR BOUND -- American Prisoners of War in Southeast Asia 1961-1973";* Naval Institute Press, Annapolis Maryland; 1998

Rutherford, Craig ; interview with John Siegfried

Schnarre, George; telephone interviews with Mike Evers 10 and 11 May; with follow on e-mails providing clarification and personal documents; 2022

Seals, Robert D.; *Operation IVORY COAST, a "Mission of Mercy";* USASOC History Office; December 2, 2020

Shields, Jim; numerous telephone interviews and e-mails with Mike Evers April – August 2022

Shorten, James; *telephone interview with Mine Evers July 26,2022*

Siegfried, John A.; *Six Degrees of the Bracelet: Vietnam's Continuing Grip;* Amazon; 2023

Summers, Harry G,; *Historical Atlas of the Vietnam War*; Houghton-Mifflin; Boston, MA; 1995

Summers, Harry G.; *On Strategy: The Vietnam War in Context*; Strategic Studies Institute; Carlisle, PA; 1982

Thorsness, Leo; *Surviving Torture, The Philadelphia Inquirer*; 2009-06-07; retrieved 2009-06-27.

U. S. Department of State Archives.; **https://history.state.gov/milestones/1961-1968/gulf-of-tonkin#:~:text=The%20Gulf%20of%20Tonkin%20inciden t,of%20the%20conflict%20in%20Vietnam.**

Veterans Law Group; https://www.Veteranslaw.com/long-term-effects-of-agent-orange-exposure/

Weist, Andrew A.; *Vietnam's Forgotten Army: Heroism And Betrayal In The ARVN*; New York University Press; New York; 2008

Webb, James; Fields of Fire; Bantam Books; New York; 1978

Wells, Thomas; **The War Within: America's Battle Over Vietnam;** University of California Press; 1994

Whitman, G. Duane; http://thelastsevendays.wordpress.com/sergeant-john-r-jones/

Wyatt, Frederick A, and Wyatt, Barbara P.; *We Came Home*; P.O.W. Publications; Toluca Lake, CA; 1977

Michael B. Evers (Mike) is a retired individual with 50 years of work experience. He served in the United States Army for nearly 20 years, achieving the rank of Major and being stationed in 15 different countries and locations, including Berlin, Okinawa, and Tokyo. After his military service, he worked for the State of North Carolina, holding positions such as the Law Enforcement Academy Director and Assistant Secretary for the Department of Correction. In these roles, he served as a sworn Commissioner on various agencies and commissions related to crime, domestic violence policies, law enforcement education, and grants. He also taught leadership and organizational effectiveness as an adjunct professor. Additionally, he served as a Liaison Officer for all Marine Corps installations in eastern states, fostering relationships with Governors and legislative bodies. Mike's passion for writing began in high school when he received his first poetry award for a piece called "Bachelors' Envy." Over the years, he has continued to write and is now in the process of compiling his writings into books. He holds a Bachelor of Science Degree from Southern Arkansas University, a Master of Education degree from Chapman University, and a Doctor Degree in Higher Education Administration from North Carolina State University. He and his wife, Yoshiko Nishimura Evers, have four adult children and four grandchildren, whom they love and are proud of.

John Siegfried, a lifelong Philadelphia native, is passionate about military history and his family. His wife, Donna, passed away in 2013. He authored Six Degrees of the Bracelet: Vietnam's Continuing Grip on 11/11/11 and has other manuscripts awaiting publication, including The New Agent Orange. His most recent work, No Greater Love: The Story of Medal of Honor Recipient Michael J. Crescenz, was released on 26 September 2022. Siegfried is a member of numerous Veteran Posts nationwide and has dedicated himself to sharing veterans' stories. He was appointed to the US Army War College in 2012 and has spoken at various venues, including events with POWs from different wars. He is also a board member of the Marine Corps Law Enforcement Foundation, supporting the children of fallen Marines and law enforcement officers. John's upcoming publications, A Wolf Remembered and The New Agent Orange, will be published in June 2023. He resides in Delaware County, PA, with his two daughters, Heather and Allison, and has four grandchildren.